D1615620

An Eye in the Sky

By the same author

Tigers: The Story of 74 Squadron RAF (Arms and Armour Press London, 1992)

A Tiger's Tale: The Story of Battle of Britain Fighter Ace John Connell Freeborn (J & KH Publishing, 2002)

Upward and Onward: Life of Air Vice Marshal John Howe CB CBE AFC (Pen & Sword Aviation, Barnsley, 2008)

An Eye in the Sky

The Royal Flying Corps and
Royal Air Force Career of Air
Commodore Henry George Crowe
CBE MC CBD (SC)

Bob Cossey

Pen &
Sword

AVIATION

First published in Great Britain in 2018 by
Pen & Sword Aviation
An imprint of
Pen & Sword Books Ltd
47 Church Street
Barnsley
South Yorkshire
S70 2AS

Copyright © Bob Cossey, 2018

ISBN 978 1 52672 596 7

The right of Bob Cossey to be identified as Author of this work has been asserted
by him in accordance with the Copyright, Designs and Patents Act 1988.

A CIP catalogue record for this book is
available from the British Library.

All rights reserved. No part of this book may be reproduced or transmitted in
any form or by any means, electronic or mechanical including photocopying,
recording or by any information storage and retrieval system, without
permission from the Publisher in writing.

Printed and bound in England
by TJ International Ltd, Padstow, PL28 8RW

Pen & Sword Books Ltd incorporates the Imprints of Pen & Sword Archaeology,
Atlas, Aviation, Battleground, Discovery, Family History, History, Maritime,
Military, Naval, Politics, Railways, Select, Transport, True Crime, Fiction,
Frontline Books, Leo Cooper, Praetorian Press, Seaforth Publishing,
Wharncliffe and White Owl.

For a complete list of Pen & Sword titles please contact
PEN & SWORD BOOKS LIMITED
47 Church Street, Barnsley, South Yorkshire, S70 2AS, England
E-mail: enquiries@pen-and-sword.co.uk
Website: www.pen-and-sword.co.uk

Contents

Foreword

For those of us who ever wondered what a career was like in the RAF as a fighter pilot and officer during the two world wars this biography will more than satisfy you. If you need facts and figures they are here. And if you need first-hand accounts they are here.

The author has made full use of his own knowledge as a military historian and the papers kept by the son of the individual concerned in the story, Hal Crowe. We follow Hal's introduction to RAF life as a young trainee Observer at No.1 School of Aeronautics at Reading in 1916 through pilot training to eventually commanding one of the RAF's elite fighter squadrons, No.74 (Tiger) Squadron. Beyond that we see Hal progress from Officer Commanding No.1 Wing at Korat in India to finally ending his career with the RAF as Air Officer Commanding No.223 Group at Peshawar in 1945 and receiving the CBE from King George VI. The fascinating account finishes with a brief chapter on what happens to an individual such as Hal Crowe when they finally leave a military career after thirty years of service.

The story throws a very personal spotlight on what it was like to serve as an observer and pilot in the First World War and after, through to operations in the Middle East, which resonates strongly with us today, and then wartime India. You also learn much which you possibly didn't know before about life in the Royal Air Force between the wars.

Group Captain Dick Northcote OBE BA (RAF Retired)

Introduction

I was first introduced to Dr Michael Crowe by his Leicestershire neighbour Michael Chapman, a member of the Guild of Aviation Artists, who was painting a scene in Malta of Hawker Demons being offloaded in Valetta Harbour in 1935. The Demons were to equip No.74 Squadron which was reforming on the island having been disestablished in 1919 at the end of the Great War, during which time they had earned themselves the soubriquet of the 'Tigers' thanks to their aggressive and fearless combat ethic. I was particularly interested as Secretary and Historian of the 74(F) Tiger Squadron Association because Dr. Crowe's father, Henry Crowe, had been No.74's Commanding Officer in 1935 and furthermore, because he had an archive of his father's writing, photographs, original cine film taken during the 1920s and 1930s with a Bell and Howell camera and personal memorabilia from his time in the Royal Flying Corps and Royal Air Force. And whilst there are some gaps in photographs, particularly from the wartime years in India, it soon became apparent to me that all that his son did have would form the basis of a biography of a man who had led an interesting and varied life spanning two world wars, serving in the United Kingdom, the Middle East and India. Parts of that story had been told in magazine articles and in books but never in its entirety. Interestingly Henry Crowe's memoir, written at the behest of his children in the 1960s, covers more than just service life, but family life too. And it highlights the advantages taken by a man with many interests of exploring the countries he was posted to as far as he was able.

It is thanks to Michael and Audrey Crowe, who have willingly shared Henry's archive with me, that this biography has been possible. Their hospitality over the past few years has been hugely appreciated and I hope that the consequence of that in the form of this book has done Michael's father's life justice.

Chapter One

Boyhood

Henry George Crowe (always known to the family as Hal) was born on 11 June 1897 in Donnybrook, Dublin, to John Joseph Crowe, a stockbroker, and Florence Helen Crowe. A year or so after his birth the family moved in to 'Carahor', not so very far away in Ballsbridge. This house was completed to the design of Richard Orpen, brother of William Orpen, a war artist during the First World War and a very successful portrait painter to the rich and famous thereafter. The Crowe family was well connected and successful. Hal's uncles Bill and Frank went to the USA, taking up business in New York and Seattle, while George and Lewis became doctors and practised in Cheshire. Hal's mother Florence's great uncle was Sir Howard Grubb, an engineer who made his name building astronomical telescopes for leading observatories, including the 28-inch refractor telescope, the UK's largest refractor, at the Royal Observatory Greenwich in 1893. He also invented the reflector sight which has been used on all kinds of weapons from small firearms to fighter aircraft and is at the heart of all modern head-up displays. He was elected a Fellow of the Royal Astronomical Society in 1870 and the Royal Society in 1883. In 1887 he was knighted by Queen Victoria.

One of Hal's earliest memories was of a great storm that hit the city of Dublin in February 1903. 'The gale must have started to get up before midnight,' he wrote later.

> The noise prevented the maids sleeping so they went down to the kitchen. The wind increased so that it was screaming round the house and as it was blowing straight onto Mother and Dad's room they moved to the other side of the house. Soon after that Cousin Di who was staying with us gave up attempts to sleep. She put on her dressing gown and just as she went on to the

landing there was a shattering crash followed by the noise of falling bricks and wood. The wind now roared louder than ever. The house was in darkness as the gas was unlit and all this made Cousin Di, an old lady, almost faint with fright.

The crash was the gable at the west window being swept away by falling bricks which smashed the wash stand in Hal's parent's room. The floor was littered with bricks and plaster and looking up they could see through the roof. They hurriedly left the room, stumbling over debris, and lit the gas on the landing and brought Cousin Di and the rest of the family down to the dining room where they lit the fire and 'we all had tea. We all spent the rest of the night in armchairs and sofas. The wind dropped at dawn and when it was light enough I went with dad to inspect the damage.'

The high chimney which served six fireplaces in the house was blown down onto the roof over Hal's parents' and Cousin Di's rooms. She had had a lucky escape for the bed she had been in a few moments before she walked out onto the landing was covered with debris. Outside, trees were down everywhere and it was days before roads were passable. Farther afield the coast was littered with the wrecks of the small topsail schooners which carried cargoes to the various small ports around Ireland. It took weeks to get the house repaired because nearly every house in the neighbourhood suffered damage.

Hal's early schooling started at a kindergarten where Swedish drill, the aerobics of the early 1900s and the foundation for modern gymnastics, and piano playing formed part of the curriculum, but he was rather put off the piano by the tutor (a *fraulein* as he called her) hitting him with a ruler on the hands whenever he played a wrong note. The boys wore sailor suits or Scottish dress. But life in Ballsbridge and nearby Donnybrook was generally pleasant. Trams ran into Dublin city centre although there were no cars to be seen. Everything was delivered by horse- or donkey-drawn vehicles and a forge halfway along the walk home from school always had a few animals waiting to be shod. Pedestrians often had to cross the narrow street in the village to avoid a sea of cow dung on market days or a fight as drunks were ejected from the local public house. At Miss Fagan's shop you could buy anything for a penny. Home life too held pleasant memories for Harold.

> Dear old nurse stayed with us till brother Cecil did not need her attentions. The last time I saw her was when I was home on leave from France before the Battle of Messines. The strain of saying goodbye was too much for her. Then Lizzie: what marvellous food she produced. She stayed on with brother Frank after both dad and mother died. Mother had several parlour maids, all very kind to us kids, and of course they were very smartly dressed on Mother At Home days when ladies arrived in carriages to take tea. Our gardener Pyne later joined the rebels but we felt sure his loyalty saved us from being molested in the Rebellion.

Hal was the eldest brother. Next came Frank and finally Cecil.

In those days the family doctor was a Dr Furlong who always arrived in a carriage and pair driven by a coachman. The doctor always wore a frock coat with a tall hat and never left the house without writing at least one prescription designed to suit the palate of the particular patient. 'I can still see his guardee moustache brushing my face as he cauterised my tonsils assuring me as the smoke came out of my mouth that there was no need to panic!'

It was always a great thrill to Hal when ships of the Royal Navy visited Kingstown. Originally called Dun Laoghaire, the port was renamed Kingstown by George IV to honour his visit in 1821. Exactly a hundred years later, one year before the Irish won their independence from Britain, it reverted to Dun Laoghaire. The battleships anchored in the Anchor Roads outside the harbour but smaller vessels and destroyers were secured to buoys inside the breakwater. Except for destroyers the ships wore buff-coloured funnels, white upperworks and black hulls and the paint was enamel. 'Later they were painted grey all over,' recalled Hal, 'and we thought this a terrible comedown.'

Kingstown Naval Base. Except for the destroyers the ships wore buff-coloured funnels, white upperworks and black hulls.

One Sunday afternoon Hal was at Kingstown with his father wearing his No.1 sailor suit when they saw a cutter being rowed to the Victoria Wharf steps, taking an officer from HMS *Melampus*, the guard ship, ashore for church. After the officer had come ashore the cutter started its return to *Melampus* but the coxswain had spotted Hal and when the officer was out of sight behind a shed he gave the order to toss oars which was a salute given to commissioned ranks. Hal returned the salute in his smartest manner. 'I never forgot that little episode,' wrote Hal, 'and later I wanted my parents to let me go for entry to Osborne which was then the naval cadet training centre.'

On occasions such as King Edward VII's visit to Dublin the fleet was illuminated while a firework display was given. Each ship was outlined with electric lights, a most impressive sight. When the king came Hal's father hired a tram which had an open top. Invitations were sent out to friends and the tram took them around the sights of Dublin where buildings were illuminated, some by electric and some by gas lamps. The tram then drove down the coast to Kingstown to see the fleet and the fireworks. Afterwards it returned to Donnybrook while the guests in full evening dress sat down to a champagne supper inside the vehicle.

In 1907 the Irish International Exhibition opened at Ballsbridge and Hal was given a season ticket so that he could visit any time and he made very good use of it. 'I learnt more at the exhibition than could have been obtained from books,' he later recalled.

> There were pavilions from every part of the British Empire. The machinery hall contained the coal fired power house for the whole exhibition as well as locomotives, racing cars, printing machinery, weaving and manufacturing processes. An art gallery, Somali village and wonder of wonders the first cinematograph in Dublin complete with a lady playing the piano. Amusements included a water chute, concerts and circus acts.

It was the sensation of the year for the Irish.

As Hal grew up activities within the Crowe family included small dances and Christmas parties when the aunts and uncles with their children came to 'Carahor' to exchange presents and eat a very rich turkey and plum pudding dinner. Home entertainment included a pianola and a phonograph which played cylinder records and on which the family made their own recordings. Theatricals were performed, cycle rides organised and holidays taken in North Wales, the Isle of Man and various parts of Ireland. 'Uncle George had a motor car. What a thrill to be given a ride in it and who cared if we were smothered in dust as we chugged along. Dad was disappointed when he asked uncle to let him take the wheel but he wouldn't let him!'

The great interest about the Isle of Man trips for the family was the journey. 'We sailed down the River Liffey to Dublin port which smelled to high heaven with untreated sewage and we would pass big four-masted square-rigged sailing ships unloading grain: and then we would spend hours watching the great oscillating steam engines turning the paddles of the steamer across to the island. At Douglas we would travel to Ramsey on the narrow gauge railway. The great wheel at Laxey, the largest water-wheel pump in the world, attracted crowds of people.'

'Carahor' was always filled with relations for the horse show and other events at the Royal Dublin Society grounds at Ballsbridge. Military tournaments in particular were splendid affairs with all the troops taking part in full dress. Tent pegging by lancers, slicing the lemon by dragoons, musical rides by artillery and hussars were most colourful. The programme usually ended with troops re-enacting some episode from the South African or Zulu wars.

Hal always acknowledged that he had a very happy, privileged life as a child but as part of that discipline was always maintained. There was no playing with trains on Sundays. And very long sermons at church which was always filled to capacity with men in frock coats and tall hats and the ladies in their satins still smelling of mothballs. But outside there was abject poverty. Hal always noticed the newspaper boys in rags with no coats or stockings or shoes come winter or summer. And this in the generally wet Irish climate.

*

After kindergarten Hal moved to St Helen's school for boys, first as a day boy and then as a weekly boarder. It was here that he met many who became lifelong friends. Life could be hard at St Helen's with punishments for misdemeanours varying from the refusal of permission to go home at half term to a severe caning, something which both pupils and parents took as a matter of course in those days. It was during his time as a weekly boarder that an aviation club was formed at St Helen's with Hal as secretary. The Wright brothers had just flown their heavier than

A Wright Flyer. This aircraft was the inspiration for the founding of an aviation club at St Helen's School, of which Hal was secretary.

air powered aircraft and so began Hal's lifelong interest in aviation and his photographing of so many aircraft types wherever he saw them.

Then the time came when Hal's parents decided to send him to England to school 'to get rid of my Irish accent'. He went first to Clive House at Old Colwyn near Colwyn Bay, a small prep school for boys. Clive House was in a converted residence facing the sea with a private path across the main railway line from Chester to Holyhead so that the boys, who came from Ireland, Portugal, China and Assam as well as from England, could walk from the house to the sea to bathe. With the Boy Scouts troop at Clive House the boys learnt carpentry and became proficient at gymnastics in the loft of the school's stables where there was room for horizontal and parallel bars.

In 1911 Hal moved to the Dean Close public school in Cheltenham, a Christian school founded in 1886 and set in extensive parkland in the centre of the city. By this time he was set on becoming an engineer with a leaning towards the Indian railways and he joined the engineering class. He took mathematics, physics, chemistry, mechanics and machine drawing and studied for the Cambridge local exams. The school boasted of having its own contingent of the Officers' Training Corps under a War Office scheme and Hal joined.

> Everyone was very keen and we took our drills, arms drill and lectures most seriously. Many of us met again during World War One. The contingent went to camp on Salisbury Plain in company with other public school OTCs in the summer holidays of 1912 and did field operations under regular army officers. We were near the Royal Flying Corps aerodrome at Netheravon and the Maurice Farman biplanes on training sorties flew over the camp in the calm air of early morning and evening.

From the camp Hal travelled to join a family holiday party in North Wales and at Portmadoc saw the then famous British aviator Gustav Hamel fly

The Cheltenham contingent, Officers' Training Corps 1912.

When at the Officers' Training Corps camp near Netheravon in 1912 cadets often saw Maurice Farman Longhorns in the air.

his Bleriot monoplane. Hamel died before reaching the age of 25, disappearing over the English Channel in May 1914 while returning from Villacoublay flying a new Morane-Saulnier monoplane he had just collected. There was speculation that the aircraft might have been sabotaged given the international tension of the time but, as no trace of the aircraft was ever found, nothing could be proved.

By 1913 Hal was a student at Trinity College Dublin studying engineering. The following year he joined the family for the usual annual holiday, a very happy one. But nobody realised at the time that it was to be the last. News became increasingly bad as the summer wore on and on 4 August war was declared against Germany. As the Crowes sailed into Dublin Bay on their way home they saw many ships waiting to take men and horses to the war. Back at Trinity Hal found that several friends had left to join the Royal Flying Corps but owing to his age he realised that the best way to follow them was to join the Army via Sandhurst. So after passing examinations and successfully completing a medical he joined the Royal Military College in November 1915. All the instructing officers

Gustav Hamel's 50 hp Bleriot monoplane at Portmadoc 1912.

and NCOs had already had war experience in France and Hal and his fellow Gentleman Cadets were so keen to go to the battlefields that their fear was that the war would be over before they had seen anything of it.

The nine-month course consisted of history, military law, writing reports, drills, PT, machine-gun and arms practice on the ranges, field engineering, trench digging, bridging, demolition and riding school. To win one's spurs at the latter, cadets had to negotiate all the jumps in the paddock without stirrups or reins and with arms folded. (Hal was proud to wear his spurs having successfully passed this demanding regime.) Another part of the course was night operations, finding their way through the local Camberley woods by compass. This helped when the cadets were called upon to search for the crew of a Zeppelin airship who were supposed to have parachuted into the woods. The cadets also had their first flight in a Maurice Farman Shorthorn biplane at nearby Farnborough. It was the first armed aircraft to engage in aerial combat during the First World War and was affectionately known as Rumpety because of the noise it made while taxiing.

Hal was very sensitive to the history of the College as a 200-year-old institution. The first Military Academy had been established in 1720

Maurice Farman Shorthorn, also known as the Rumpety, at Farnborough. Hal and his fellow cadets at Sandhurst had their first flights in this type.

The Royal Military College at Sandhurst 1915: the New Building housing C, D, E and F Companies.

at Woolwich to train cadets for commissions in the Royal Artillery. In 1799 a school for staff officers was established at High Wycombe and in 1801 this became the Senior Department of the newly-established Royal Military College. A Junior Department was established at Great Marlow a year later to train Gentleman Cadets for the infantry and cavalry regiments of the British Army. In 1812 this Junior Department moved into buildings designed by James Wyatt at Sandhurst and was joined a few years later by the Senior Department, which in 1858 changed its name to the Staff College and subsequently became independent of the Royal Military College in 1870. The Staff College now had its own Commandant and Adjutant, although it continued to be administered by Sandhurst until 1911.

The Royal Military College at Sandhurst 1915: equipment issued to cadets.

The Royal Military College at Sandhurst 1915: ascending a small mineshaft.

Life at Sandhurst was often tough. Each cadet had a separate room leading on to corridors with ex-soldiers acting as batmen, each to so many cadets. The batmen did all the cleaning of boots, buttons and equipment but the rifles and bayonets were the cadets' responsibility and if not found to be spotless on parade punishment was by what was called a puttee parade which meant, after dining in full mess kit, doing a rapid change from dinner jacket to breeches and puttees and dashing down to the company anteroom. The first to arrive absolutely correctly dressed in every detail was let off. The others had to do arms drill for fifteen minutes. If a cadet did something which was judged to have let down the company he was sentenced to an ink bath and was made to strip and get in to a bath polluted with ink and then had to run the gauntlet naked down the corridors past each cadet who could have a flick at him with a wet towel. 'On one occasion some fools put chemicals in an ink bath which turned the cadets' hair white,' remembered Hal. 'A heck of a row over this caused the Company Commander and Commandant to be moved elsewhere. But life was not all thus. There

The Royal Military College at Sandhurst 1915: the lake on which the band played on as their sabotaged raft slowly sank.

were excellent concerts in the gym and the band played in the mess on guest nights.'

There were amusing moments too. 'As part of the field engineering course cadets had to construct a raft out of tarpaulins stuffed with hay as floats, many of which were then lashed to spars and planks to form a decking. The band was playing on one of these rafts in the shallow lake near the College one calm summer evening when cadets in boats lay alongside and without being seen made cuts in the tarpaulins. The result was a wonderful sight of the band slowly sinking, the men wading ashore and the big drum floating away! We all had to subscribe to new skins for the drums.'

Chapter Two

Rebellion

'A lot has been written about the Easter Rising of 1916,' recorded Hal in his memoirs, but this is not the place to do other than give a broad overview and to put his experience of it into context. The rebellion was an armed insurrection by Irish republicans whose objective was to bring to an end British rule in Ireland and establish an independent Irish Republic. It was organised against the backdrop of Britain's heavy engagement in the war on the Continent and elsewhere and with a promised supply of arms from Germany which would enhance the chances of success. In this hope the organisers, the Military Council of the Irish Republican Brotherhood, were wrong. Originally intended to begin on Easter Sunday, the rebellion was postponed until Easter Monday, 24 April. Members of the Irish Volunteers, led by activist Padraig Pearse, and James Connolly's Irish Citizen Army occupied key locations in Dublin but not before the British had seized the shipment of German arms to the rebels a few days before, which greatly reduced the scale of the rebellion outside the capital.

When it began there were just 400 British troops in Dublin to confront the rebels but reinforcements were quickly sent from England who disembarked at Kingstown on the morning of 26 April and advanced towards the city. They were repeatedly caught in crossfire at the canal at Mount Street with the rebels killing or wounding 240 men for four of their own dead. However, after five days, with up to 20,000 troops backed by superior artillery, the British army took control of Dublin. Although most of the leaders were court martialled and executed, ultimately the rebellion succeeded in encouraging active support for Irish Republicanism and the later Irish War of Independence in 1919.

Hal's term at Sandhurst had been given Easter leave and he had arrived home before Good Friday to find that his father had joined a voluntary organisation helping wounded men from France who were being landed from hospital ships at Dublin's port. He carried stretcher cases all Easter Sunday and when he came home that evening he told the family that there were rumours of serious trouble breaking out and that he would not be required at the docks on the following day. When the maids came back from early morning Mass on Easter Monday they nervously told of rumours of fighting in the city. Shortly afterwards scattered rifle fire could be heard close to 'Carahor' but being a bank holiday shops were shut and most people in the area stayed at home, so nobody really knew what was happening until one of the Crowes' neighbours managed to get a stop-press edition of a newspaper which headlined with the news that rebellion had broken out and that 'Roger Casement, the Irish nationalist and activist, had landed in Kerry from a German submarine to lead it which was startling news to everyone who heard it' as Hal wrote many years later. He wasn't entirely accurate though. Casement, who for twenty years had served in the British consular service before becoming absorbed in Irish nationalist politics, was convinced that an Irish-German alliance was a way of securing full Irish independence and had organised the shipping of 25,000 captured Russian rifles and a million rounds of ammunition to Ireland aboard the *Aud*. Casement persuaded the German authorities to carry him to Ireland by submarine, his idea on the face of it being to rendezvous with the *Aud* and supervise the landing of the arms. It turned out that his actual intention was to meet the leadership of the Irish Republican Brotherhood to persuade them to abandon the planned insurrection which he was convinced was doomed to failure as he didn't consider the arms shipment to be enough to sustain it. He was arrested on 21 April hours after landing on the Kerry coast and the Royal Navy captured the *Aud* on the same day.

On the Tuesday after the bank holiday Hal and his brother Frank did a recce on their bicycles around the neighbourhood and tried to get bread from a bakery in Ballsbridge, but shops remained shut. As the week wore on rumours were rife and the noise of firing intensified and came much closer with a few spent bullets hitting the house. Troops destined as reinforcements for France were diverted to Kingstown and passed 'Carahor' on their way to the city. 'Mother and other ladies brought tea and sandwiches to the roadside for the men,' Hal wrote.

They were amused to find the troops trying to talk French to them thinking they were in France. Those same units went on towards the city and got caught by rebel machine-gun fire at Ballsbridge and suffered serious casualties. A naval gunboat, HMY *Helga*, was sent up the river to attack Liberty Hall which was said to be the rebel headquarters but a large lattice girder railway bridge was in the line of fire and the gunboat's shells did more damage to the bridge than to Liberty Hall.

Liberty Hall was the headquarters of the Irish Transport and General Workers Union and the headquarters of the Irish Citizen Army at the time. Until the insurrection it had been a munitions factory where bombs and bayonets were made for the impending rebellion and it was on the street in front of the building that the leaders of the rebellion assembled before their march to the General Post Office on Easter Monday. Although the *Helga*'s bombardment had failed, the building was completely demolished by British artillery a few days later.

When Hal's leave was up he had to negotiate his way safely back to Sandhurst. He and a few other cadets put on their uniforms and so got through the military roadblocks and on to Kingstown to catch the mail boat to Holyhead. The family fully expected to hear that Hal had come to harm on the way but as he said 'these things always seem worse from a distance'. In fact the journey was largely uneventful, although not without its moments of apprehension. The cadets were closely questioned by their colleagues about the rebellion on their return to Sandhurst and were thought lucky to have seen real fire in anger.

*

At last, training complete, in early July 1916 the day of the passing out parade arrived. King George V and Queen Mary inspected the parade 'and I remember thinking how small they both were'. The cadets knew by then which regiments they were to be appointed to. Hal had completed a 'first appointments' form on 19 July 1916 in which he had stated his preferences as to which he wanted. These were the Royal Irish Regiment, the Royal Dublin Fusiliers and the Royal Inniskilling Fusiliers. Hal got his first choice and was commissioned as a second lieutenant in the Royal Irish Regiment and joined the 3rd (Reserve) Battalion in Dublin. The regiment was an infantry regiment of the line in the British Army, first raised in 1684 and which saw service for two and a half centuries before being disbanded following the establishment of the Irish Free State in 1922. They were the first British Army troops to attack the Irish rebels during the 1916 uprising. Hal received his uniform complete with regimental buttons and badges and was issued with a 'holdall' containing all that a soldier would require for personal hygiene in barracks and in the field, including a shaving brush, safety razor, comb, soap, toothbrush, shaving mirror, spare boot laces, knife, fork and spoon and facecloth. In the field the holdall would be carried in his haversack. Wrapped within the holdall was Hal's 'housewife'. This was a pouch containing every-thing required to carry out repairs to clothing – a thimble, two balls of grey darning wool (for socks), fifty yards of linen thread wound around card, needles and spare buttons. On top of this Hal received a valise, sleeping bag, camp bed, washstand and bucket as well as a sword and revolver holster. This all amounted to a lot of gear and much of it neither he nor his colleagues ever took on active service.

The morning Hal reported for duty in Dublin to start earning his 7/6d (37.5p) a day, he went from 'Carahor' by horse-drawn cab (with the driver complete with his bowler hat) and received the correct salute from the armed sentry at the Richmond Barracks gate. He reported to the adjutant, Percy Martin, an old friend of the family, and the Commanding Officer. The senior officers of the battalion had served in the South African War and saw to it that the mess was well run. The band played during dinner on guest nights and at the end the pipers in their saffron kilts marched round the table playing 'Garry Owen', the regimental march. Finally the pipe major drank a pint of Guinness at one go beside the Mess President.

The 3rd (Reserve) Battalion's role was two-fold: home defence and the training of officers and men to keep them occupied before posting

Second Lieutenant Crowe trying out his newly-issued respirator in 1916.

to the regular battalions of the regiment overseas. Some of these men had just come off sick leave after wounding or illness. Junior officers' duties, Hal's included, were the taking of parades, looking after the men in every respect (including inspecting their feet, socks and boots, all three of which were very important to infantrymen of course), paying the men, inspecting their meals and dealing out punishment, escorting officers under close arrest and sitting on courts martial and courts of enquiry. 'We had been told at Sandhurst that it was unusual for an officer to be under close arrest,' recalled Hal, 'so I was surprised to find that six officers *were* under close arrest. They were all wartime reserve officers and bounced cheques and drink spelt their undoing.'

At the end of August 1916 the Reserve Battalion was ordered to move to Templemore, southwest of Dublin. Hal went with the advance party to help get the old barracks there into shape for occupation having been unoccupied for many years. The main party moved by rail, boarding the train as laid down in the drill manual. 'The non-corridor train was ready at the platform when we arrived with all doors open. The men were then told off so many to each compartment and on the command "entrain" they all got in, the doors slammed as one at the same time and the train could proceed.' But Hal was not long at Templemore because he was posted to the 6th Battalion in France. The battalion had suffered severe casualties at Loos in the spring and early summer of 1916 before it was sent to the Somme where it played a prominent role in the September battles of Guillemont and Ginchy.

Hal's experience of war on the ground was to cover the period September 1916 to September 1917. He was 19 and was 'thrilled and excited at the prospect of seeing something of the real thing when I was posted to the 6th Battalion.' For us looking back to those times a century ago it is difficult to understand the enthusiasm of so many young men for throwing themselves into the fray. But that is with the benefit of hindsight. They weren't to know the full horror of what they would experience despite the losses already incurred by 1916.

Hal took a small draft of reinforcements from Dublin to Dover where they embarked in a convoy of old cross-channel steamers, some of them

Hal in July 1916, just prior to going to France with the Royal Irish Regiment.

paddlers, and were escorted by destroyers and a small airship to Boulogne. It was his first visit to France so, the war notwithstanding, everything was of great interest to Hal with his enquiring mind, as indeed was all that he was to encounter on his postings abroad over the next thirty years. On disembarking he and his men entrained in dilapidated old carriages with broken windows and goods wagons for the Base Depot at Étaples, fifteen miles south of Boulogne, where they paused for a few days and where they were given their steel helmets and gas respirators, attended lectures, were trained in bayonet fighting and exercised in a gas chamber to give them confidence in their respirators. And all the while they could hear the artillery barrage (called drumfire because it sounded like rolling drums) on the Somme where the battle was raging.

Étaples was the principal depot and transit camp for the British Expeditionary Force in France and also the point to which the wounded from the front, as well as newcomers to France, were taken. The place was notorious, for the conditions were awful. The camp had a justified reputation for harshness and the treatment received by the men there eventually led to the Étaples Mutiny in September 1917 when worsening relations between personnel and authorities at the camp led to a corporal of the Gordon Highlanders being shot by a military policeman trying to disperse an angry crowd of around a thousand soldiers in the town protesting about conditions. An innocent bystander, a French woman, was killed too.

Chapter Three

To the Front

Hal and his men eventually entrained for Bailleul, one of the railheads for northern France. At Bailleul there was also an air depot and hospital centre. There is no doubt that from the British point of view the First World War was a railway war in so much as the Army depended on railways to maintain its lines of communication and supply. Virtually all goods were moved from the Channel ports to the railheads by standard-gauge rail and from there to the front, very often by temporarily constructed narrow-gauge railways when the mud of Flanders and France stopped motor and horse-drawn vehicles. Hal's train hurtled along at a good 15mph towed by an ancient locomotive, 'fearfully and wonderfully made as were all French engines'. From the railhead they were transported by old London buses to where the remnants of the 6th Battalion were billeted in farmhouses. These were often old and dilapidated with extremely crude latrine arrangements, each farm having a large square pond which was universally called the 'rectangular smell'. That part of France had not yet been overrun by the enemy and the farmers and their wives worked hard in the fields with the front line not so many miles away and all the paraphernalia of the approaching war around them, using their huge cart horses for ploughing and windmills to grind the corn.

After a few days Hal marched to Locre in Flanders. Marching on the French paved roads was tiring and they rested often. More reinforcements started to arrive to build up the battalion's strength before taking their place in the front line. Their turn soon came to take their place in reserve and they marched to Kemmel in bodies of men no more than half a platoon (around twenty five men) in size and well separated in case the road was shelled. At Kemmel they were billeted in an empty château and some old huts, sleeping on the floor. The horse-drawn field cookers were parked at the château and produced dixies of bully-beef stew and gallons of tea. While there, as an officer Hal had to attend the funerals of men recently killed in the trenches, the bodies sewn in blankets and buried in Kemmel cemetery.

The changeover of units in the front line was carried out by night but first Hal wanted to see what conditions were like by day and so he was given the job of going into the trenches in daylight to take over the stores, familiarise himself with orders and garner information about the enemy from the outgoing battalion. It was a quiet afternoon when he did so with only the occasional trench mortars being lobbed over. He could see the projectiles tumbling over in the air which he soon learnt meant he could judge where they *might* fall and explode like a small thunderclap. 'It was always said that you never heard the bullet that hit you,' explained Hal, 'that when you heard a loud crack the bullet had actually already passed by.' If you didn't hear the crack the odds were it had hit you. With shell-fire it was different.

> The smaller field-gun shells we called whizz bangs because you heard the gun fire then, seconds later, there was a noise like a violent escape of steam followed at once by an explosion in the air. A shower of shrapnel, bullets and bits of shell than spattered down. The large guns and howitzers shelled the back areas and one heard the shells passing high over the trenches.

Hal's descriptions of conditions at the front and in reserve pulled no punches. 'Owing to the high water table it was not practicable to dig trenches in the Kemmel area so rough breastworks of sand bags were used,' he wrote. These were about seven feet high. At the front line duck-boards resting on frames were necessary to enable men to move easily without wading in the mud and water in the bottom of the trench. Officers wore trench boots modelled on Canadian boots as worn by trappers – big leather boots up to the knees so that the wearer could be in water without getting wet. No deep dugouts were possible in the trenches and instead semi-circular corrugated metal shelters were used. Men slept in them on rough wooden frames covered with rabbit netting. Stores and other gear were kept fairly dry on boxes. Coke-fired braziers were provided for cooking (and for keeping warm when it grew cold). Eggs and bacon could be fried on the braziers and rissoles (a mixture of bully beef, crushed biscuit and potatoes) heated up.

The routine was normally four days on the front line, four in the support line (a little farther back from the front) and eight in reserve. In reserve men slept in tents or Nissen huts and they could get baths in the convent at Locre thanks to the kindness of the nuns there. Clothing was deloused at a special unit equipped with steam compartments. Men could not, of course, undress during the eight days on the lines but if things were quiet during the day they were able to take their boots off and massage their feet with whale oil. Being in reserve was not all beer and skittles for Hal and his men. They had duties to undertake each night for the Royal Engineers, taking engineering stores of all kinds up to the front on trucks which were pushed along the narrow-gauge railways built to ease the supply problem. Frequent derailments involved unloading, re-railing and desperately trying to catch up on lost time. This was not helped by enemy shelling causing further delays and which meant that they seldom got back to camp before dawn.

For the men, entertainment in the form of a travelling cinema run by the YMCA visited reserve units. Officers though could have the use of a horse to ride into Bailleul officers' club for a good meal. The enemy shelled the town several times and on one occasion caught a party of officers leaving the club which was how one of Hal's friends, Kit Baldwin, lost his arm. On another visit the horse Hal had took fright on the way back to Locre when shells fell near and no matter what he did he couldn't prevent her galloping all the way back to her stable without stopping!

On 14 October 1916 Hal wrote home to his parents after he had completed another four days on the front line.

We are now out of the trenches and I have come out unwounded. I was only hit by bits of earth sent up by shells where they burst and by stones. Of course I can't tell you a lot of the things we did but the whole time I never felt a bit funky. When I was on duty in the daytime I used to watch our shells bursting on the Huns. It is lovely hearing the rush of our shells whispering through the air and then a huge mass of earth is shot into the air and sandbags, trench boards and pots etc. are hurled into the air and then gradually come down. The Germans have big trench mortars which do a lot of damage to the trench and give shell shock easily. I was within ten yards of a big [minenwerfer] burst one day and it covered me with clods and dust and suffocated me with smoke and stuff. Martin came out all right, also Malcomson who is bothered with neuralgia a lot poor chap. Malcomson had a letter from Freddy Pryce and Pryce had a letter from the doctor of HMS *Hampshire* saying that he was a prisoner in Berlin. As you know the *Hampshire* was the ship that Kitchener was going to Russia on. So perhaps Kitchener is a prisoner! I wonder, is he?

When he wrote this Hal had not heard that Field Marshal Lord Kitchener, Secretary of State for War, was dead. HMS *Hampshire* was sailing on 5 June 1916 from Scapa Flow to Russia when she is believed to have struck a mine laid by a German submarine off Marwick Head to the west of the Orkney Islands. The ship's doctor may have been a prisoner in Berlin but he wasn't on the *Hampshire* when she sank as all 643 hands were lost. He presumably was a previous doctor on the ship.

I have strong reasons to believe that I either killed or wounded a German the other night. He was firing for several days from a certain place and I had him well marked with sandbag sights and a compass bearing, then when I waited for him to fire his evening hate I let him fire several shots and had the rifle absolutely laid on him. Well, he has never fired again. Malcomson had shots at another man and we believe he got him too. In Martin's sector they got a sniper with a machine gun. I hope my chap was badly hit. The next day he never moved or was seen, so I have had a smash at the Huns at last.

The rats are great. One sees a thing as big as a rabbit and we fire our revolvers at them and we blow them to bits.

The things I don't like are the rifle grenades. One can't see them coming (as one can a trench mortar). We had several casualties from rifle grenades (I won't tell you the dates we were in the trenches). When I have been looking over the parapet I have had the sandbags round me cut to pieces by bullets. I don't care a bit about bullets, it's the rifle grenades I don't like, but at the same time they don't do very much damage.

Thanks awfully for the papers you have been sending. They were most useful and interesting. When we had read them they did to light fires etc. etc. The concert went off fairly well. The man that arranged it didn't work it properly and all the turns had been gone through in so short a time that he had to fill up the rest with some Australians.

You might send me the waterproof cover for the hat please. I'll be away on a short course from 17th to 23rd so it is as well that you don't send me anything to arrive between those dates as I may not get anything you send then. When you are sending the cap cover please send me some envelopes (the foreign sort). I can always get paper but envelopes are scarce.

We had several black kittens in the trenches. Lucky signs. One of the Tommies brought one back here with him. It is in my tent now sleeping beside me.

Surprise attacks were always expected after dusk and before dawn under the cover of darkness, so every man was at his post on 'stand to arms' morning and evening with rifle loaded and bayonet fixed. Stand to arms lasted between half an hour and an hour. At 'stand to' the German machine gunners used to traverse the parapets, their bullets ripping through the sandbags to try to catch someone's head as Hal alluded to in the letter above. Rum was issued by officers after dawn 'stand down'. It was a great tonic. By day and night officers patrolled up and down the front-line trenches. Hal had a case of a sentry being found asleep at his post, a crime punishable by death. He was detailed to prosecute at the soldier's court martial and 'lost the case I am glad to say'.

Despite the grim conditions humour was sometimes not very far away, but it was humour often as not unintentional as intentional. Hal tells the story of a well-known and slightly eccentric general.

> Going up the line on inspection he found as he entered the communication trench that he had left his gas mask behind. It was an order that everyone had to carry their respirators at all times in the line. However, he met a sergeant coming out of the line and he borrowed his. The General in due course found a man without his respirator and ordered 'gas alert' and the wretched soldier made a mess of putting it on. He got ticked off and the general told him he would show him the correct drill. 'You see I have my respirator in the alert position with the flaps tucked in. When the gas gongs sound I put both thumbs under the flaps, flick them open, then put the thumbs in again and flick out the respire …,' but he could not finish the sentence. He flicked out a pair of the sergeant's dirty socks!

On another occasion the same general was again visiting the front line but had chosen a day when one of the tough characters had got at the rum jar and was drunk.

> He could not be left in the front line in case the General spotted him so it was decided to send him down to the support line on a stretcher covered with a blanket like a corpse. But the General was early on his inspection and met the stretcher bearers carrying the man in the narrowest part of the trench. He stopped, made his aide de camp stand aside and springing to attention said, 'I, General Sir Aylmer Hunter-Bunter CB DSO MC, salute you the gallant dead.' There came a voice from under the blanket: 'what the hell is the old b****r blathering on about now?'

Patrols ventured into no man's land by night to get information and repair the barbed-wire entanglements which were always being broken by shells or mortars. When a Very light or star shell lit up the scene the patrol stayed stock still until the light went out, for if anyone moved it was easier for them to be seen and sniped at. No man's land at Kemmel was a mass of shell craters, usually full of water with parts of dead bodies and the nauseous sweet smell of death. The bodies of men wounded or killed there were always brought in eventually although corpses often had to be left for days, hanging perhaps on the barbed wire. It really was hell on earth. Conditions were bad enough during the spring and summer but as autumn turned into winter with its long nights, rain, wind and snow, they became intolerable.

> During one's patrols and after months of being in and out of the line it became almost impossible to believe that at that moment people were dancing and dining in comfort in Britain. Mail of course was a great joy, brought up as far as possible by battalion horse transport whence it was carried in bags up to the line. We had to censor the men's letters but for good conduct a reward of one green envelope a month was given. This allowed the man to send an uncensored letter although a proportion *were* censored at Base and if any vital information was given away in it a Court Martial resulted. Leave home was granted that winter to as many as possible and how welcome it was. But I met many men who on returning to join the unit seemed to have a premonition that they would not survive the next engagement. Often they were right.

In his memoir Hal writes that he became the Battalion Intelligence Officer but there is no date to go with the statement. It was not a role that would typically be given to a newly-commissioned officer but would instead go to someone who at least had some experience and had completed a Battalion Intelligence Officers' course. There is no indication that Hal undertook the latter and he wouldn't have racked up a huge amount of experience in the short time he had been in France and Belgium. An Intelligence Officer's duties would typically be collecting information by personal observation or talking with front-line troops, snipers, scouts, patrols and observers. He had to keep himself fully briefed about the military situation by liaising with neighbouring units in the line. He supervised the distribution of war news and intelligence throughout the battalion and kept the war diary. He would also be required to keep a map of all enemy dispositions as far as they were known: familiarise himself with no man's land and make any reconnaissance the battalion commander required: prior to an advance or raid collect all information regarding enemy positions: compile daily intelligence reports under the direction of his Commanding Officer and send them to Brigade Headquarters: see that snipers were constantly employed: and carry out the training of company scouts and patrols as required.

This is an onerous set of responsibilities and perhaps it was its very nature that prevented Hal from doing more than simply noting that he was the Battalion Intelligence Officer and leaving it at that.

Chapter Four

The Battle of Messines

On 9 June 1917 Hal wrote home again.

Well, now that the great event has come off I can tell you my experiences of the great battle. I expect you have seen in all the papers that we have captured the Messines-Wytschaete Ridge. Well, I was right through the thing. Please keep the accounts in the papers as I would like to keep them and any photos that appear. I needn't say how the show went as the papers tell everything on that score. My job as Intelligence Officer was purely one of observation. I had to watch every stage and thing happening. I had two of my observers and my servants with me and we all came through without a scratch I am glad to say. I was out watching when the great mines went up. I have never seen such a sight in my life and may never see such a one again (it is fully described in the papers). You can't imagine all the curtain of debris, fire, smoke …

Well my shortest way forward was down a tunnel in the front line: we had a block in the tunnel, anyway at last we got out and I saw a sight I don't want to see again. There had been a crowd outside and a shell had burst, such mutilation was bloody awful. Then I went over the top and saw scenes just like the Somme films, huge mine craters, lines of prisoners coming back, signallers and wires all over the place, above aeroplanes with their hooters and lights, in front the intense barrage and curtain of MG fire, frightful row, and behind, the tanks. I never saw such an impressive sight: they came out over the hill out of the morning mist, slowly creeping. I needn't go on, you've seen the tank films. The tank officer was out in front of the tank guiding it on the best way. The sights of wounded etc. and bits of Hun blown up in the mines were bloody. Everyone did well, the whole line surged forward and won the ridge and well beyond it so that in the afternoon I was back with advanced Battalion HQ in a German dugout. I was going to get souvenirs and could have done by the hundred but I can't send them home, so what's the use.

I saw about 60 tanks altogether. My old Sandhurst tunic I lent to Lt Turner who was wounded badly. A sergeant and I got our tunics and two old poles and we rigged up a sort of stretcher (a trick I learnt in the Scouts). We got Turner some distance like this. At last we got a stretcher and I gave the tunic to him as a pillow forgetting that I probably would not see it again, so I've lost it. I lost my compass, fountain pen, pocket book, some letters. Luckily I took out my cheque book and advance Field Pay Book so I am alright. Please send my other tunic I have at home, also a whistle and lanyard as soon as possible. If Dad has an old Pocket Book he might send it too. The poor little magnifying glass has also gone west.

I have never spent such a long morning in my life and I don't want another battle either. With the continuous shelling, sights, want of sleep, responsibility etc. one feels very, very tired and shaken. The Huns came over in hundreds. I hope this is alright telling you all this. Anyway I thank God I came through alright as a good many others do too.

In the spring of 1917 rehearsals had begun for the Battle of Messines in June.

We marched for two days into the back area near St Omer. The contours of the ground where we rehearsed were similar to the Messines ridge but none of the Generals seemed to realise how our advance would be affected by the mine craters after they had been blown.

To put that into context, behind the actual front-line mine shafts were being dug by the Royal Engineers under no man's land to a point beneath strongly defended positions in the enemy lines. 'But the Germans were also "playing mole" and mining under us – we could hear them. Daily checks by Royal Engineer officers reassured us as to how far they had got.'

This was all a prelude to the Battle of Messines, fought and won by the British Second Army under General Sir Herbert Plumer. The preparation for this had begun as long before as June 1916 with the digging of shafts as part of a plan which was not executed then. A year later, on 4 June 1917, it did begin with an intense bombardment of the German lines, a bombardment which continued until 02.50 on the morning of the 7th. By this time 100,000 British, Australian and New Zealand infantrymen were lying in position on a clear moonlit night waiting for the signal to advance. The sudden silence after four days of constant bombardment unnerved the Germans who began firing flares in an effort see what was happening. They were soon to find out for after twenty minutes of waiting a huge explosion rent the air, followed by eighteen more explosions which devastated the German front-line defences and killed huge numbers of German soldiers. Then the barrage began again, this time a creeping barrage which covered the British troops as they secured the Messines Ridge, supported by tanks, cavalry patrols and aircraft. The success of the assault was in large part due to the explosion of nineteen mines in the Royal Engineers' tunnels – explosions heard back in England. This was not surprising given the size of the charges placed in the tunnels which ranged from 14,900lb to a massive 95,600lb. The craters produced by each exploding mine were up to 260 feet in diameter. In fact several mines failed to explode and one has still to detonate.

Casualties on both sides were high in the battle: 7,354 German prisoners were taken; 10,000 were reported missing and over 6,000 died. British casualties were far from light with 24,562 men killed, wounded or missing with half of these casualties being Australians and New Zealanders of II ANZAC corps. Fifty years later Hal wrote an account of that terrible day.

Before zero hour we ordered everyone to crawl out of the trenches into no man's land because it was expected that the mines would demolish the breastworks and bury the occupants. The Germans had not expected our attack on the 7th June – they thought it would be later. So all was quiet. But precisely at zero hour about sunrise the mines were blown. What a fantastic sight it was. Like the eruption of a volcano. Great curtains of scarlet and purple flame, smoke, debris and earth soared upwards hundreds of feet and then the artillery and machine gun barrages opened up. It was said to be the most intense artillery concentration of the whole war and that was saying something.

The 16th Irish Division went forward on schedule with the Ulster Division on our right. But we got held up by the huge mine craters with their lips 20 or 30 feet high and had to go round them. It was the first time we had seen tanks in action. It was an unforgettable sight to see them coming out of the mist and smoke with their sleeve valve engines pouring oil smoke astern and their guns spitting flame and fury. They had a hard time negotiating shell holes and I saw at least one on fire.

The Mk IV tank used at Messines was more comfortable than the earlier versions and was equipped with Lewis guns and the armour had been upgraded to withstand current German armour-piercing rounds. There was a crew of an officer and seven men but they could travel at no more than 2 mph. The so-called males were equipped with two 6–pounder guns and four Lewis guns whilst females were equipped with six Lewis guns. Female tanks were lighter than males. By the end of the war tank technology had developed to a point where it was decided that they should be both male and female (that is equipped with both heavy armament and lighter machine guns) after which the terms were discontinued.

As the day wore on and the lines of the barrages lifted we were mistakenly shelled by naval guns from the coast. Follow up units came through us and we consolidated a sort of a line in case the enemy counter attacked. We spent that night in the old German lines. Their dugouts built in concrete on piles were much better than ours. They had that strange cheese like German smell and vibrated when shells fell near giving a drumming effect on the ears. There were several alarms during the night. By morning we were all pretty tired after sleepless nights and I suppose the effects of being so close to the artillery barrages.

*

The Battle of Messines ended on 14 June. On 31 July the rains came. It rained day and night for weeks on end, it seemed, turning the shell-torn ground into a great slimy bog in which men drowned and guns and vehicles disappeared. The 6th Battalion was by now very under-strength and it was used on casualty evacuation duties and also to relieve units in the front line for a short while before being brought back behind Ypres for a short rest before repeating the performance. Actually there was no recognisable front line, just a rough line of occupied shell holes, and there was nothing to be done but crouch down in them in the pouring rain hoping for the best. The rum ration saved the day.

We used to crawl round to each shell hole at dawn with a couple of men and the rum jar. For food we had the bully beef and biscuits from our iron rations. The biscuits were like the old dog biscuits about four inches square and thick. It took a long time to eat one biscuit but that passed the time. Just to vary the treatment German low flying aircraft machine gunned us at intervals.

Moving into or out of the line, the infantry used the paved Ypres–Menin road. But off the road the men sank in the mud. Wrecked vehicles, dead horses and corpses littered the verges and the smell was 'not pleasant'. Marching on the road it was a question of whether to go fast or slow because, in either case, one might be just where a shell burst, for the Germans shelled it continually and the battalion suffered many more casualties. Hal admitted to being lucky not to be wounded himself but 'owing to a lack of green vegetables I had a series of boils, some very painful, especially one in the nostril which our excellent doctor lanced in the front line while his orderly held my head between his knees'.

With the increasing losses the battalion was so understrength that they were moved south to occupy positions opposite the famous Hindenburg line. The heavy casualties the German Army incurred on the Western Front as a result of the fighting on the Somme induced them in September 1916 to shorten their defensive lines and thus save manpower by withdrawing to a newly-prepared position in the rear of the Somme battlegrounds. Constructed between late September 1916 and March 1917, vast quantities of materials and manpower, including the forced labour of civilians and Russian prisoners, were used in the Hindenburg Line's building. When they withdrew to it the Germans left behind every sort of booby trap and many more casualties resulted.

Hal's final duty into no man's land was to guide several individuals (male or female he never knew, disguised as they were). 'I wished them good luck as they left me to go through the German lines at a quiet spot and then on to carry out whatever task they had bravely volunteered to do.'

*

After Messines Hal had applied to be seconded to the Royal Flying Corps. He was called for interview and on 5 September 1917 his posting came through. He returned to England for air training via the RFC's Headquarters at Hesdin in the Pas de Calais, a focal point for all RFC operations in France as a support base. There is no indication in surviving correspondence or memoirs as to why Hal made the decision to join the RFC. Could it have been that one trip in a Rumpety at Sandhurst that spiked his interest? Or was it the air activity over the trenches that he had seen which made him begin to think that service in the air would be preferable to enduring more of the war on the ground? He had been exceptionally lucky to have survived a year on active service at the front, for the average life of a second lieutenant was literally a matter of days over the whole period of the First World War. Perhaps it was a realisation that the longer he was a soldier the less his chances of survival. Being an airman certainly wouldn't mean immunity from death but there was a perception that the odds of survival were greater.

Or perhaps it was simply a desire to be a part of this exciting new form of warfare as many of those of Hal's generation thought.

Chapter Five

No.20 Squadron

'The family were rather horrified that I had volunteered to join the Royal Flying Corps,' wrote Hal. 'But it was my decision and led in after years to a long career in the Royal Air Force. I should explain that I was seconded, that is lent by the Army [i.e. the Royal Irish Regiment] to the RFC. In 1917 officers seconded had to start their flying career as observers so that the Service could benefit from their war experience. Those surviving six months on active service with the RFC were then released to train as pilots if they were still fit.'

After passing medical examinations and a short leave Hal completed a course at the No.1 School of Military Aeronautics at Reading, a training school for the RFC which was formed in 1915 as an instructors' college but expanded in 1916 into a full training school for cadet pilot and observer training. Here they were taught theoretical aspects of flight including map reading, gunnery and mechanics. For the observers the school had a room mocked up for artillery observation with a light-studded map painted onto the floor and a mock fuselage hanging from the ceiling. At Reading Hal was issued with his flying kit which consisted of a leather helmet and goggles, leather coat and gauntlet gloves and thigh-length fleece-lined rubber-soled flying boots, this type of clothing being essential given the open cockpits of the day. Aircrew all rubbed castor oil into the leather to take the new look off and thus give the perception of experience rather than being a novice! Flying pay was now added to their 7/6d a day and they also received rations in kind and were entitled to free accommodation and rail travel.

From Reading Hal's course moved to Hythe near Folkestone where the No.1 (Observer) School of Aerial Gunnery was based in the Imperial Hotel which the RFC had taken over in its entirety, including the staff. It provided accommodation for 170 officers ('what a contrast this was

No.1 (Observer) School of Aerial Gunnery Course, Hythe, October 1917.

to life in the trenches') whilst other ranks were billeted in the town. The school was responsible for the training of RFC, Royal Artillery and other observers, the subjects taught including aerial fighting, photography and map reading from the air. Ground and sea ranges belonging to the school were established on the coast between Hythe and Dymchurch. All on Hal's course were familiar with the Lewis machine gun which they would be operating in the air but they had to train in the use of a special sight 'to allow for the movement of our own and the enemy aeroplanes while the bullets were in their flight'. They flew in the Royal Aircraft Factory R.E.7 (designed as a light bomber and reconnaissance aircraft) after which they wrote recce reports: and the Vickers F.B.5 Gun Bus, armed with a single Lewis gun operated by the observer in the front of the nacelle, for air firing training against targets floating in the sea and those towed by other aircraft. The observer had no safety harness in the Vickers (or in the Bristol Fighter, which Hal flew in later in France). 'In aerobatics one had to just hold on jolly tight. Centrifugal force helped to keep one in when looping.' Aircrew had no parachutes; only observers in kite balloons had them and they were of the static line type.

Hythe 1917. Second Lieutenants Crowe and Woods.

Hythe 1917. Royal Aircraft Factory R.E.7.

Hythe 1917. Hal and a pusher-prop Vickers Gunbus. The engine is a 100 hp Gnome Monosoupape 9-cylinder rotary.

On 28 November 1917 Hal was posted to No.20 Squadron in France (it was to be the highest-scoring squadron of the First World War with 620 victories) and he was thrilled at the prospect. The squadron had formed on 1 September 1915 at Netheravon, moving shortly afterwards to Filton and then on 16 January 1916 it flew across the Channel in its

The course at Hythe operated from other Kent airfields. This is Dymchurch aerodrome 'taken from the fort'.

F.E.2a aircraft to Clairmarais, operating in the fighter-reconnaissance role. By the time Hal joined the squadron it had converted to the Bristol F.E.2b and was based at Ste Marie Cappel near Cassel behind the front where just a couple of months previously he had been serving in the infantry. The Bristol F.E.2b was:

> a splendid new 2-seater fighter with a Rolls Royce engine. Like all aircraft at that time it was made of wood with metal fittings and undercarriage and wire bracing. Covering was of best Irish linen sewn on and tightened with dope.

It was often simply called the Bristol Fighter or, more popularly, the Brisfit. Despite being a two-seater it was an agile aircraft, able to hold its own against opposing single-seat fighters, and so solid was its design that it remained in military service into the 1930s. Armament consisted of a Vickers machine gun firing forward through the propeller actuated by Constantinescu oil-pressure gear and a Lewis gun mounted on a Scarff ring for the observer. A few double gun mountings were later issued for the Lewis guns.

> All aerodromes were grass fields. No thought of runways in those days. Ste Marie Cappel was large enough to operate four squadrons. We lived in Nissen huts and had individual messes. We were most comfortable with linen sheets and pillow slips. Everything was kept clean by one batman per hut. The aeroplanes were housed in canvas hangars camouflaged beside the aerodrome and had to be manhandled on to the airfield for flight. Engine changes were carried out by the squadron but any major repairs had to be done at the Aircraft Depot at St Omer. Offices, the armoury, photo section, bomb and ammunition stores and transport were of course necessities. Leyland lorries and Crossley tenders made up the unit's transport.

During the wet winter of 1917 No.20 Squadron was employed on offensive patrols, usually flown at about 17,000 feet and designed

The Royal Flying Corps in 1917, somewhere on the Western Front. Top row: seven B.E.2s and a R.E.7. 2nd row: eight B.E.2s. 3rd row: three Shorthorns. 4th row: one unknown, two Avro 504s and four Bleriots. 5th row: seven Caudrons.

No.20 Squadron at Ste Marie Cappel aerodrome in November 1917. Hal is sitting on the chair on the extreme right.

to establish Allied air superiority, thereby giving some protection to reconnaissance and artillery observation aircraft flying at lower altitudes. They seldom did more than one high-flying sortie a day but when the squadron later switched to low-flying attacks in March and April 1918 they did as many sorties as possible, aircraft flying at daybreak to the aerodrome at Bruay, west of Lens, from where operations were conducted, returning to Ste Marie Cappel at dusk. Hal quickly put his training into practice in the Brisfit, operating the rear gun, navigating by map, operating the camera for vertical photos, compiling recce reports and dropping 20lb and 112lb bombs (when carried). Bomb dropping was not normally a function of a fighter squadron as they had no bomb-sights so the bombs were simply released as the target was seen to pass under the leading edge of the lower mainplane. If aircraft became embroiled in a fight before they reached the target area they always released the bomb because of the danger of it exploding while still on the bomb rack if hit by enemy fire. Hal also had to learn some rudimentary flying skills as there was a joystick in his cockpit and a rudder control which would enable the observer to get the aeroplane down in emergency, which usually meant if the pilot was incapacitated. Having mastered all these skills, before observers could wear the coveted 'Flying O' badge they had to complete so many hours flying (or serve six weeks with a squadron) and to have had at least two successful air combats. In addition they had to pass a practical exam demonstrating their memorising of a map of enemy aerodromes in a proscribed area. On top of this the observer's CO had to recommend that he be awarded the badge.

Each evening the squadron commander (Major E.H. Johnson) arranged the flying programme for the following day with the flight commanders. Pilots would be with the fitters and riggers in the hangars and observers would be overhauling their guns and magazines in the armoury. Before flight, crews were briefed for the operation. Then aircraft usually took off individually and formed up as they climbed to operating height. Squadron and flight commanders wore coloured streamers on their struts to identify them.

The prevailing wind over northern France was from the west which was always a danger as in a dogfight aircraft were apt to get blown far over the enemy lines and consequently not always have fuel enough left to reach their side of the lines again. Pilots and observers each kept a continuous lookout for enemy aircraft. An enemy diving on you from the direction of the sun was often not seen or spotted until you saw his tracer or heard the crack of bullets. A much quoted mantra was 'Beware the Hun in the Sun'.

When the squadron's leader decided to attack he gave a pre-arranged signal and dived on the enemy firing his front gun. Then as he turned away to repeat the attack his observer perhaps engaged the enemy with *his* gun. Hal graphically described this type of air tactic as one that

> would be carried out as opportunity presented itself. By then both our own and the enemy formations would get split up and the whole would develop into a dogfight. It was often very

difficult for the observer in a scrap of this sort. For a start guns often developed stoppages during firing and this might force us to withdraw from the fight to clear the trouble. Also it was often bitterly cold in the open cockpits with the wind howling around us and communication between me and my pilot was impossible as we had no intercom and your voice couldn't be heard above the noise. So observers used to hit the pilot over the head to draw attention to anything! Most dangerous of all, the aeroplane would be flown into steep turns with excessive increases in the forces of gravity which often forced one down on one's knees on the floor of the cockpit. With no safety harness and an open cockpit one had to hold on tight with one hand to the gun mounting to avoid being thrown out. One small observer I knew *was* thrown out to the top of the fuselage but was able to climb on board again.

After the dogfight the formation would reform and aircraft were counted (there might well be somebody missing). If fuel was running short the CO would decide to return to base. If needed, aircraft would land for fuel at a forward aerodrome and damaged aircraft might have to land to be checked over. Those who made it back would be debriefed in the Operations Room. Claims for enemy aircraft shot down were not allowed unless confirmed by at least one other crew. Damage and casualties and troubles with guns or engines would be discussed and action taken. Later any air photos would be shown after processing to the crews concerned.

On 10 December 1917 Hal excitedly wrote home:

Well I had my first trip over the lines … today. (I shan't give details of anything so that I shan't be giving away information.) My machine was alone, we dived at a Hun (the pilot using his gun) when the Hun split – and before we knew where we were we had three Huns of terrific colours on our tail. I fired a whole drum of ammunition into the nearest chap. All this time we were splitting and stunting. At last we got away. We did a vertical dive from 14,000 ft. to 3,000ft at 300 miles an hour [sic]. They didn't follow probably thinking they had done us in. The whole flight did not take 2 minutes. I honestly enjoyed it immensely, it was topping. The wind was terrific in the big dive.

We afterwards found that our tail had been shot about a bit and a few missed the petrol tank. I am looking forward to the next scrap. Owing to mist and the dive into the clouds I couldn't see if I had hit the Hun and downed him. I don't think I have given away anything in telling you this.

Second Lieutenant Cooke was Hal's pilot on this occasion as he was four days later when, on his second operational sortie, the squadron was suddenly dived on by three Albatros fighters, all painted in startling colours. ('German pilots were allowed to paint their fighters in this manner hoping to scare their opponents rather like Red Indians painting their faces and bodies with their war paint.') On this occasion they only did slight damage to the tail-plane of his aircraft and they escaped unscathed too. 'I failed to hit any of them,' Hal bemoaned.

In January 1918 cold weather set in. Pilots and observers suffered from frostbitten faces and hands and to help prevent this they rubbed in whale oil and then smeared on Vaseline. The guns often froze too and the observers fired short bursts at intervals to try to keep them free. Even with the radiator shutters tight shut and lots of revs it was very difficult to keep engines warm enough when descending to give the necessary power. And blood coming back into the hands when descending could be excruciatingly painful.

13 January 1918:

Well I have just come down from a most successful time. In plain language we got a Hun. This is officially (my first) but unofficially my second as my last crashed but we did not claim it so we didn't get it credited to us. This afternoon we saw a beautiful white fat Hun nosing around in the mist, so we dove on him, the pilot firing his gun. The Hun circled round to the left with

No.20 Squadron: Second Lieutenants Cooke and Crowe.

smoke coming out of him: my gun got in a burst of a whole drum and presently we had the satisfaction of seeing him crash to the ground on fire. We got Archied like anything after this but the pilot split and zoomed about so that we arrived back safely. You can't imagine how bucked we were, so we looped and stunted out of sheer light heartedness. The scrap only lasted about three minutes.

(Archie was anti-aircraft (AA) fire. There are two explanations as to where the term originated. Firstly that Archie was the 'A' (A for Archie) in the contemporary phonetic alphabet used by the British Army; secondly that a British pilot reacted to enemy anti-aircraft fire by singing the chorus from a popular music-hall song of the day called *Archibald Certainly Not*. This caught on and was inevitably shortened to Archie.)

22 January 1918:

Well today I had another topping scrap. We got over the lines (somewhere) about 11 am. We were meeting some other machines and with these up came about twenty Huns [flying Albatros scouts]. They got up to within about 40 yards of me before I saw they were Huns – I suddenly saw the iron crosses on their heavily camouflaged wings. I got the old gun going. I hadn't time even to nudge the pilot, telling him the Huns were near. When he heard the gun going he banked and split. Well there was a great scrap, Huns and our machines doing individual scraps. I was switching the gun all round the place and fired about 130 rounds into him when he suddenly went topsy-turvy and so down, completely out of control. My pilot then saw one beneath him all on its own and dived. At the same time another Hun got near us. I gave him a burst and he sheared off. The Hun my pilot dived at burst into flames and crashed in Hunland [east of Moorslede]. I then saw a Hun downing one of our machines and fired at long range but the gun broke (I had a broken return spring). Suddenly a Hun dived at our tail. I barged the pilot and signalled this startling bit of intelligence to him. He dived and I pointed the broken gun at the Hun and do you know he actually cleared off and we got over our lines to remedy broken parts. So I guess this old Hun had the wind up all right. These Huns were painted all the colours imaginable. Later on in the morning my pilot and myself were all alone as we lost the others in the scrap and we got high above us another Hun. I fired with the mended gun but he funked scrapping and dived for his own lines. Later on we came home. It's been the best and most sporting scrap I've had and we all heartily enjoyed it. We got umpteen Huns and they got only one of our boys, so who says we're losing the war eh?

Well now, to turn from the battles in the air to a more quiet mode of amusement. We have a most topping concert party here belonging to the Division. They give a very good show and two of them make very excellent girls. Their togs cost from 20 guineas upwards so they do it in style. They have limelights and all the usual theatrical effects and properties, really a topping good show.

There were plenty of opportunities for recreation. No.20 Squadron had four horses which officers took turns to ride. The handling of the reins was thought to be somewhat similar to flying the rather sensitive First World War fighter aeroplanes! There was also table tennis and physical training exercises in a large hut. On non-flying days visits to other squadrons were both valuable and good fun. 'On one of these visits I remember seeing the first jazz band drums being played by an American,' said Hal who always enjoyed music and theatre. Transport was provided for sampling the fleshpots of St Omer and Cassel. Each flight commander saw to it that the 'other ranks' were well looked after too. A large wooden building was used at Ste Marie Cappel as a cinema and theatre. The latest Charlie Chaplin films from Hollywood were seen, even before they reached London. Army concert parties composed of professional actors, but no actresses, presented popular shows and sang the latest hits from the London theatres. But such diversions were only temporary and the reality of the war soon re-established itself.

On 23 January 1918 Hal was awarded his Observer's wings and was appointed Flying Officer (Observer) RFC. (Hal's Army service record shows that they had promoted him to lieutenant in his absence on the 19th). Five days later the squadron Operational Record Book records another victory when Hal shot down a triplane which he watched cork-screwing to the ground near Albert completely out of control.

In March 1918 a series of major offensives broke the stalemate of trench warfare on the Western Front. The German spring offensives which began on 21 March 1918 involved sixty German divisions attacking along a fifty-mile front between St Quentin and Arras. They penetrated British defences on the Somme and in some places they advanced almost forty miles – quite remarkable after three years of virtually stationary trench warfare. The British Army retreated over a wide front and all fighter squadrons were at once switched to ground

Two 112lb bombs exploding on German line near Armentières.

attacks, dropping 20lb bombs and machine gunning the advancing enemy.

Surviving letters from Hal to his parents tell the story of the spring of 1918 from his perspective, beginning with 28 March 1918:

I saw some English papers lately and one would think by them that we were losing the war. Well we're not so you can take it from me we're not losing at all. By the way I've been having a priceless time lately shooting at Hun infantry and cavalry etc. Also dropping the odd egg on the beggars. But it's a bigger strain on us than usual high flying. Cooke is on leave at present so I've been flipping with Lindup, a very good chap. In my Bristol Fighter we had just attacked some cavalry who were in the open country when tracer bullets streamed up at us. A few hit the cockpits but did not wound us. Suddenly we were enveloped in steam. The radiator had been hit and we just managed to make a 'drome near the lines [it was Marieux] before the engine seized. We thought the machine was on fire. Retreating soldiers crowded round us. They had thrown away their arms and were thoroughly demoralised and seemed to be on the point of hooking it so we prepared to burn the machine, but they didn't hook it in the end. Officers were trying to hold them and get them to stop and eat their rations. That night enemy bombers bombed us and added to the confusion. Dumps of ammunition could be seen being blown up and the flickering light of star shells showed how near we were to the front. It was a startling experience to see men so much at the end of their tether. With the help of a tank fitter we got the radiator repaired and eventually landed back at Ste Marie Cappel to find that we had been posted as missing so they were astounded when we arrived back safely. I don't think I'm giving away any information by telling you this.

Hal said quite a lot in his letters at times which seemed to escape the censor's eye! On 27 March No.20 Squadron was set upon by three bright red triplanes over Cambrai, part of Baron von Richthofen's circus, and got badly shot up. Hal was short of ammunition having expended it on ground targets during the low-level sortie but nevertheless got in a few bursts at them.

> We attacked some Fokker triplanes since the last adventure, Lindup got one then we had three on our tail, they were all bright red and belonged to Baron von Richthofen's bunch, hellish nutty they were. I gave two of them what they wanted but they beat it and didn't crash that I could see, but one stuck to us, we split about like anything, my gun jammed so I had to watch this chap coming up at us with tracer spitting out of his machine going all round me. I could hear the bullets hitting the machine and I wondered if I was hit or if I would wake up and find I was dead. At last he stopped firing (we were now about 500 feet up) and came up right beside us, so close that I could see the pilot's face, with a clean shaven big mouth, goggles and all. He must have come up to see if we were dead or not.
>
> We got back to our 'drome [Bruay] OK. The machine was a bit shot about, but both of us were unhit. We got a tyre punctured, two struts shot through, aileron controls shattered, main spars of bottom planes shot away, one rudder control gone, one flying wire gone and some cross members of the fuselage smashed (all by bullets). One set of bullets came in through the ring of the mounting, past me and through the floor. It sounds bad but we were very lucky and gave them by far the worst of it.

The Brisfit had to be written off but it said much for the design that it could stand such punishment. 29 March 1918:

> I enclose a cutting from *The Times* giving the official version of this big battle in which we had our scrap and had the pleasure in firing at Boche infantry and cavalry and artillery etc. It was fine being able to dive on the Huns to about 400 feet firing all

the time, seeing them scatter and fall. I got one priceless burst of fire at about 40 Hun cavalry on a road. They simply went hell for leather galloping like smoke and I'm pleased to say the whole 40 did not gallop away. The cutting says that Baron von Richthofen achieved his 69th and 70th aerial victories. He darned nearly achieved his 71st! His 71st would have been me in the scrap with his old red triplane, but all the same the aforesaid gentleman must have got a lot of holes in him and lost a few of his pilots I guess. There's no doubt we the RFC cleared the sky of Hun planes and absolutely have superiority over him in the air. As you see by the papers, the King sent a special message of congratulation to the RAF on its work. [Somebody here is pre-empting the formation of the RAF by a couple of days. It didn't officially happen until 1 April 1918.] Of course as you can see by the papers the war in the battle zone is open warfare and travelling as fast as we do it seems like a huge cinema picture with artillery simply firing in the open. In short we are having a simply priceless time but it is rather a strain on the pilots.

30 March 1918:

I've just returned from another little show. This time we got a lot of Archie in an oil tank and got covered with oil of the thickest blackest variety, lovely! We managed to make an aerodrome and they sent us a new tank and some Air Mechanics to put it in. Luckily the engine did not seize. This is the third mishap to me and Lindup in three days. So I guess now that we've had three that will finish it. Anyway I hope so. Cheers.

But on 2 April there was another. While on an evening patrol at about 15,000 feet in perfectly clear weather with not a sign of trouble Major Dennistoun, Hal's pilot (who was also his flight commander), had forgotten vigilance was key and was flying on a straight and level course.

Suddenly a German anti-aircraft shell burst just below us with a huge zonk and close enough for the black smoke to be smelt. It was a lucky shot but German gunners were good and had good predictor instruments. Immediately the machine was seething in petrol and so were we, both tanks having been ripped open. The major held his head to the side of the machine to avoid being gassed. He switched the fuel supply off and we went into a steep dive, turning and twisting violently as we did and made it to our side of the lines with a barrage of AA shells following us. We saw a ploughed field which we decided to land in, so we glided down to this. The prop stopped and we did a small pancake on to the field. She ran a few yards then quietly, gracefully tipped up on her nose to the vertical then settled backwards to about 60 degrees. (This was my first actual crash landing.) We got out with the Lewis gun in double quick time.

Neither of us were hit, hurt or thrown out. Of course immediately we were surrounded by a battalion of infantry who were in rest nearby. But German artillery had seen our landing and got the range accurately, destroying the aeroplane in minutes. We found on examination that both tanks were hit and also the engine. This was quite an exceptionally good stroke of luck for the Archie people. Eventually we went home in a staff car.

On 10 April 1918 the Germans launched a second major attack. Subsequently known as the Battle of the Lys, they came over at dawn in thick mist against an Allied line running for twenty-five miles south from a point east of Ypres. This front was held by the Belgians in the far north, by the British Second Army in the north and centre and by the British First Army in the south. The latter was a relatively weak force including two divisions of the undermanned Portuguese Expeditionary Corps which was due to be replaced the day of the German attack. Morale was low in the Portuguese ranks and when the attack came they were overrun and withdrew from the fight, losing 7,000 men killed and wounded in the process. Hal was far less charitable. 'They ran,' he said.

Shellfire over the battlefield.

But it was thick mist and fog all day and we could do nothing to help. But the next day was clear and we did as many low flying sorties as possible. I had to map the position of the enemy advance along miles of front for Second Army Headquarters. We flew low enough to see blood on the faces of the wounded. At the big locomotive repair depot near Hazebrouck we saw engines being blown up. Quite a sight. The situation became chaotic and it looked as if the Germans would be able to advance to the Channel Ports of Boulogne and Calais. On the evening of the 12th Ste Marie Cappel was being shelled and we were ordered to fly to an aerodrome further west [Boisdinghem]. We all took off individually in the gathering dusk. It was too dark to read a map and we had no night flying lights but I had marched when in the infantry along the road from St Omer to Boisdinghem, closer to the coast in the Pas de Calais. We flew low along this road and were the only crew to land at our destination that night. When I say land we hit the ground hard and did some terrific bounces before stopping. The Bristol undercarriage had a good test that night.

Chapter Six

The Royal Air Force

'On April 1st 1918 the Royal Naval Air Service and Royal Flying Corps were combined to form one flying Service to be called the Royal Air Force. It took us a long time to get used to this change but Parliament had decided.'

The squadron continued to fly low-level sorties from Boisdinghem until Hal left on 13 May 1918. It was an eventful month for him. In his record of service book, entries made by his CO, Major Johnson, are brief in words but tell succinctly of Hal's successes after 28 March. The book also tells of Hal's promotion to lieutenant on 22 April 1918. (RAF ranks were not introduced until 1 August 1919.)

21–4–18	*Albatros Scout.*	*Out of control north of Wervicq*
3–5–18	*Triplane.*	*In flames south east of Hollebeke*
3–5–18	*Albatros Scout.*	*Out of control south east of Ypres*
8–5–18	*Triplane.*	*Crashed north of Wervicq*

Lieut Crowe especially good at reconnaissance.

Hal's letters home fill in some of the gaps. 15 April 1918:

Well I suppose you have seen in the paper about the Hun doing a push up my way and in a part of the country I know so well from having been there in the infantry. I have been very busy lately and had a special mission the other day locating the Huns. We had to go over at 400 feet in mist and rain. It was very bumpy indeed and we could feel the thud of field guns and shells at that height quite distinctly. We were so low at one point of our flight that one could see the blood on a man's face who was being carried away. At one place Cooke managed to help a platoon of ours in its attack by machine gunning the Huns they were attacking. I bet the Hun was using all the swear words he knew. A few days later Cooke and I had to do another mission low down but this time in clear weather. We saw the battle as one sees it in the cinema. Huns and our men in the open, a stretcher here and there, houses on fire and in the background towns in flames gushing forth great columns of dense black smoke. Here and there our shells would blow up a Hun dump so that a sheet of smoke and flame would go up like nothing on earth. A most wonderful panorama. While low flying the same day we got some hot machine-gun fire from the ground and our radiator was shot through (but we made our aerodrome). An explosive bullet burst in the cockpit, a small piece of which gave me a tiny wound on the leg. The windscreen got a bullet burst on it and was smashed but being Triplex glass it didn't break. The machine is to be rebuilt before further use. We fought four Huns as well that day and they went hell for leather away when we started firing. That day I did five shows and we all felt like fifty years old that evening. I think it's all right to tell you these experiences as I am not giving away any information by so doing.

22 April 1918:

While flying we recently ran into three snow storms but got out of them alright and didn't get lost. While photographing the other day we had a fine scrap with Albatros scouts with bright blue wings and bright gambooze [sic] tails and fuselages [possibly gambooge, a greenish yellow colour]. I kept on taking pictures and during the scrap I got a photo of seven of the Huns underneath us. I may be able to get a copy, possibly from the Photo Officer. We dived on one chap and he turned on his back and tail slid slowly into the ground so that adds another to our list of Huns. Cooke got this with his gun. I was too busy with the camera. The same day we met twelve Fokker triplanes, all black, but they went away after a short shoot and we were too far over to follow. I fired at them in turn, 300 rounds in all just to sting them up and break up their formation. I see that Richthofen has at last been brought down on our side. He certainly was a fine chap. I see that his machines are always painted red and so that must have been him that Lindrup and I scrapped down in the Cambrai battle.

25 April 1918:

The CO has just been in to congratulate Cooke and myself on our each getting the MC. So we are celebrating this tonight. All well. We are very bucked etc. over it.

The award was gazetted three months later on 26 July 1918, the day Hal was at Buckingham Palace to receive it from King George V.

Lt Henry George Crowe, R.Ir.Regt and RAF. For conspicuous gallantry and devotion to duty when taking part in many low flying bombing raids and reconnaissance as an observer. On every occasion he brought back very accurate and valuable information. On three occasions his machine was shot down by enemy fire, but he continued his work, and his great fearlessness and fine spirit have been an invaluable example to others. He has taken part in several air combats and been responsible for the destruction of many hostile machines.

'He spoke to me in a gruff Teutonic voice,' Hal later recalled, 'and asked how long I had been flying and wished me luck. None of the family were able to be present as war time travel to and from Ireland was difficult.'

4 May 1918:

We went on another show in the afternoon in which I brought down a triplane in flames. Cooke got an Albatross in the morning out of control. Our patrol ran into some triplanes in the afternoon and we started business. I had fired about 250 rounds at various people just to keep them at a safe distance when one cheeky beggar (painted green on the top plane, bright blue on the centre plane and green on the bottom plane and fuselage) came up very near. I gave him about thirty rounds (taking about one and a half seconds to give him them) and he immediately went down in a straight dive (evidently in trouble and hoping to reach earth in time). When he was about 5,000 feet off the earth we saw a flash of flame from him which then went out. He burst into flame again just before crashing to earth, then again he burst up in a flare (evidently petrol tanks bursting). After seeing him crash we turned again and were joined by umpteen of our scouts and together we drove the remaining bunch way over until it was time we finished our patrol. It was a most successful day for us as well as the squadron. The total was something like six Huns down during the day to our bunch alone, let alone other bunches. So you see we have the Huns cold meat in the air – for example, the Hun's patrol which is meant to stop us coming over we simply passed over them yesterday (ignoring them), did what we had to do far over, then on our way back we still saw the patrol so we dived and chewed the patrol into cold meat, five of the patrol of Huns being driven down, no losses to us. Our infantry must have seen this scrap so I hope it bucked up the poor devils. That means my 7th officially.

6 May 1918:

Lately Cooke and I have been taking photos. I work the camera and take the photos and direct Cooke. He simply works the machine and keeps his eyes open. Lately we took a continuous series of overlapping photos of a stretch of country thirty miles in length, luckily with no breaks in it at all. We got congratulated by the Wing Colonel and Brigadier on the remarkable series and managed to be mentioned in the Intelligence Summaries for it. The CO was bucked as it gets the squadron a good name. I have done 130 hours over enemy lines now.

*

By May 1918 Hal had been on the squadron for six months and his CO agreed it was time to put him forward for pilot training. But a certain amount of subterfuge had to be used to get Hal back to England, for the only way was to be evacuated via hospital. So it was that Hal became a patient in No.24 General Hospital at Étaples, a so-called base hospital, part of the casualty evacuation chain farther back from the front line than the casualty clearing stations, and which Hal had previously encountered on his way out to join the 6th Battalion in 1916. The siting of these hospitals was critical. They needed to be close to a railway line so that casualties could be brought easily to them (although some also came by canal barge). They also needed to be near a port where men could be evacuated for longer-term treatment in Britain. At their busiest during the offensive the extensive group of buildings that made up Étaples hospital catered for a remarkable 22,000 casualties.

From Étaples Hal was speedily transferred to the RAF Hospital at Hampstead where he was passed fit for pilot training. Whilst waiting for this to begin he stayed with his uncle George at Didsbury on leave, which was great fun and the perfect antithesis to life on the front.

How we sang all the musical comedy numbers round the piano in the evenings. The songs included *Oh What a Lovely War*, *If You Were The Only Girl in The World*, numbers from *The Maid Of The Mountain* and *Chu Chin Chow*. I saw the latter show every time I was on leave – I must have seen it six times and it ran for years. There were various adaptations to some of the songs which being rather vulgar could not be sung in front of the ladies!

An AD Flying Boat designed by the Admiralty's Air Department to serve as a patrol aircraft with the RNAS. Hal probably saw N1522 at Felixstowe while he was stationed just up the Suffolk coast at Orfordness.

When the date of Hal's pilot's course came through it wasn't until August 1918 and would mean a return to Reading where he had begun his observer training with the No.1 School of Military Aeronautics the year before. Until then he was posted to the Aircraft and Armament Experimental Establishment at Orfordness on the east coast of England. It had been decided that the single Lewis gun in the rear cockpits of fighters and bombers did not produce sufficient firepower and should be duplicated, thus allowing for stoppages in one gun and bringing down more enemy aircraft. Rotatable mountings for two, three or even four Lewis guns had been produced and an observer with recent war experience was asked for to test them and Hal was that man. Various spring-loaded devices to enable the observer to swing the guns against the slipstream at high speed were deciding factors in the tests. Trials were conducted in many of the experimental types of aeroplane available and other factors such as fields of vision were assessed. Trajectories of tracers (incendiary and armour-piercing) and standard .303 ammunition were carefully tested and filmed against ground and air targets under the direction of scientists of the National Physical Laboratory, who also supervised other trials at Orfordness. Hal was involved in these as well as with the first turn and slip indicators to assist flying in clouds and with testing various designs of camouflage painted on the upper surfaces of aircraft. Orfordness was important to the War Office who had bought a large part of it for the RFC in 1913 but had soon acquired the whole area. The Ness is a long shingle spit off the Suffolk coast, separated from the mainland by the River Alde. It can only be reached by ferry from the little town of Orford so was ideal for secretive work such as early experiments in long-range radio navigation and the first purpose-built experiments on radar. In later years the Atomic Weapons Research Establishment had a base on the site and in the 1960s experimental over-the-horizon radar, Cobra Mist, was built on the spit. More recently a powerful medium-wave radio station was used for transmitting BBC World Service programmes. Nowadays, in the twenty first century, the spit is a nature reserve. When the War Office bought the site they built airfields on it and in 1915 the first incumbents were aircraft of the Central Flying School's experimental flying section which moved from Upavon. Many highly significant advances in warfare were made there in those early days and, apart from those Hal was briefly involved in, they also included the testing of parachutes, aerial photography and bomb ballistics.

At the end of August Hal's pilot's course at Reading commenced. Those on the course were all billeted in Reading itself with lectures taking place in the university. Practical rigging of aircraft and the running of all types of engine then in service was conducted in hangars at Wantage where there was an RAF training camp for officer cadets. The lectures covered theory of flight, engines, instruments, wireless (including learning the Morse code up to receiving at 12 words a minute and transmitting at 18), semaphore, compass swinging and navigation. Radio telephone was just being developed at that time but only in one direction – in other words the leader of the formation could transmit only and the other aircraft in the formation could only receive. Morse was used for artillery observation work.

Ealing 1918. The RAF Armament School: Instruction on 'hanging nose pistols'.

From Reading the students moved to Ealing for an armaments course – the RAF's Armament School was at Uxbridge with a detachment in Ealing. Lectures and practical instruction covered all types of bombs, their filling, fusing, loading and their suitability for various types of targets. Bomb-sights were used in an early type of simulation trainer with a moving map which could be stopped when the imaginary bomb was released, enabling accurate use of the sight to be judged. At Ealing Hal was billeted with another officer in great luxury in a house which he discovered in later years was next to his future wife Nora's barrister uncle, Sir William Jarratt.

It was whilst in the middle of a morning lecture at Ealing on 11 November 1918 that news came through that an armistice was about to be declared and, sure enough, at 11 o'clock the sirens gave the 'All Clear'. The students assembled in the dining hall for the CO to make the official announcement.

I remember that in his speech he said we must *not* think that this would be the end of all wars and how right he was for within twenty years we were involved in the Second World War. But for the moment, as people realised that the armistice meant that the war was over, they thronged into London to celebrate. That evening I was in Piccadilly with other chaps.

Ealing 1918: Hal at nearby firing butts at Perivale.

Ealing 1918. Bomb types at the RAF Armament School.

It was raining when suddenly a great wave of cheering came to us and down the street came an open landau with two horses with King George and Queen Mary sitting there in the rain smiling and waving. Immediately behind the landau came a taxi with an officer in his Scottish uniform standing on the roof embracing two chorus girls still in their frilly stage costumes, getting soaked of course! In the theatres the shows could not go on because the audiences danced on the stage with the actors and actresses. It was free drinks everywhere for anyone in uniform. People bathed in the fountains and generally made whoopee.

But after a few days the rowdy elements started playing havoc and London was put out of bounds to all service personnel.

Chapter Seven

Ireland Again

In December 1918 Hal's course ended and he, with some others, moved to the new Collinstown aerodrome, the site of the modern Dublin International Airport, for flying training – in fact it was so new that construction of facilities there was still underway and the hangars were incomplete. Designated No.24 Training Depot Station and specialising in day bombing, it was part of No.3 Training Wing of the RAF. Initial training was carried out on the ubiquitous Avro 504 which Hal recalled fondly in later years as

the finest training aeroplane. The instructor sat in the front seat with a voice pipe to the pupil in the rear seat who did his first solo flight from there. The engine was of a type never seen in later years. Called a rotary engine it was of French design. In it the crankshaft was stationary and the crankcase with cylinders and airscrew attached revolved around the crankshaft. The explosive mixture entered by the crankshaft and the burnt gases were exhausted through a valve in the cylinder head. Castor oil was used to lubricate the engine and it sprayed out of the cylinder head valves covering the fore part of the fuselage and giving a wonderful smell of partly burnt castor oil. Our flying clothing and seat cushions got liberal doses of oil which may have been good for the bowels? To start the engine one shouted 'switch is off, petrol on, suck in'. The mechanic repeated this and swung the propeller round a few turns. Getting the propeller in the right position on compression he would shout 'contact!' The pilot repeated this and switched on. The mechanic then gave the propeller a smart pull down using both hands and stepped aside to

Collinstown. Hangars under construction. Personnel unknown.

avoid being hit if the engine started. There was no throttle.
The switch was used to give bursts of engine when taxiing or
landing.

The amount of dual instruction on the Avro varied according to the
proficiency of the pupil but about eight hours was the average. Every
aerial manoeuvre was taught and take offs, approach-and-landings and
aerobatics practised until the instructor deemed them satisfactory. After
some twenty hours on the 504 newly-qualified pilots went on to the type
for which it was thought they were most suited. In Hal's case it was the
Bristol Fighter with which he was already so familiar as an observer.
Training on the 504 was the only dual instruction that Hal ever had. For
all the many other types he flew until he left the RAF on retirement it
was solo from the word go.

Hal's pilot training was on the Avro 504, a line-up of the type here taken from the cockpit.

Training often meant accidents such as this crashed Avro 504.

Collinstown was a very good posting for Hal. If he was not on duty he could cycle home to 'Carahor' at weekends, sometimes staying a night, and his routine settled into a comfortable one of service and domestic life intertwined. But this wasn't to last. The Ireland he had gone back to was still riven by Republican troubles. The Irish

An unidentified pilot extracts himself from the crashed 504.

Republican Army, the IRA, had evolved from the Irish Volunteers who had staged the 1916 rebellion. Three years later the Irish 'Republic' was established by *Dáil Éireann* (Assembly of Ireland) – a breakaway government formed by Sinn Féin, the Irish Republican party – and the IRA, the army of the *Dáil*, waged a guerrilla campaign against British rule in Ireland from 1919, a campaign which came to be known as the War of Independence which ended in 1921 with the signing of the Anglo-Irish Treaty.

On the clear moonlit night of 20 March 1919 Hal was Orderly Officer at RAF Collinstown. He left the Officers' Mess at about 11.15pm and walked the few hundred yards up the main road to turn out the guard at the main entrance. When he got there he was correctly challenged by the armed sentry. The guard paraded and Hal inspected the men before dismissing them back to the guardroom and signing the guard report. All was in order and he wished the men goodnight and walked to his quarters and went to bed. He later recalled that as he walked away from the guard-room he heard a whistle and then another from a different point and in

Once qualified on the Avro 504 Hal went on to qualify on the Bristol Fighter.

A Bristol Fighter with the top cowling removed at Collinstown.

the light of what happened next realised afterwards that this was a signal that he, the Orderly Officer, had turned out the guard and would soon be out of the way. Next morning when his batman woke him with a cup of tea Hal learned that the aerodrome had been raided during the night. He hadn't heard a thing and no one had called him.

He dressed hurriedly and rushed to see the Commanding Officer and Adjutant who told him what had happened. At about 11.45pm a man in British uniform had walked up to the 19-year-old sentry at the main gate and asked him for a match. When he put his rifle aside to get out his matchbox he suddenly found a revolver pointing at his head. More men appeared and gagged and bound the sentry while masked men dashed into the guardroom and overpowered the twenty-one men of the guard whom they also gagged and bound and tied with ropes to the roof beams so that they were suspended above the floor. The intruders then left. The corporal of the guard immediately found that by nudging the man next to him he could swing on the ropes and he swung for over an hour until the rope holding him chafed through and he fell to the floor. He rolled to the stove and managed to chafe through the rope binding his hands too. This enabled him to free his other bindings and release the rest of the guard. The corporal tried to telephone the CO but found that the line had been cut. He also found that all the rifles and ammunition in the guardroom had been stolen so, with nothing to defend himself, he ran down to the CO's quarters and alerted him. The CO woke the Adjutant in turn and they, with the now released guard, toured the camp looking for signs of the intruders. There was no sign of them but what they did find was that all the telephone wires had been cut, that the armoury and ammunition stores had been broken into and all the rifles, machine guns, revolvers and ammunition taken. Furthermore, the petrol pipes of the twenty or so vehicles on camp were cut, thus preventing any pursuit of the raiders. But no damage had been done to any of the aeroplanes.

Once the news of the raid reached RAF Headquarters in Merrion Square in Dublin the balloon went up. A battalion of infantry with armoured cars immediately set up a defensive position at Collinstown but there was nothing left there that the raiders would have wanted so that it

Collinstown. The guardroom from which the IRA stole rifles and tied up the twenty-one men of the guard.

was something of a 'horse has bolted' situation. Despite the surrounding area being scoured by troops and police nothing was found of the raiders or the stolen weapons. A court of enquiry was held during which the guard was disciplined for allowing such a thing to happen – in fact there was an unspoken suspicion of complicity. But Hal was not asked to give evidence because he was deemed to have acted strictly in accordance with regulations.

To put the raid into perspective, the IRA was short of armaments and it was the 1st Battalion of that organisation that executed it to help rectify the problem. The raiding party of twenty-five men dressed in khaki and equipped with masks divided itself into two sections. While the sentries at the guardroom were overpowered by the first section and the entire guard disarmed and secured to the beams of the guardhouse, 200 men of the RAF remained asleep nearby, Hal included, oblivious of what was going on. The second section collected all the arms and ammunition it could and loaded them onto a convoy of vehicles. The total haul was seventy-five rifles and 5,000 rounds of ammunition.

There were frequent visiting aircraft to Collinstown such as this Sopwith Camel.

Other visitors included S.E.5s. These had come to grief in a crosswind.

Righting an S.E.5 after an unsuccessful crosswind landing.

Flying training continued normally at Collinstown for a week or two afterwards but in April it was transferred to Baldonnel, also near Dublin, an airfield complete and fully built in all respects. At Collinstown it was decided to cease all building work and close down

the station. Dublin airport opened there in January 1940 with a flight
a day to Liverpool.

A selection from Hal's photographic record of Baldonnel

DH.9A H3586 at Baldonnel in 1921.

DH.9As about to take off from Baldonnel to formate and overfly the funeral in
Dublin of British Army officers killed on Bloody Sunday, 21 November 1920.

Hal with a DH.9A at Baldonnel.

An interesting Baldonnel visitor in 1920 was Handley Page 0400 J2259.

Entry to a Handley Page 0400 was by a trapdoor beneath the fuselage. J2259 again.

Hal didn't see much of Baldonnel and although he didn't mention it in his memoir his photographic record suggests he did visit the airfield before being posted at the end of April 1919 to No.106 Squadron at Fermoy in County Cork (as he does record in his memoir) and with them, he says, he remained until November 1921. However No.106 Squadron disbanded on 8 October 1919. In the official records (but not in his own memoir) Hal is listed as being with No.2 Squadron which was reformed from No.105 Squadron at Oranmore in County Galway on 1st February 1920, but in between times it seems he was with 105 Squadron as a detachment of the disbanded 106 Squadron and when No.2 Squadron was re-formed from No.105 Squadron, the men of 106 Squadron then became in effect a detachment of the new No.2 Squadron! Throughout all these changes No.106 Squadron personnel could well have referred to themselves as '106 Squadron' instead of '105 Squadron' and '2 Squadron'. It was probably the easiest thing to do given the confusion of numbers!

In October 1918 a Defence of Ireland Scheme had been formulated. It is instructive to devote a few paragraphs to this as it throws light on the British government's view of what they were up against in Ireland and how they would deal with any given situation. Copies of the scheme were sent to all commands, districts and sub-districts and their components in the country. That for the Fermoy Brigade was signed by Brigade Major Pearson on 28 October 1918 and No.2 RAF Squadron was also forwarded a copy. Within the pages of the document '106th [sic] Squadron Royal Air Force' is also specifically listed as a unit within the Fermoy Brigade. It begins with an assessment of the state of the country which it says is 'on the whole quiet but although on the surface conditions appear normal and quiet there is a very intense feeling underneath. The rebels have a thorough system of organisation, the utmost secrecy is observed and there is little doubt that, but for the presence of troops, organised trouble would soon recommence.'

The threat of German intervention in Ireland in support of the rebels, even so close to the end of the war, was still perceived as being very real. In addition to having to face the possibilities of a German invasion, the fact that it would be the signal for an organised rising by 'Sinn Féin Clubs and Irish Volunteers' was to be contemplated.

The document expands on this. The Defence Scheme had been drawn up to deal with 'certain contingencies', these being a local rising, a general rising, a German landing or a combination of the latter two, which was considered to be the most serious threat and 'must therefore form the basis of the scheme'. The Navy was responsible for watching the coast both at sea and on land, coast watchers on land being supported by the local police. Military units were given responsibility for the defence of important towns, the railway system and 'vulnerable points'. In the main these were cyclist brigades. Infantry would be based at sub-district headquarters and would be available to support the cyclists if necessary.

Were an invasion to happen the document spends considerable time outlining the means of communication. The Post Office's telegraph, telephone and postal services were to form the primary means – 'it is considered that a large percentage of the PO Engineering staff is loyal' – but this was to be backed up in the case of the breakdown of the Post Office system for any reason. This back up consisted of:

> Visual signalling but 'owing to the nature of the country and climate this is not to be relied upon.'
>
> Despatch riders who 'must not be sent with unimportant messages over roads where they are likely to be attacked.'
>
> Carrier pigeons, remembering that 'certain birds are trained for certain places and it is pointed out that if birds are trained to fly say from Templemore to Kilkenny they will not find their way to the latter place if liberated at Cahir.'
>
> Wireless, remembering that 'when a message is handed in to go by military wireless it must be in code or cipher except in cases of extreme urgency.'

Almost as a last resort aeroplanes should be used 'in the event of a breakdown of the ordinary means of communication [to] convey messages to units by dropping them in weighted bags to which long coloured streamers are attached'. Squadrons were ordered to select dropping grounds as near as possible to their headquarters and mark them with a circle at

One of the Defence of Ireland Scheme's methods of communication – carrier pigeons.

'Wrapping a pigeon in newspaper before dropping the basket from the air. This procedure begs many questions!'

least fifteen feet in diameter. The orders very specifically detailed how such circles should be created 'by beating ashes or stone into the ground and painting or whitewashing them white'. The dropping circle should be located in the centre of a field with no object that was likely to camouflage it. Also the surface of the field must be of a uniform colour and not partly of grass and partly ploughed for 'it must be remembered that this circle looks very small from a plane at 5,000 feet'. That was not all. Aircraft dropping a message were instructed to circle low over the dropping ground and sound a klaxon before throwing message bags over the side. If it was all clear to drop, the receiving unit was to place a thirty-foot-long strip (perhaps of painted tent canvas) across the circle: if it were under attack or 'hard pressed' it would place no such strip or alternatively fire a magnesium rocket. 'The best time to fire a rocket from the aircraft's point of view is when the aeroplane is between the sun and the firer and at an angle of 45 degrees from the firer.' This particular instruction ends with 'message bags dropped from aeroplanes must be returned at once to 106 Squadron RAF Fermoy'.

The IRA continued to gain in strength after the Collinstown raid. They and the Irish Volunteers before them had been drilling secretly for years and arms had been smuggled into the country as well as being stolen from the British military. They were well led and organised and, as they wore no uniforms, could disappear by mingling with ordinary civilians, so were difficult to engage let alone apprehend. Rebellion prevailed until in 1922 the British government sanctioned the provinces of Munster, Leinster and Connaught becoming the Irish Free State. Only part of Ulster remained in the UK, the counties of Donegal, Cavan and Monaghan seceding from the Union to become part of the Irish Free State too.

To augment the police and the army the Royal Irish Constabulary Special Reserve (RICSR) – the so-called Black and Tans – and Auxiliary Division of the Royal Irish Constabulary (ADRIC) were formed. The RICSR was composed of former soldiers and ADRIC of former officers. The term 'Black and Tan' came from the mixed uniform that the first recruits received which included elements of RIC rifle-green (which was almost black) and Army khaki. The first RICSR deployed were in County Limerick where the colour combination reminded people of a local hunt's pack of hounds, which were known as the Black and Tans. The name stuck.

ADRIC was formed in companies and was a quick-reaction force. Its members, all former officers, wore either their own Army uniforms with a beret or blue English police uniforms with a bonnet. Air co-operation with them was provided by detached flights of eight aircraft each at various places and No.106 Squadron had them at Galway, Castlebar and Fermoy. Actually the flight at Fermoy was established on the racecourse nearby with the aircraft housed in canvas hangars with surrounding high breastworks to protect them from small-arms fire. Everyone slept in tents with messes and recreation rooms made up of disused aeroplane cases. The whole camp was surrounded with barbed-wire fences with gates to move aircraft onto the airfield. In fact No.106/No.2 Squadron were in tents for two years with a few bits of furniture bought in the town to give a semblance of home comforts. There was one hurricane lamp per tent but no heating and in the wet Irish climate there was always a feeling of dampness. Huts were provided in 1921 after questions were asked in Parliament, but it was almost too late for Fermoy closed not long afterwards.

Fermoy was a particularly troublesome place for the British government. It was the scene of the first attack by the IRA against British troops to capture badly needed weapons, preceding the Collinstown raid. It had taken place on a Sunday morning in early September 1919 as an armed detachment of fifteen soldiers were marching to church in the town. Twenty-five members of the local IRA company with only six revolvers between them were waiting for them. The British were called upon to surrender. They refused and there was a struggle in which a soldier was killed and three were wounded. The IRA captured fifteen rifles which were taken away by car. The Army immediately began searching the surrounding countryside and the following night soldiers from the barracks invaded the town of Fermoy and looted shops in the main streets. They returned two nights later but were forced back by

An aircraft packing case used as the Officers' Mess at Fermoy in 1919.

What a contrast! Fermoy Officers' Mess in 1921.

Officers' quarters at Fermoy in 1919.

townspeople armed with sticks and stones. The Fermoy reprisals were the first such revenge raids by the Army.

Hal was to see at first hand reprisals by the Army. On 26 June 1920 Brigadier General Lucas of 16 Infantry Brigade was fishing on the banks of the River Blackwater. A man, George Power, approached him, drew a gun and ordered him to put his hands up. Lucas hesitated briefly then dropped his fishing rod and complied. He was disarmed and marched back to his fishing lodge where he found that two other prisoners had been taken on the riverside that afternoon – Colonel Danford of the Royal Artillery and Colonel Tyrrell of the Royal Engineers. The motive of the IRA for capturing Brigadier General Lucas, the most senior British officer in Fermoy, was to use him as a hostage to secure the release of one of their comrades who was on hunger strike in Cork jail. Hal takes up the story.

There was great excitement when we heard the General had been kidnapped. The Army were understandably furious and

The site on the River Blackwater where Brigadier General Lucas was captured by the IRA while he was fishing in June 1920.

were determined to find out where he had been taken to. They thought they could force the inhabitants of Fermoy to give them this information by going from house to house and bullying the occupants to tell them. What a hope. The Army told us about their plan which we thought was crazy but they were set on seeing it through. It was agreed that RAF airmen should be allowed to co-operate with the soldiers if they felt so inclined and no questions would be asked. McKeever and I went into the town in mufti [civilian attire] to see what would happen. Like all such situations it began quietly. The soldiers walked down into the town from the barracks with their officers also in mufti and we followed. Then someone shouted 'put that bloody light out.' A brick shattered a street lamp. Then it started. The troops ran into the town square. They threw bricks at shop windows shattering the plate glass with a sound like shrapnel. Householders came to their doors and were questioned without result. Then the soldiers started looting. Some stole from grocers' shops. Some threw trays of trinkets from jewellers' shops into the river.

Some threw cycles into the river until one officer found he had thrown his own motor bike in – it had been down at the garage for repair. Some tried to set fire to draperies in the town centre while the owner watched from an upper window. The situation was now completely out of control and so McKeever and I went back to camp. It really was a disgraceful affair. Every shop window smashed and nearly every store looted. The end of it was that the IRA chased the troops out of the town and the Army still did not know where their General was being held. Days later he escaped and made his way to safety. Then the row started. Questions in Parliament. An Army enquiry. An Air Force enquiry. A search of the barracks and aerodrome for loot but none was found. And so it all came to nought. Compensation was paid, out of which the shopkeepers did pretty well and were quite happy. And boys were diving for jewellers' items in the river for weeks afterwards.

*

No.106 Squadron, and No.2 Squadron, were equipped with the Brisfit. The aircraft were used for the daily dropping of bags of mail at army and police detachments and barracks, the reconnaissance of roads and railways for signs of damage and escorts to road convoys, all of which involved low flying. Other duties included passenger flights for VIPs which often meant landings in very small fields guarded by troops and with armoured cars present during landing and take-off. And there was the dropping of propaganda leaflets plus the delivery of baskets of carrier pigeons to police posts. One aircraft with its crew was kept ready for immediate take-off for action when reports of attacks on barracks came in. Crews often saw burnt-out cars and buildings and some dead and wounded but they never saw armed IRA men. At one stage bloodhounds were flown in from England and taken to various points by the squadron in an attempt to track the rebels down but they were not much use.

We were a cheery bunch of officers who came and went, some to be demobilised, others to return to their homelands in Canada, Australia and South Africa. I was the only one with a regular Army commission and I wanted to follow this up with a permanent commission in the RAF. There was much discontent after the war at the slowness of demobilisation and we heard of mutinies at aerodromes abroad and in England but at Fermoy we only once had a refusal to go on parade which was quickly withdrawn when we officers paraded wearing our revolvers.

Despite the potentially heavy tasking of the squadron, in actual fact life was fairly uneventful and Hal bemoaned the 'absence of many air adventures'. His memoir records more of the day-to-day aspects of life at Fermoy although a total eclipse of the sun could hardly be described as a day-to-day occurrence!

Bristol Fighter (Brisfit) F640 at Fermoy.

The cockpit of Brisfit E2553.

Taking off on bumpy grass on a gusty day. Hal's accident in Brisfit H1590.

It was a cloudless sunny day and I was escorting a military road convoy near Tipperary. The effect from the air was a period of twilight and the air that had been slightly bumpy became calm. The bumps returned after the eclipse. On the ground poultry went to roost at the start and cocks crowed after the eclipse as for a new day.

Hal and Brisfit E2553

But the IRA were never very far away and local populations were often caught up in their activities. Hal and three fellow officers were introduced to a family with four daughters and a young son who farmed a dozen miles from Fermoy and they started going across to see them for convivial evenings of singing and dancing. However, before long their reception on

A J-type Brisfit at Fermoy.

Several garish camouflage schemes were applied to Brisfits. This is F4383.

their frequent visits was less welcoming and ultimately something happened which put a stop to them altogether. Two of Hal's fellow officers went over to the farm one evening in a motorcycle and sidecar. Come the following morning they were not in the mess at breakfast and their beds had not been slept in. Hal feared they had had an accident or the motorcycle had broken down and he drove out to look for them. But passing through the village before the farm he became aware of sullen looks from the locals and, reaching the house, one of the girls waved from a top window and shouted at him to go back to Fermoy. She was in an agitated state and whilst Hal's instinct was to stay and find out what had happened he did drive back to the aerodrome and was relieved to see that his friends had by then made their way back by train. The pair had enjoyed the usual entertainment of song and dance and had left the farmhouse at about 10.00pm and stopped in the driveway to relieve themselves. As they did so they saw that a tree had been cut down blocking the way and almost at once they were set upon by several masked men. They thought it was a joke and still thought so even when taken to a barn and told not to move. Two of the men guarded them until dawn when they left and Hal's friends, by then stiff and cold, went to check that everything was alright in the house. The doors were locked but they got in through a kitchen window and crept upstairs to find the girls sitting up in bed with their brother on the floor with a golf club acting as a guard. To their horror they saw that the girls' hair had been cut off. The girls were terrified that the RAF's presence in the house might cause them further trouble and they insisted that the two men leave which is when they found that their motorcycle and sidecar had been burnt out. They walked to a nearby station and caught a train back to Fermoy. Some days later Hal found out how the girls had been dragged downstairs and had their hair cut off with sheep shears. They had been told that if any of the RAF men ever went to the farm again it would be burnt down. It was very evident that the RAF were not always welcome in Irish communities and that fraternisation with them could easily lead to warnings like this – or much worse.

Hal had to give lectures on air co-operation at various times to the Army. One such lecture was given in Cork barracks and afterwards Hal went with the troops on a raid, the objective being the capture of rebel leaders who were thought to be hiding in the hills west of the city. They left the barracks at 2.00am in a column of open vehicles with armoured cars as escort. At some time after 3.00am they left the vehicles and marched several miles across country led by guides familiar with the area. Eventually they halted and police with troops crept up to a house which was just visible in the darkness. A knock at the door produced no answer but then men were seen running away from the back of the building. Police, troops and Hal gave chase but lost them. As it grew light they advanced across the hills in open order in case they stumbled across any enemy – and quite suddenly came under machine-gun fire. 'We took cover. I went over a high bank like a Grand National winner,' Hal recalled.

> It was in that burst of firing that we had three officers killed. But we could see columns of black smoke in the valley and thought another part of our force had found a rebel hideout and burnt some vehicles. We found later that by pure chance the rendez-vous for our transport had been fixed just where the rebels had set up an ambush. It was our cars we could see burning and when we got to the position we found the drivers' dead bodies lined up by the roadside.

If the Army had asked for the air co-operation that Hal had been pro-pounding a few hours before, the operation might not have ended so disastrously.

Chapter Eight

Moving On

Hal was awarded his permanent RAF commission on 17 November 1921 (it was gazetted on 13 January 1922) which meant that he now had a secure career to look forward to and a few days later he left the squadron at Fermoy for No.39 (Bomber) Squadron at RAF Spitalgate, near Grantham in Lincolnshire. On 30 August the following year he was promoted to flight lieutenant.

No.39 had just been re-formed, having disbanded at the end of the war, and was waiting for its aircraft. To keep themselves current flying-wise they had Mono Avros – Avro 504Js with the Monosoupape engine were known as such. The aircraft the squadron was waiting for were de Havilland DH.9As, an American Liberty-engined day bomber fitted with a forward-firing Vickers gun on the port side of the forward fuselage, a single or double Lewis gun on a Scarff ring on the rear cockpit and the capacity to carry up to 660lb of bombs under either the lower mainplanes or the fuselage or both. The aircraft were actually on the airfield but in store in a dismantled state and as there was a shortage of riggers the pilots took on the job of erecting the aircraft allotted to them themselves and fitting modifications. This took many months and it was nearly a year before all twelve machines were available and serviceable. Hal recorded one criticism of the DH.9A when he got to fly them – a weak undercarriage necessitating making a near perfect landing dead into wind to avoid a minor crash.

On 24 June 1922 he took part in the rather wet RAF Pageant at Hendon in north London, the airfield only having recently been taken possession of from its private owners, the Graham White aviation company, by the government. The first pageant had been held in 1920 and in the inter-war years it became a major annual event, known from 1925 as the Royal Air Force Display: that in 1938 was the Empire Air Day.

RAF Spitalgate in 1922.

The annual display was intended to show the public what they were getting for their money and to encourage competition among squadrons. From its earliest days the pageant featured a grand finale and in 1922 it was 'an Eastern drama, depicting the attack and destruction of a desert stronghold intended to illustrate the work that was done by the RAF in the East'. A Bristol Fighter returning from a reconnaissance made a forced landing near the stronghold which opened fire on the grounded aircraft. An armoured car section returning from a raid passed close by and drove to the rescue using their heavy machine guns to keep at bay the stronghold's garrison, described colourfully in the pageant's programme as 'Wottnotts'! An RAF bomber squadron then appeared and attacked the stronghold under heavy fire from an enemy anti-aircraft battery mounted on lorries. The bombs found their target and the stronghold was soon in flames. The showing of the destruction of a village of aggressive tribesmen was very up to date as the RAF had just assumed overall military control of the Iraq mandate where it was using bombers and armoured cars to bring the area under air control. For Hal this was all very prescient for he would be in Iraq within a few years doing that very thing.

Hal and DH.9A E8725 at RAF Spitalgate.

The RAF Pageant 1922. The 'desert stronghold' which would be bombed by Bristol Fighters and strafed by armoured cars during the pageant.

Hal (and No.39 Squadron) wasn't involved in this set piece but he did participate in the 'Standard Avro' race in which twelve aircraft were lined up into wind with the pilots on the ground a hundred yards away. When the starting pistol was fired they ran to the machines, climbed in and strapped up. A fitter swung the prop and immediately the engine started the pilot took off as the fitter dived under the wing! Usually the aircraft became airborne within seconds of each other so it was a case of close formation around the markers of the course, jostling for position and a final dive over the finishing line. There were several heats with Hal winning the first but coming second in the last because his engine would not start first time. Aside from participating, the pageant also gave him the opportunity of capturing many of the attending aircraft on his camera as his albums show. Hal was to be heavily involved in the displays a few years later as CO of No.23 Squadron.

Aircraft at the 1922 RAF Pageant

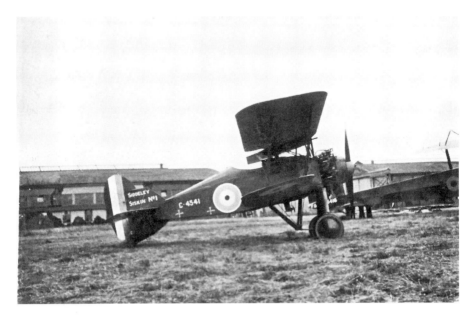

An Armstrong Whitworth Siskin.

There were civilian types too at the pageant, such as this Bristol Tourer Puma.

A DH.4 flown by the Belgian air attaché at the pageant.

A de Havilland DH.9C.

A de Havilland DH.10A.

A Martinsyde Buzzard plus a relaxing RAF officer!

A Parnall Puffin amphibian

Preparing a Vickers Vimy for the pageant.

A Westland Weasel with a Bristol Jupiter engine.

Hal's Avro 504 under the guard of the local constabulary (and two small boys) after his forced landing near Herne Bay.

*

'I had one forced landing while in No.39 Squadron,' Hal later recalled.

I was ferrying a Mono Avro from Manston in Kent to Grantham and when near Herne Bay the engine suddenly vibrated and then there was a violent explosion followed by violent vibration. I switched off and stalled, stopping the propeller revolving. I then

Pointing out the missing cylinder of the Monosoupape rotary-engined Avro 504 which caused Hal's forced landing near Herne Bay.

picked a field and did the usual series of S turns followed by a side slip and landed in a field of cows. Inspecting the engine on the ground I was amazed to find that one cylinder had blown off together with its piston and connecting rod without damaging the aeroplane. The engine was a French Mono rotary.

Hal was aware that now he was commissioned he could earn an additional year's seniority if he took a technical course and later a Staff College course, provided of course that he passed. He was not slow in applying for an air photography course to fulfil the technical course requirement. This was something of a logical choice as he was interested in photography as a hobby and it seemed to him a natural thing to do to capitalise on that interest. Indeed Hal's legacy to his family, and to historians, has been a collection of photographs from the 1920s and 1930s taken at home and whilst on overseas postings, not only of rare RAF subjects but of another of his interests, archaeology. He also owned an early Bell and Howell cine camera which he used extensively in a similar way and that is still with the family in working order, as is his original projector.

His application for an air photography course was successful and he was formally posted to the Staff School of Photography, Maps and Reconnaissance at Farnborough on 9 April 1923. Since October of the previous year it appears he had been seconded to the school on a supernumerary basis too so that when the course proper started he was well placed to tackle the syllabus. At the same time he had an eye to the future for he acquired some of the books required for the RAF Staff College examination which he was to take a few years hence and started reading them.

New cameras were being developed at Farnborough and Hal fitted one of the new 6/18 compasses into one of the school's Bristol Fighters (he was always demonstrating his technical and engineering abilities). The 6/18 was a compass which settled onto a true course after a turn without over-compensation which had been a problem hitherto. He practised hard with the new cameras and the 6/18 until he could cover a specified area with an accurate mosaic of photos. So successful was he that once the course was complete Hal became an instructor for the school for a while.

This period of Hal's career marked increasing opportunities to use his camera. Several visits to Manston whilst with No.39 Squadron included a Blackburn Dart.

The Dart's cockpit.

Also at Manson, a Vickers Vimy.

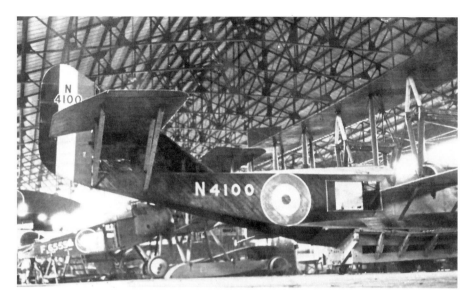

Felixstowe F.5 flying boat N4100 with a Sopwith Salamander in the background.

The Sopwith Salamander showing its armour plating.

A Sopwith Cuckoo

RAF Halton was another airfield visited. Here Hal captured a Sopwith Snipe.

RAF Cranwell, where Hal found a Westland Walrus.

Hal over the Hampshire countryside whilst with the School of Photography, Maps and Reconnaissance at Farnborough in J6689, a dual-control trainer version of the Bristol Fighter.

Hal's posting to RAE Farnborough produced another crop of photographs and not just of aircraft. These are 9-inch howitzers.

And it led directly to his taking part in a survey of Dartmoor with the Royal Engineers and the resulting production of a six-inch-to-the-mile map.

There were other things that Hal became involved with while at Farnborough. For example, he was detached with two Brisfits to Gosport to photograph bombing trials against an old battleship, HMS *Agamemnon*, whilst she was underway and radio-controlled from an accompanying destroyer. *Agamemnon* had been stripped of her flying deck, sea cabins, the main derrick, lower conning tower, masts and yards, torpedo equipment and most of her crew amenities. The 12-inch turrets remained intact, although all actual armament had been removed. Hatches, coamings, scuttles and lifts were dismantled or plated over. Before Hal's time she had been exposed to a cloud of poisonous gas to determine its effect on a battleship. Then she was subjected to machine-gun fire by strafing aircraft. When it came to Hal's involvement his photography was invaluable in assessing damage when 6-inch, 5.5-inch and 4.7-inch rounds were fired at her by battlecruisers. These tests showed that well-protected ships would

A kite balloon in the 'main street' at Farnborough.

obviously suffer damage to their upper works if shelling was accurate but because of their construction and plate armour protection for the hull and other key areas they would not have their steaming or fighting capability seriously impaired.

Whilst Hal was at Farnborough Lawrence of Arabia was also there but under the name of Aircraftsman Shaw. Hal's memoir rather gleefully records that Shaw was on the CO's parade soon after his arrival

A kite balloon cable lorry.

An Avro Aldershot at Farnborough in February 1923.

and, inspecting the men, Hal ticked him off for untidiness and ordered him to get his hair cut! But that was before they knew who he really was. Lawrence served in the RAF from 1922 to 1935 having enlisted under the assumed name of Ross first of all and later Shaw, formally adopting the second by deed poll in 1927. He had moved to Farnborough on completion of the recruits' course at RAF Uxbridge but undesirable

A Boulton and Paul Bourges at Farnborough in February 1923.

A Nieuport Nighthawk at RAE Farnborough in February 1923.

publicity – he was exposed by the press as Lawrence of Arabia – led to his discharge and joining instead the Tank Corps at Bovingdon in 1923. He was subsequently reinstated in the RAF two years later. When he first

Prototype Victoria 1 J6860 at Farnborough in 1923.

met Aircraftsman Shaw, Hal wasn't to know how the next stage of his RAF career would also take him to the Middle East.

Chapter Nine

Iraq

By the end of the First World War the power of the Ottoman Empire had been broken but not without great cost in lives lost for the Arab states. The price of victory was their independence and Britain had guaranteed this in return for their assistance during the war. However, the Turks may have been broken but they were not totally subdued and in the aftermath of the war they continued to exploit the weakened state of the Arab world by undermining the influence of the British who, with the French, were faced with the job of reconciling the nationalist demands of the Arabs with the need to ensure that their independence would be based on constitutional methods of government.

In May 1920 at a peace conference in San Remo, Britain inherited responsibility via League of Nations' mandates for the newly-created territories of Palestine, Transjordan and Mesopotamia, an area encompassing much of present-day Iran and Iraq. France inherited Syria and Lebanon. The mandates included administrative and internal and external security responsibilities. Alongside this Britain had to consider her own interests in the area. The Middle East was an important staging post to the Indian sub-continent and Far East: and she had oil interests in the area too. She had to ensure therefore that Arab nations would be friendly after independence.

The position in which Britain found herself in Iraq couldn't have been less encouraging. British ability to impose control over its mandated territory was hampered by very extended lines of communication, difficult terrain and the fact that troops *in situ* were not enough to deal with all contingencies. Furthermore, in Iraq there was a growing dislike of British control and this led to rebellion. That this should have happened was an embarrassment for the British and as an official document of the time stated:

it was a clear indication that a system of constitutional, indigenous government dependent on effective security control by military forces was the only clear way of introducing the desires of the progressive Iraqis to the methods of modern statecraft.

But this would take time, whereas Iraqi nationalists had wanted immediate independence. In this they were encouraged by the events in Syria where there was stiff nationalist resistance against the French. Unrest in Iraq spread very quickly, fanned by the oratory of religious leaders of both the Sunni and Shia sects. Within a month of Britain's acceptance of the mandate, by June 1920 widespread disturbances had broken out in the Middle Euphrates area and in Baghdad there was a strong undercurrent of revolutionary activity. By July British soldiers were fully engaged in the rebellion and suffered heavy casualties. In the north there was unrest amongst the Kurds who suspected British motives and feared an extension of Arab authority into their country, not helped by the fact that the British didn't make clear their intentions for the future of Kurdish Iraq. The Turks meanwhile, encouraged by the problems the British were suffering, were threatening Mosul, Kirkuk and Erbil.

In short the country was strife-ridden from north to south. British political officers were being murdered as were the entire crew of the British gunboat *Greenfly* on the Euphrates. Slowly though order was restored, albeit only to a degree, and by September 1920 something approaching calm returned. But the damage was done. Back home calls were made in the press for the ending of the British mandate. Winston Churchill, the newly appointed Colonial Secretary, summoned British military leaders and civil administrators to a conference in Cairo in March 1921 to discuss the situation, although it had already been decided in London before he travelled to Egypt to end the unpopular mandate and to install Faisal bin Hussein bin Ali al-Hashimi as King Faisal I of a newly-created Kingdom of Iraq. Once installed, he would sign a friendship treaty with Britain.

In a major policy change it was also decided that whilst an Army garrison would remain at strategic points, security in the Middle East should be transferred to the Royal Air Force. This needs to be put into context.

At the end of the First World War the infant RAF had teetered on the edge of annihilation in the face of opposition from the Army, Navy and politicians in high office. By January 1920 over 280,000 men – officers, cadets and NCO ranks – had been discharged. Enter Winston Churchill, who was appointed Secretary of State for War and Air in January 1919, and Air Chief Marshal Hugh Trenchard, who was re-appointed Chief of the Air Staff (having previously resigned from that position) at the same time. Churchill's and Trenchard's relationship was often a stormy one but between them the basis for a restructured RAF was agreed, albeit on a restricted budget. This included an RAF College at Cranwell, an Air Staff College at Andover and an RAF Aircraft Apprentice School of Technical Training at Halton. At the same time a Short Service Commission scheme was introduced. Of the twenty-six squadrons that would form the post-war RAF it was envisaged that nineteen would be based abroad in India, Egypt and Iraq, with all reporting to a headquarters in Cairo. The justification for this was that Britain needed to garrison its still huge empire and Trenchard was of the robust opinion that a few squadrons would be able to control vast areas from the air without the need for large numbers of expensive boots on the ground. When Churchill moved to the Colonial Office in March 1921 he supported Trenchard in his views, especially as far as Palestine and Iraq were concerned.

The shifting of military control of Iraq from the Army to the RAF as agreed at the Cairo Conference was accordingly completed by late 1922. Foreshadowing the 'show of force' policy of air arms in recent conflicts in the Middle East and in Afghanistan, the RAF in the early 1920s would quickly prove its ability to deal with lawless Arab tribes by simply being there and overflying trouble spots and indicating an ultimate solution by the dropping of bombs or the firing of guns. The threat that they could and would if necessary do so was usually enough to defuse a situation.

They were not tasked solely with quelling disturbance or intervening in hostile rebellion but also in establishing permanent communication routes, air mapping and pioneering future long-range civil airline routes. All this would be done in the harshest of conditions by largely poorly-paid servicemen living in sub-standard conditions with little in the way of diversion other than what they provided for themselves. Yet in the true spirit of a British serviceman's determination to enjoy himself come what may it is recorded time and time again that bonds of true comradeship were forged in the grim conditions. It was almost a case of the worse the conditions the more determined men were to ignore them and 'carry on regardless'. This was especially true at squadron level where officers and men formed integrated, cohesive units with a shared will to succeed. As Chaz Bowyer says in his book *RAF Operations 1918–1938*:

> Death and injury were no strangers to men flying over the ... baking plains and deserts of Iraq. Crewing aircraft of ageing design, backed by minimal maintenance facilities, in climates and conditions never envisaged by the machines' designers years before, all aircrews were well aware of the hazards involved but accepted these as routine facets of their duties.

And again:

> On the first-line squadrons ... every man, of whatever rank or trade, quickly formed a tightly knit, interdependent unit community ... without corrupting necessary overall discipline so vital for ultimate efficiency ...

According to Hugh Trenchard, effective control in the Middle Eastern theatre could be achieved by four squadrons of single-engined two-seater aircraft, one single-seater squadron, one reconnaissance squadron and two twin-engined bomber squadrons, the latter also to be convertible to transports for moving men and materiel. The squadrons would at all times be based outside troubled areas, either at Baghdad, Shaibah or Mosul, or at advanced landing grounds. A well trained and equipped military force would protect flying stations and landing grounds supplemented by armoured car companies. The fact that the aircraft were 'of ageing design', even antiquated, was a result of continuing restricted budgets, as much a product of the prevailing economic situation as the continuing infighting amongst the three services for available funds. Throughout the 1920s aircraft such as the DH.9A and Bristol F.2b continued to be in front-line service overseas.

Finally the matter of command was carefully considered. Trenchard's view was that to render the Air Force scheme of control a success it was absolutely essential that the command of all the forces in Mesopotamia be invested in an Air Officer who should serve under the superior political authority. In October 1922 Air Vice Marshal (later Marshal of the RAF Sir) John Salmond was appointed Air Officer Commanding Iraq Command. The lack of experience among RAF officers overall was realised and so it was agreed that initially it would be necessary to attach Army officers to the RAF for administrative purposes. There were other areas too in which Army personnel were retained – intelligence for instance – where their presence was valued for many years. As an anonymously prepared outline history of the 'RAF in Iraq' in the National Archives comments:

> The scheme for Air Control was a bold and indeed a revolutionary venture which typified the outlook and spirit of the junior Service. It gave great confidence to the pioneers of Britain's new air power which was to be so magnificently justified in similar and greater undertakings.

There is no denying the seriousness of the situation when the RAF took over. Local unrest was everywhere. In the north, Turkish penetration towards Mosul and anti-government agitation in Kurdish areas continued to destabilise unity. There was an intensity and bitterness in the lawlessness of local tribes and factions. It was AVM Salmond's job to restore order and establish security and respect for authority over a huge area. Throughout the course of its operations in Iraq the RAF was active either in the internal disorder of the deserts of the south, the external threat of Turkey in the mountainous north and inter-tribal raids across the Iraq-Nejd (modern Saudi Arabia) border. Initially the Turkish threat was the most pressing and the AOC decided to concentrate his forces in the Mosul area and thus call the Turks' bluff. 'The arm in which our force was strongest was aircraft,' he said in a later report.

> It was only, however, if we had a considerable ground force in the forward area that we could safely concentrate a large force of aircraft where they would be within reach of the enemy's distant bases and lines of communication: that is to say it was only by a forward policy that we could place the weapon in which we were strongest where it could best strike the enemy.

So concerned was he about the situation, King Faisal placed the Iraqi army under the command of AVM Salmond and operations began in March 1923 and were totally successful. The threat of the Turks was eradicated and consequently the political outlook of the people changed – they now anticipated fair dealings from the British and the new Iraqi government. Over the country as a whole the strength of British airpower was perceived as a means of supporting (and backing) friendly tribes against those less friendly, although this was mainly in the south where in the first half of 1923 continuous tribal disturbance threatened to end in fighting. Brigandage was rife and some sheiks obstinately defied central government. Political officers' jobs again became difficult and dangerous. But the deployment of aircraft, often working in co-operation with police patrols, defused situations. RAF policing of the southern desert against raids by tribes from across the Nejd border ensured the security of Iraqi tribes.

*

Although there remained much to be done it was clear that by 1924 the government had extended and strengthened its control over the greater part of the country. Respect for the power of the RAF meant respect for the government and rebellious sheiks learned that if they ignored this retribution would be swift. It was into this scenario that at the end of 1924 Hal learned he was to be posted to Air Headquarters Baghdad.

On 27 February 1925 he was appointed as Photographic Officer HQ Iraq Command to take the place of a man invalided home. He would spend the second half of the year and the largest part of 1926 both at RAF Hinaidi and in travelling the country. A report by Air HQ Baghdad summarising events of 1926 giving the wider picture of the situation in which Hal found himself is instructive.

> **Political.** The decision of the League of Nations to fix the Iraq-Turkey frontier ... though not immediately accepted by Turkey, brought relief to Iraq. It meant the passing of the worst external threat to the country and resulted in greater confidence in exerting further efforts towards internal reconstruction and administration.
>
> **Internal Security.** In October 1925 a party of about 150 Shammar tribesmen from Iraq carried off about 600 camels from Kuwait territory. They were pursued relentlessly by armoured cars and police on the ground and by aeroplanes in the air. 47 raiders who desperately resisted capture were killed and 27 were captured: the remainder escaped across the Syrian frontier. 350 camels were recovered and restored to the Sheikh of Kuwait: about 200 died or were killed in the fighting and the rest were taken into Syria by the remnants of the raiders. The story of the suffering and losses of the raiders, harried day after day by land and air ... is reported to have had a salutary deterrent influence on all other would-be raiders. [Inter-tribal raiding was made illegal by government decree in 1926.]
>
> **Kurds.** Properly established police posts, readily assisted by the RAF, enabled the administration ... to be maintained and consolidated. The brigands were for the most part under constant surveillance from the air, or at any rate thought they were, and so their operations were restricted. Mahmoud was reduced to a life of a wandering fugitive. In June he engaged a small force in the neighbourhood of Penjwin, but his attack was repulsed by reconnaissance aircraft, one of which was forced to land in

tribal territory and the crew were captured. Later in the year further attempts by the same sheikh to enter Iraq were thwarted and he was finally allowed to see the High Commissioner after his air force prisoners were returned. On the northern frontier there was no change in the refugee problem which continued to hamper internal administration. [In 1919 Sheikh Mahmoud Barzanji rose up against Iraqi authority in British Mesopotamia and later the British Mandate in Iraq as a consequence of which he was imprisoned. When he was released he rebelled again and declared himself to be the ruler of the Kingdom of Kurdistan. This lasted until July 1924 when superior British forces defeated him once more. Mahmoud retreated to the mountains, only emerging to make further sporadic attacks until eventually he reached terms with the Kingdom of Iraq in 1932.]

Relations with Turkey. In June the Ankara treaty was concluded which defined relations between the two countries and thereafter there was improvement in the frontier situation.

Relations with Arabia. Improved relations were continued though tribal raids with the Shammar as the main offenders demanded the attentions of the RAF whose co-operation with the military and police security forces had already made a deep impression on the tribes.

Relations with Syria. Inter-tribal strife continued throughout the year and aircraft were frequently operating in support of armoured cars. There were no major operations.

Relations with Persia. Persia had still not formally recognised the state of Iraq. Relations were on the whole good and only minor incidents on the frontier occupied small numbers of aircraft. Internal disturbance, however, still threatened to have serious reactions inside Iraq.

Levies. [The Iraqi Levies was the first Iraqi military force established by the British in the new state. Its members were used mostly for the guarding of RAF bases.] The force was reduced during the year by one cavalry regiment. There was no change in the role of the Levies which continued to operate in [the Kurdish city of] Sulaimaniya area and in the territory of the Sheik of Barzani.

Dulaim Camel Corps. The newly formed Camel Corps of the Dulaim tribes were in action during the year and co-operated successfully with aircraft in intercepting a large raiding party returning from Kuwait with looted camels.

*

But we are getting ahead of ourselves. In the late spring of 1925 Hal sailed with a few other RAF officers in the Anchor Line freighter SS *Circassia* from Birkenhead en route for Bombay (Mumbai today). She was an old ship, powered by steam turbines fuelled by oil and manned by white officers, Indian crew and Goanese stewards. The *Circassia* cruised at 12 knots and hugged the coasts of Portugal, North Africa and Malta to Port Said where she took on more oil. During refuelling Hal and his fellow officers went ashore to the newly opened Simon Arzt store, which traded day and night the year round for the convenience of ships' crews, to buy lightweight pith helmets which they hadn't been able to get in England.

On posting overseas men were expected to buy tropical and formal kit from their tailors. This included:

- a khaki pith helmet with RAF flash
- khaki shirts with spine pads, worn to protect the back from the intense heat that was thought to cause heat-stroke.
- drill trousers, tunics and shorts, breeches and puttees and stockings
- black footwear
- a white mess-kit jacket with blue shoulder straps, gold badges of rank and wings
- miniatures of medals

SS *Circassia* en route to Bombay.

- brass buttons
- overall trousers
- blue cummerbund, white shirts and butterfly collars
- mosquito boots
- cold weather blue uniform

Port Said.

Ordinary clothes were also packed for a tour abroad. All kit was packed in tin uniform cases which were proof against white ants. Any cases the contents of which would not be wanted on the voyage were wooden crated to avoid denting in transit.

With the pilot aboard and a searchlight rigged in the bows, the *Circassia* entered the Suez Canal with its speed limited to 5 knots to avoid the wake damaging the canal's banks. The 'all clear' had to be obtained from each signal station along the length of the canal to proceed and if a large vessel was coming up as they sailed down they had to secure to bollards on the bank to let it pass, as they did a P&O mail steamer. Repair work on the canal banks and the dredging out of sand went on continuously by teams of workmen. Entering the Red Sea they had changed into tropical kit and air scoops were fixed in the portholes to create a draught. No fans were fitted. It was extremely hot and the heat brought out large brown cockroaches in the cabins. Whenever possible men slept on mattresses on deck during the hot nights but had to be up at dawn when the decks were scrubbed. If the light was turned off Hal could see the phosphorescence in his salt-water bath and the sea was brilliant with it at night. By day flying fish, schools of dolphins,

Hal in tropical kit, all of which was acquired before travelling to Iraq – except for the pith helmet which he bought in Port Said.

The Suez Canal.

sharks and electric eels were regularly seen. Hal spent some time studying Arabic during the voyage, trying to learn enough to use.

> The Bombay Pilot came on board on our 30th day out from
> Birkenhead and tugs took us alongside Ballard Pier near the
> Gateway to India. The Frontier mail train was on the pier ready
> to take passengers from a P&O liner which had just docked to
> the North-West Frontier where a tribal war was raging. The
> three of us bound for Iraq had to wait for a week in Bombay

for sea passages up the Persian Gulf. We were lucky enough to be invited to stay at a friend's flat on Malabar Hill overlooking the city where the air was fresher. But it was near the Towers of Silence where the Parsee sect expose their dead to the fowls of the air to be picked to bits. 'Souvenirs' often fell from the vultures into our garden. The pavements in the city were stained by smelly red spits from the betel nut chewers. Thousands slept the year round on the sidewalks and horribly deformed beggars pestered one for alms.

When they did sail for the Persian Gulf it was in the British India Steam Navigation Company ship SS *Vasna* which was also carrying large numbers of natives, pilgrims and others to Karachi, Bushire and Basra. They lived on deck where they cooked their food on charcoal braziers and where latrines to suit each religion were provided. It was again very hot in the Gulf – 120 degrees with high humidity. Hal was given a tour by the Chief Engineer of the boiler and engine rooms where it was even hotter and the crew wore only shorts and canvas shoes and also a hood over

The Indian Marine Dockyard, Bombay.

Bombay. Hal (left) and his friend 'Doc' on Malabar Hill where they stayed whilst waiting for a ship for the Persian Gulf.

their heads to avoid the constant drip of water caused by condensation on overhead beams. They entered the Shatt al-Arab river 120 miles south-west of the confluence of the rivers Tigris and Euphrates. The smell of the great oil refinery at Abadan hung in the air long before they could see it. From Basra just up-river they travelled to Baghdad on a metre-gauge

The opportunity to sightsee in Bombay was not to be resisted, especially as Hal had his camera with him.

railway. Stops were made for water and fuel and, as it was a non-corridor train, passengers also took the opportunity to leave their compartments for the dining car. The journey took about twenty-four hours and when the train pulled into Baghdad West at dawn they were met and driven into the city which looked just like the pictures of the Arabian Nights with a few golden domes and many blue ceramic domes of the mosques. There were crowds of Arabs, camels, donkeys and Kurds carrying huge loads on their backs. We crossed the River Tigris by the famous Maude bridge of boats to Air Headquarters at Hinaidi.

The aerodrome at RAF Hinaidi was some miles outside Baghdad. It was established as the main British base in Iraq after the First World

Whilst at Hinaidi Hal photographed much that he didn't later record in his memoir. He entitled this 'A typical Kurd'.

War, initially under British Army command until the Royal Air Force took over in 1922 when it accommodated Air Headquarters Iraq, five squadrons, an aircraft depot, units of RAF armoured cars and an RAF hospital. There were extensive barracks, recreational facilities, communication facilities, maintenance units, hangars and a civil cantonment all surrounded by a bund high enough (in theory) to protect against floods and wide enough to drive lorries on top .

Hal on arrival at RAF Hinaidi in 1925.

The AOC at Air HQ Iraq was AVM J.F.A. Higgins. Reporting directly to him was the Chief Staff Officer, Air Commodore H.C.T. Dowding, and reporting to him were the heads of two Air Staff Sections, 'I' and 'O'. Group Captain K.G. Brooke commanded 'O' and reporting to him were officers responsible for operations, signals,

Hal's quarters at Hinaidi.

Hinaidi was a large base and a narrow-gauge railway was used both to move supplies around and to bring them in from outside.

Winters in Iraq could be extreme. This is a view from Hal's quarters after periods of heavy rain.

armoured cars and training. The photography section came under the latter and was headed up by Squadron Leader G.E.H. James MC and it was to him that Hal, as Photographic Officer, reported.

In the RAF of the time, one of the requirements for those holding permanent commissions was to specialise and the areas in which they could specialise included armament, engineering, signals, navigation and photography. Once qualified the new skills learned could be applied as an instructor, staff officer or directly as a practitioner. On a squadron the specialist officers ensured that all pilots were up to date in their relevant fields and they acted as the officer in charge of that discipline on the unit.

Hal's training in all aspects of photography at the School of Photography at Farnborough had led directly to his appointment as

Winter in Iraq.

DH9A H3510 of No.84 Squadron. As photographic officer Hal borrowed DH.9As as he undertook his duties.

DH.9A J7852 of No.84 Squadron came to grief at Hillah aerodrome, 75 miles south of Baghdad. Hal wasn't the pilot on this occasion but accidents were relatively common in the Middle East because of conditions, the serviceability of aircraft or their suitability for operation in a hostile environment. Hal saw many examples of aircraft that had come to grief and of course he photographed them. He wasn't immune himself to experiencing the occasional problem.

Photographic Officer at Hinaidi. As part of his responsibilities Hal flew DH.9As borrowed from the resident squadrons (such as Nos.30 and 84) and, apart from undertaking strategic reconnaissance, he covered the country from Mosul in the north to Basra in the south for mapping purposes. Geologists at that time were on the hunt for oil and he put in a lot of flying time taking aerial photographs of hills which later proved to be where vast oil deposits were discovered. In addition, survey fights for new road and rail communications were an important part of Hal's duties.

> In the hot weather we got up before dawn and flew up to breakfast time while it was still cool and the air calm. Then up to noon we did administration and maintenance. After lunch in the heat of the afternoon when dust storms often occurred we slept under ceiling

An example of Hal's aerial photography. A French Nieuport Nighthawk over Hinaidi with rifle ranges, photo hut, defences and tennis courts beneath.

fans in our rooms and got eaten by sand flies if there was a power cut. Our Assyrian servants brought us tea about 4pm and then we played tennis or cricket till sundown. Evening baths laced with Jeyes fluid to disinfect the insect bites preceded dinner in mess kit with perhaps a visit to a concert party afterwards. We slept on the roofs of our mud hut quarters with the legs of the bed in tins of paraffin to discourage creepie crawlies. I got sand fly fever when it was 122 degrees in the shade and had a spell in hospital.

Many opportunities presented themselves to Hal beyond his RAF duties and Hal was of course there with his camera when they did.

More examples of Hal's photography. Inhospitable territory. An old Kurdish mountain stronghold.

The mosque of Khadimain (now Al-Kādhimiya), Baghdad.

Soon after his arrival at Hinaidi Hal was to see the Italian aviator Francesco De Pinedo who in 1925, accompanied by engineer Ernesto Campanelli, flew a fragile SIAI S.16 single-engined biplane flying-boat, then being built for the Italian Navy, from Rome to Australia to Tokyo and back to Rome, covering 55,000 miles in six months. Hal saw De

A dust storm approaching Hinaidi.

Pinedo and his aircraft in Baghdad as it landed on the River Tigris (and collided with a gunboat as it water taxied) on his return flight to Rome.

Then in late March 1926 a pair of specially prepared Fokker CVs flown by Captains Botved and Herskind of the Royal Danish Army Air Corps, each with a mechanic on board, arrived. They were on a flight from Copenhagen to Tokyo and back. All military equipment was replaced with extra fuel, oil and supplies for the crew.

Three months later Hal was at Shaibah when a modified Potez 28 (the fuselage was fitted with additional fuel tanks) landed after setting a new world distance record with a non-stop flight from Paris, piloted by the brothers Ludovic and Paul Arrachart. Leaving Paris on 26 June they landed at RAF Shaibah with a broken fuel pipe, having covered a distance of 2,680 miles in 26 hours 30 minutes. A few days later on 30 June, Alan Cobham and his mechanic A.B. Elliot left England on a survey flight to Australia in de Havilland DH.50J G-EBFO equipped with floats. Over Iraq Bedouin tribesmen fired at the aircraft, breaking a fuel line and wounding Elliot who later died in hospital. Cobham landed on the Tigris at Baghdad to fix the fuel line and to recruit Sergeant Ward of No.84

Gertrude Bell at Hinaidi in November 1925, photographed by Hal.. She was the English writer, political officer, archaeologist and spy who explored and made contacts in the Middle East during the First World War. She was an important and influential figure, more so in many respects than Lawrence, and she played a major role in establishing the modern state of Iraq thanks to her knowledge of and relations with tribal leaders throughout the Middle East. Unusually for the time for a woman she was highly thought of by British officials and was empowered to act on behalf of the government. She was also held in esteem by the Arabs.

Squadron as a replacement for Elliot. They arrived at Port Darwin on 5 August. When he flew back to England Cobham became the first pilot to make a return flight from England to Australia in the same aircraft.

Hal had taken one of his father's shotguns with him to Iraq 'and we had splendid weekend shooting parties in the ruins of Babylon and down

King Faisal exiting a Vickers Vernon at Hinaidi in November 1925.

The Italian Francesco Pinedo's SIAI S.16 flying-boat which he flew from Rome to Tokyo and back in 1925. Hal photographed it on the River Tigris in Baghdad.

One of two Royal Danish Army Air Force Fokker CVs, this one carrying the serial R1, at Hinaidi on its flight from Copenhagen to Tokyo in 1926.

Alan Cobham's DH.50 had 'SIR CHARLES WAKEFIELD FLIGHT TO AUSTRALIA' sign-written on the forward fuselage. Sir Charles was the sponsor of the flight.

the Tigris by launch to the Ctesiphon Arch' which lay south of Baghdad. This is the first of many mentions in his memoirs of archaeological sites he visited whilst in the Middle East and later in India, obviously of considerable interest to him. (Ctesiphon was the imperial capital of the Parthian and Sasanian Empires, was one of the great cities of ancient Mesopotamian and was twice the size of Imperial Rome.) But on this occasion it was the shooting that came first.

We would be out on the sandbars before dawn and then as soon as it was light the sand grouse flew over us in clouds. One did not aim at individual birds but just browned the mass. We hired Arab boys to fetch the fallen to be brought back for the squadron messes. Duck and geese and even gazelle were brought home on occasion. The gazelle had to be shot with a service rifle from a moving car.

Drama at Hinaidi. Two unidentified DH.9As destroyed by fire after a bomb one was carrying exploded.

A shooting party on the Tigris. Hal had one of his father's shotguns with him, taken for this express purpose.

A Vickers Vernon of No.45 (Bomber) Squadron at Hinaidi. 45 Squadron operated an air service between Baghdad and Cairo.

Hal also recorded things that were not directly connected with his own RAF duties but which piqued his interest. For example he was interested in an air service which operated between Baghdad and Cairo using Helwan-based twin-engined Vickers Vernons (the first dedicated troop transport for the RAF) of No.45 Squadron. This service had started in July 1921 and incredibly, but necessarily, a track, visible from the air, was created across the desert from Baghdad to the eastern edge of the desert in Jordan to act as a guide for the pilots. The route between the two cities was 866 miles long with the western third mostly over the well-populated coastal plains between the Nile and the Dead Sea where there were plenty of landmarks by which to steer. But the eastern section was over the Jordanian and Iraqi deserts, uninhabited except for nomadic tribes and with few landmarks, so the track was laid by the wheels of an armoured car or by a plough pulled by a Fordson tractor, depending upon the nature of the terrain. Twenty-six emergency landing grounds were created along the route, several of which included spare tanks of fuel. And of course the problem of finding a force-landed aircraft was overcome by simply following the track.

This service provided useful training for aircrews and it meant that a limited number of important officials, mail and parcels could reach Iraq (via Egypt) more quickly. A Vernon could carry seven individuals plus mail, which was charged at 3d (1p) an ounce. The number of passengers was reduced for longer flights or if parcels were carried. Sometimes the eastbound flight brought boxes of kippers from cold storage in Cairo which was a great treat because everyone got rather tired of Tigris mud fish, caught by the natives by throwing pieces of chapatti 'doped with something that made the fish faint and float to the surface' where they could be gathered into nets!

When the snow melted in the Caucasus Mountains in 1926 the rivers Tigris and Euphrates burst their banks, flooding vast areas from north of Baghdad down to Basra. Baghdad city and the Hinaidi cantonment were surrounded by a huge lake and what had been desert became a sea with 'white horses' when the wind blew. So serious was it that it was feared the waves would wash away the soft muddy banks

Vickers Vernons formation flying near Hinaidi.

Hinaidi floods: stores being brought across to the bund from the submerged railway station.

Hinaidi floods: repairing the bund.

of the bund and so Indian sappers and miners were drafted in to place sheets made from dried palm leaves along the high water mark to stop the erosion. Hal took many photographs of the extent of the flooding and also a cine film which he sold to Pathé Gazette (the original name of Pathé News).

Towards the end of his year in Iraq Hal and two colleagues took ten days leave in Beirut, which in those days was in Syria, later becoming the capital of Lebanon when that country won its independence in 1943. They crossed the desert from Baghdad by Nairn Transport, a company which operated a Beirut-Haifa-Damascus-Baghdad and return route known as the Nairn Way, taking about thirty hours for the run. The vehicles were open American Cadillac cars driven by tough Australians who had to be stewards to their passengers as well as drivers. The schedule meant they reached the Syrian border at 2.00am after which they had to drive on the right (by virtue of French control of Syria) as opposed to the left in Iraq. It was hot. A tank of water on the back seat had a long tube so that each occupant could take short drinks *en route* although the water became unpleasantly warmer as they proceeded. On the return trip their convoy was escorted by French Foreign Legion troops in armoured cars

Nairn Transport operated a cross-desert route known as the Nairn Way using American Cadillacs.

because of possible bandit attacks but 'they left us when it was thought danger of a shoot up was past.'

Having reached Beirut all three enjoyed the chance to swim in the clear waters of the Mediterranean and sunbathe – but they overdid it and had to stop after a few days when their skin blistered. And again there were sights to be seen, including Baalbeck (known as Heliopolis during a period of Roman rule), famous for its ruined temples and for the largest quarried stone in the world, weighing in at 1,200 tons.

There is little doubt that Hal and his friends took full advantage of the ancient land in which they found themselves and they visited many of the key sites as he was quick to mention. Indeed at one point in his memoir Hal writes: 'it may be of interest to record the places in Iraq which I flew over or visited on the ground which are mentioned in the bible or in fiction.' [The author's notes are in italics.]

- Nineveh, once capital of Assyria (*which lies across the river from Mosul*).

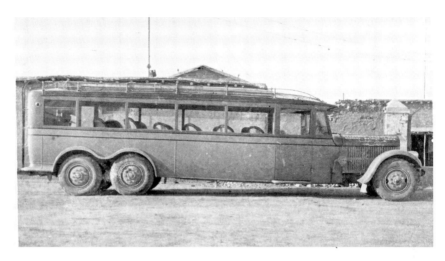

Nairn Transport also had larger vehicles on charge. Inscribed on the bonnet of this monster is 'Overland Desert Mail Baghdad-Beirut-Haifa' with Arabic script beneath.

The French escorted the Nairn cars in the Syrian desert. Hal and two colleagues used the service to get to Beirut for a spot of leave.

- Erbil (*which dates back to at least 6000 BC and is one of the oldest continuously inhabited cities in the world*)
- Kirkuk (*the supposed site of the burning fiery furnace*)

Whilst on leave Hal visited Baalbeck. Indeed he took full advantage of the opportunities which presented themselves to photograph many archaeological sites in Iraq.

Excavations at Babylon. Another of the dozens of photographs Hal took from the air.

The walled city of Samarrah taken by Hal. It stands on the east bank of the Tigris 100 miles north of Baghdad. The tower in the foreground is a spiral minaret.

- Hit, bitumen wells which furnished pitch to build the walls of Babylon. (*Hit is a small walled town built on the site of the ancient city of Is. The bitumen wells have been used for at least 3,000 years*)
- Babylon. (*King Nebuchadnezzar, in a reign of more than forty years, was the ruler who destroyed Jerusalem and carried off the Jews into their Babylonian captivity. And he created the Hanging Gardens. As a city Babylon is known to have existed for fifteen centuries BC*)

The Ctesiphon Arch, south-east of Baghdad.

- Kish, (*inscriptions in the ruins tell us that it was the first city founded after the Flood and was the traditional first capital of the Sumerians*)
- Ur of the Chaldees, the birthplace of Abraham
- Basra, the port of (*the fictional*) Sinbad the Sailor.

Chapter Ten

No.14 Squadron

O n 18 October 1926 Hal left Hinaidi having completed what was for those days a short tour in Iraq. He, and those who travelled with him having also completed their tours, left by train for the Persian Gulf, stopping for refreshment at Ur of the Chaldees. From Basra they took a stern-wheeled river steamer down the Shatt al-Arab to the harbour bar where the *Assaye,* an old P&O troopship, was anchored, her draught being too great to come up to Basra. 'All the way down the Shatt al-Arab from Basra to Abadan and beyond the banks are lined with forests of date palms with date packing stations at intervals, opposite which steamers were loading the fruit for worldwide markets,' remembered Hal. 'The hornets which frequent the palms are large insects with trailing antennae. One sting and you are in hospital.'

The *Assaye* already had a large passenger component on board, including wives *en route* from England to India 'all wearing the latest fashion in short skirts which we had not seen before. This caused quite a stir!' The voyage to Karachi was otherwise uneventful. Once there, men travelling on to RAF units in India left the ship and then, after a further few days, tour-expired personnel bound for the UK disembarked. For those left on board

> snake charmers showed their skill on the wharf and several turtles were brought on board for cooking. Newly born baby turtles were also brought to the ship. We put numbers on their shells and organised races on deck. We caught lots of fish in the harbour, among them puffer fish which blow themselves up like a balloon once they are landed in the boat. Coming up the Red Sea I got shots of dolphins swimming and jumping right in front of the bow.

The stern-wheeled river steamer which took Hal from Basra down to the P&O troopship, the *Assaye* that would take him on to the southern end of the Suez Canal.

A date-packing depot on the banks of the Shatt Al-Arab.

Men bound for Egypt and Palestine were landed at Suez at the southern end of the canal to save paying canal dues. That included Hal who was bound for Palestine to join No.14 Squadron as a flight commander. He travelled by train to Kantara (nowadays Al Qantarah El Sharqiyya) to catch the night mail for Lydda (Lod) and woke at

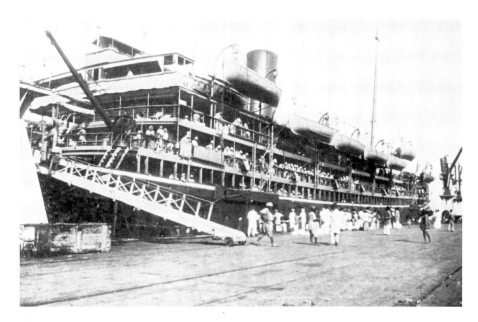

The *Assaye* alongside at Karachi. RAF wings can just be made out in the centre of the bridge behind the derrick.

dawn the next day as they were passing through huge plantations of orange trees 'the scent of which was delightful at the open window'. From Lydda he drove to Jerusalem in an RAF Rolls Royce armoured car which was on a duty run. Security of RAF airfields and bases in the Middle East was the responsibility of armoured car companies and No.2 RAF Armoured Car Company was based at Amman from 1922. Other duties for the cars included rendering assistance to downed aircraft, often escorting lorries carrying spares long distances to them.

Hal was excited at the prospect of seeing Jerusalem.

> It came fully up to expectations but I was to see lots more of it in the following years. It was a glorious day and I shall always remember the view from the top of the Mount of Olives over the Garden of Gethsemane towards the walled city of Jerusalem and also eastwards over the Dead Sea valley to the Mountains of Moab.

An RAF armoured car and wireless transmission in the desert. Armoured Car Companies were provided for the security of RAF airfields across the Middle East.

Making his way to Ramleh, Hal was flown from there by an old colleague of his, Flight Lieutenant Philip Wigglesworth (later Air Marshal Sir Philip Wigglesworth), to Amman, the air headquarters of the dual mandated territories of Transjordan and Palestine, where he joined his new squadron. He was fascinated by what he could see on the flight: 'from about 12,000 feet above Jericho one could see four seas – the Mediterranean, the Red Sea (Gulf of Aqaba), the Dead Sea and the Sea of Galilee.'

No.14 Squadron had been re-formed on 1 February 1920, having been disbanded a year earlier, by the renumbering of No.111 Squadron at Ramleh. It was initially equipped with Bristol Fighters and by 1922 had moved to Amman whilst retaining a detachment at Ramleh, re-equipping at the same time with the de Havilland DH.9A. This was a far more capable aircraft than the Bristol Fighter for the squadron's role of peace-keeping from the air as it had a longer range and could carry bombs. Hal already had some experience of the DH.9A of course, briefly with No.39

Squadron and more extensively and recently at Hinaidi. Colloquially known as the Ninak from the phonetic alphabet treatment of its designation 'nine-A', there was one flight of four at Ramleh and two flights each of four at Amman. Amman aerodrome was situated on the edge of a cliff and in certain wind directions pilots had to touch down a few yards from the edge in order not to overrun the landing area. Hal was confident that this 'was not really a problem for we were all in such good flying practice that we could put the old 9A down in small places'. In 1927 a survey was carried out of all the aerodromes and landing grounds in Transjordan and Palestine. Amman was the main one and the survey recorded that it held stores of 10,000 gallons of aviation petrol (sic), 3,000 gallons of MT petrol, 2,000 gallons of aviation oil, 2,000 gallons of MT oil and 2,000 gallons of castor oil. It was noted that:

> this aerodrome is marked with a circle. It drains from the hangars in a direction east. The hollow east of the circle is therefore always wet for some time after rain and dangerous to land upon. The best part for landing is between the hangars and the circle, as near as possible to the hangars. The whole aerodrome goes out of action for one or more days after heavy rain.

Interestingly one of the responsibilities of the CO of No.14 Squadron was the quarterly inspection of all Transjordanian and Palestinian landing grounds and ensuring that stocks of fuel and oil at them were maintained at the prescribed levels.

Amman in those days was nothing like the city it now is. A military report on Transjordan revealed that there were 800 mainly stone-built houses and the population was a mix of 'Circassian Mohammedans (sic), Arab Moslems (sic) and Christians'. There was a significant amount of livestock – the report's anonymous author counted 1,500 cattle, up to 300 horses and 4,000 sheep and goats. It was the main commercial trading centre of northern Transjordan and was the chief seat of government with the Emir having a palace there. A 'reasonable hotel' had recently been built and there was a desire to develop the tourist trade in future

Amman as it was in the 1920s, taken from the amphitheatre.

years 'there being many antiquities worthy of a visit in Transjordan'. Amman was connected by railway to Dera'a and Ma'an and a metalled road led to Es Salt and Jericho. Otherwise it was 'fair weather tracks' to other villages and settlements. Finally the report said Amman was in communication telephonically and telegraphically with both north and south Transjordan.

Hal was to command the squadron's C Flight and he was pleased to discover that he had an excellent group of men under him and that competition between the two flights at Amman – the other was A Flight – was keen. (B Flight was at Ramleh, still flying Brisfits, until it too moved to Amman in August 1927, having by then re-equipped with DH.9As.) If an aircraft became unserviceable the ground crews worked day and night to repair it (provided the spares were available).

Serviceability, given the often harsh conditions, was generally good: Hal only had one forced landing whilst he was on the squadron and this was due to a sudden breakage of a rocker arm. He landed on a mud flat on the Sinai Peninsula and lived in the desert for about a week until repairs could be made and he could fly back to Amman. It wasn't the

North of Amman lies Jerash and this is an aerial view of the site that Hal took. He landed nearby and took more photographs.

most comfortable of experiences. Each day when the heat built up, sand devils, pillars of sand sucked up in vortices, swept over the landing area. Mirages appeared at the same time. But he wasn't alone. Apart from his observer, a donkey appeared from nowhere then wandered off after staying a few nights! They made a tent of sorts by hanging a blanket from the leading edge of a lower main-plane and sleeping under the wing. A heavy dew often caused water to drip from the trailing edges and this could be collected with a sponge to get enough water for shaving. They had a week's rations in tins and had water bottles and a water tank on the port wing. (In particularly hot weather the DH.9s also carried 'chargles', canvas bags full of water, lashed to each lower wing tip and these always produced a cool drink on landing.) Cooking was done on a Primus stove and in the evening they sat on the ground round a fire made from sage bushes which they had collected from the surrounding desert. They avoided bringing camel thorn close to the aircraft as it could puncture aircraft tyres – indeed to lessen the chances of this the DH.9As were later

Jerash: carrying water.

fitted with thorn-proof tyres. Aircraft carried a lot of survival equipment on cross-desert flights and necessarily so. This included a spare wheel bolted onto the fuselage (in some cases rather illogically *under* the fuselage where it could be difficult to get to depending on the nature of a

Jerash: excavations in the Main Street.

mishap) while a bedroll, a water bag (usually made from an animal skin), emergency rations and the crews' personal kit were attached or hung in cages on various points around the fuselage or under the lower wings. Loaded like this the DH.9A wasn't the most spritely of aircraft and one pilot reported he found it difficult to overtake or fly above flights of pelicans cruising comfortably along at about 70mph!

*

Within the complicated Middle Eastern political framework following the First World War and the Cairo Conference of March 1921, although Transjordan, ruled by the Hashemite dynasty, became a British protectorate under the British mandate for Palestine, it had a fully autonomous governing system. Both Transjordan and Palestine came under the aegis of one High Commissioner based in Jerusalem. Transjordan, known simply as Jordan from 1946, had a border with Saudi Arabia and it was seen as a buffer between that country and Palestine. The Emir Abdullah of Transjordan, the brother of Iraq's King Faisal, relied heavily on British financial and military support to control tribal conflicts within his

Jerash: the Senate House.

C Flight No.14 Squadron Amman, December 1927. The officers left to right are Flying Officer Cooke, Flight Lieutenant Crowe MC (Flight Commander), Squadron Leader Hopcroft DSC (Squadron CO), Flying Officer Festing Smith, Flying Officer Moritz.

No.14 Squadron flew the DH.9A. This is ER959 at Amman, Hal's personal aircraft.

kingdom. Responsibility for its defence was, as with that of Iraq and Palestine, handed to the Air Ministry and specifically to No.14 Squadron which operated in the Transjordan and Palestine mandates throughout the 1920s and 1930s having already served in the area during the First World War. To facilitate the execution of their new tasking, during the years after 1918 airfields and landing grounds were built across the Middle East.

Hal and DH9A ER959 at Amman. Note the squadron shield screwed to the fuselage side above his head. The aircraft didn't always carry this shield as other photos show.

Hal's groundcrew, LAC Worsdale (fitter) and LAC Layton (rigger) in front of Hal's ER959.

For the British, Transjordan was something of a different proposition to Iraq. For a start internal law and order in this rather more developed country was up until 1926 chiefly the responsibility of the Arab Legion and police forces and from 1 April 1926 also by the Transjordan Frontier Force. They would be supported by airpower if necessary. The Legion was financed by Britain and commanded by British officers and was formed as an internal security and police force to keep order among the tribes of Transjordan and to guard the important Jerusalem-Amman road. The Transjordan Frontier Force was an Imperial Service regiment, also financed by Britain and commanded by British officers – a lieutenant colonel, five majors, eight captains, three lieutenants, ten warrant officers and four staff sergeants: there were seventy-eight local officers and NCOs and ultimately 625 troops forming three cavalry squadrons and an infantry unit. A camel squadron and mechanised units were later added. The Force was used in the defence of both Transjordan and Palestine.

No.14 Squadron dealt in the main with incursions from outside the border although there were other duties too – ferrying officials, flying patients to hospital and carrying despatches and mails for example. Air policing involved flying twice-weekly sorties with three aircraft to observe tribal movements, often with Arab Legion officers as passengers. These patrols focused either on the Syrian border or the desolate expanses of south-east Transjordan. In the former case it was to dissuade Transjordanian tribes from incursions into Syria: in the latter it was to keep an eye on anything that might be stirring in the desert and to watch out for Imperial Airways aircraft that had force-landed and looking for and assisting cars on the desert tracks that had got lost or run out of petrol. This 'southern recco' as it was dubbed was not popular as crews found it tedious. In his history of the squadron, Michael Napier describes such a patrol which involved leaving Amman at first light to take advantage of the clear smooth air and flying about sixty miles south-eastwards to the desert fort at Qasr Tuba. The next landmark was the white chalk of the three peaks of the Jebel Thuleithuwat ten miles beyond which was the Arab Legion post at Ba'ir. The patrol then flew east to another post at Imshash on the Arabian border where they would land for a rest 'so that

The Transjordan Frontier Force on parade at Amman.

Hal's C Flight at Aqaba.

the crews could enjoy a breakfast of sausage and beans washed down on some occasions with an illicit bottle of beer'. The next leg was south to Hausa then east to Ma'an where the DH.9As landed on the 4,000-foot-high plateau. During the summer months it was too hot in the afternoon for the aircraft to take off again, so the crews resorted to taking a siesta until the cooler evening air when the Liberty engines generated sufficient performance for them to get airborne and return to Amman.

'There were several scares when we had to search for Wahabi raiders coming north from Saudi Arabia,' Hal wrote in his memoir. The fanatical Wahabis were much feared because they enforced their Sunni Islamic beliefs in a brutal way.

> Running low on fuel on one of these patrols I landed my flight at Aqaba. I had warned the police beforehand and they had camels waiting for us to ride into the village police post. The camels were nice to ride and we only went at walking pace along the shore of the Gulf [of Aqaba]. The animals were used to walking in the water but only scraped under the palm leaves which leant over the sea and we had to duck to avoid being swept off. One of my officers did get left on a tree and had to drop into the sea.

A Sunday morning spring clean at Amman. The Wahabi standard was captured by the RAF in 1924. The Wahabis were a feared Sunni sect.

In the spring of 1927 it was learned through intelligence agents that the Wahabis were planning to raid Jordan and No.14 Squadron responded by increasing their patrols of possible routes and wells that might be used. These continued through the early summer until on 10 July meteorological reports forecast heavy rains which would have put Amman aerodrome out of action. Hal's C Flight was at stand-by so the CO, Squadron Leader Edward Hopcraft, decided to send it to Ramleh (Palestine), which would remain useable. The rains duly came and turned Amman into a bog. After forty-eight hours the weather cleared and C Flight conducted a desert patrol from Ramleh without seeing anything unusual. The next day was fine too and the crews were all in the ground floor ante-room of Ramleh Mess having a pre-lunch aperitif with windows open and sun beating down when, with no warning, the pictures came off the walls and the place shook. Within a few seconds the whole flight launched themselves through the windows into the garden with their drinks still in their hands looking at a great column of dust from Ramleh village where an earthquake had wrecked native houses, killing 500 people. Buildings at Ramleh aerodrome were not particularly damaged but aircraft in the hangars had moved, some against the hangar sides thus damaging wingtips. The

Hal's flight was caught in a fierce gale at Ma'an in the spring of 1927. Hal resorted to slashing the fabric of the wings to stop the aircraft 'flying away'.

Ma'an. Hal's DH.9A after the 80mph gale. The struts have been knocked out by one of the other aircraft which were blown away.

earthquake affected a large area of Transjordan overall with property in Amman and Es-Salt particularly affected (not to mention scores of villages) and in Palestine at Lydda and Nablus as well as Ramleh.

A further signal about the Wahabis was received after the earthquake and Hal took his flight to Ma'an where the landing ground was of black basalt gravel and was, in contrast to many desert airstrips, serviceable after rain. They completed a patrol before landing but saw nothing untoward. That evening the weather became very oppressive and there was a dead calm. As was usual practice the flight secured their aircraft with screw pickets (to fix the aircraft to the ground) and ropes on the wings: the flying controls were secured and chocks firmly placed at the wheels. There were no meteorological reports to worry them and they went to their hotel about a mile away from the landing ground for a meal, leaving an Arab Legion guard and two airmen with the DH.9As. But the crews had hardly finished their meals when the wind started to roar, increasing in intensity all the time. A tender skidded to a halt outside the hotel with a very frightened corporal reporting that the 'kites were moving'. The wind was even worse on the exposed landing strip and the men could hardly walk against it. Clouds of dust with hail embedded in it added to their troubles. The aircraft wings lifted in the gale, tearing the screw pickets out of

Ma'an. Dismantling the aircraft and holding back the wings to prevent their blowing onto the fuselage.

Ma'an. Three damaged DH.9As on a train for Amman at Kutkani station.

the ground and blowing the aircraft tail first across the ground until they came up against a small hill where they remained with tail skids broken. There was no means of preventing them being blown farther away. It was impossible and certainly too dangerous to start the engines even if there had been any shelter to go to, so the crews slit the fabric on the lower wings

During his tour with No.14 Squadron Hal sailed home on P&O's SS *Naldera*, seen here at Marseille, for three weeks' leave.

to try to reduce their lift factor and then simply hoped for the best. There was no sleep for anyone that night and when day broke the wind was still blowing fiercely. 'This was a disaster indeed,' said Hal afterwards, 'and the Met Office got into serious hot water for failing to send me any weather report. And I had no barometer with me to warn me of the approach of bad weather.'

The aircraft were dismantled and taken by rail back to Amman. After fitting new wings, the squadron had all four aircraft flying again after about ten days. Fortunately the Wahabis, whom C Flight had been sent to look for, never materialised.

*

Shortly after this Hal was due for leave as he had been in three 'hot weathers' in the Middle East since coming out from England. He sailed from Port Said by P&O for Plymouth, had three weeks at home and then returned overland to Trieste and then by sea to Alexandria. And from that point 'life went on again,' said Hal.

Annual bombing and gunnery training was scheduled and completed. Two Spanish aviators came down in the desert and when reported missing the squadron was sent to look for them, a task made no easier by the fact that the pair had left their aircraft and walked away from it. Both were eventually found. (In May 1928 Sergeant Grayson and Flight Lieutenant Wigglesworth were presented with the Silver Cross of Military Merit by the Spanish consul for their part in the search for them.) The squadron helped in the survey for the oil pipeline from Iraq to Palestine built by the Turkish Petroleum Company. And there were medical emergencies at Amman.

The French *Corps d'Aviation* in Syria often visited in their 'lumbering old Breguets'. Their method of starting engines was rather dangerous but typically French.

> The mecanicien having set the propeller dashed from one wing tip, seized the propeller blade in both hands and pulled it smartly down. This worked with the low compression French engines but when they tried it on one of our high compression Libertys the motor started but the following blade caught the mecanicien and he went to hospital.

When Imperial Airways started their Middle East mail and passenger service with DH.66 Hercules three-engined biplanes they proved to be unreliable and often force-landed in the desert, necessitating the need for the squadron to look for them and assist in getting them back into the air by organising the ferrying of spares and fuel to them.

In November 1927 No.14 Squadron themselves became directly involved in mail flights when they were instructed to undertake a weekly Amman-Cairo-Amman service. The order for this has survived. Instructions were that one DH.9A be detailed weekly by the flight commander of the duty flight and the timetable to be followed was leave

Amman for Ramleh at 1230 on a Wednesday, depart Ramleh at 0500 the following morning for Gaza where the crew would wait for any mail for Imperial Airways before departing for Heliopolis. On the Friday the return flight would take off at 0700 for Ramleh and from there continue on to Amman at 1230. A route following the railway was to be strictly adhered to – Amman to Ramleh, Gaza, the police post at El Arish, Romani, another police post at Kantara, Abu Sueir, Tel El Kebir, Bilbeis and Heliopolis – and the same in reverse order on the return. The crew were to carry a revolver and ammunition. If a forced landing was necessary the crew were to carry out a thorough examination of the aircraft (assuming they were uninjured and were able to). If communication could be made with 'a RAF station' via police posts or railway stations, information should be given as to the cause and extent of damage, whether the aircraft could be flown after repair, the spare parts required, water, food and blankets required, the bearing and distance of the nearest police post or railway from the downed aircraft, whether road transport could get near to the downed aircraft or whether another aircraft could land safely nearby. If the forced landing was in a remote area and communication couldn't be established, as soon as the aircraft was reported

Amman. DH.66 Hercules G-EBMW. This type was used by Imperial Airways on its Middle East mail and passenger service but proved to be unreliable.

as being overdue attempts would be made to obtain any information from police posts or railway stations *en route*. Search aircraft would be despatched as soon as possible. Force-landed pilots were to adopt various methods of attracting attention, either by use of a hand signalling mirror, a bonfire of scrub, an oil or petrol fire 'using as a container the half petrol tin carried in the aircraft', or smoke bombs.

*

Whilst the squadron carried on with its general tasking 'we had to compete with the eccentricities of our Group Captain', Hal later rather fondly recalled.

> He had his own aeroplane and every time he flew we watched in trepidation. He finally turned it over on the aerodrome but remained in the cockpit timing the ambulance. When it arrived he said: 'Good heavens. Three minutes twenty seconds. Might have been dead by now.' His passion was archaeology and he planned the patrols by the armoured cars so as to visit old Roman remains. Flint arrow heads were a special joy to him. When out with the cars he liked to go for walks in the desert naked except for a pair of shoes, a prismatic compass and field glasses!

This rather colourful description refers to Group Captain Lionel Wilmot Brabazon Rees VC OBE MC AFC who took command of RAF Transjordan and Palestine in 1926. The interest in archaeology Hal refers to manifested itself in the taking of some of the earliest archaeological aerial photographs of sites in eastern Transjordan and the publishing of articles in learned journals about his findings, for which reason he is considered a father of the archaeological studies of the area and a pioneer of aerial archaeology. He had won his MC in 1915 when in the RFC and his VC when with No.32 Squadron during the Somme offensive in 1916.

*

In 1927 large numbers of refugees fleeing from the Druze revolt in French-controlled Syria had been permitted to set up a camp at Azrak but it soon became evident that the camp was also becoming a safe retreat for armed Druze fighters. To put an end to this Group Captain Rees, with No.2 Armoured Car Company and companies of the Transjordan Frontier Force, occupied Azrak in April 1927 and 'undesirable' Druze men were rounded up. No.14 provided constant air support and reconnaissance throughout the operation.

A 'Military Report on Transjordan' for 1927 and an entry in the squadron's operations record book summarised the Azrak situation:

> In the spring of 1926 while the French were operating in the Jebel Druze against the Druze revolt, a large number of Druze refugees, mostly old men and children and the families of the fighting men who had been killed, crossed the frontier

Group Captain Brabazon Rees was prone to crash landings, including one in DH.9A E870 at Burka, thirty miles north of Jerusalem, in June 1928. No.14 Squadron flew to the rescue.

E870 was dismantled and taken back to Amman by a Morris six wheeler.

into Transjordan. The Druze chiefs asked the Transjordanian authorities for permission to establish a camp at Kasr Azrak to accommodate them. This was granted on the understanding that they would assume responsibility for the good faith of the

Actually, forced landings were common. On the occasion photographed here, Flying Officer Cooke had force-landed near Yebnah in Palestine, his wheels sinking into mud after ten days of heavy rain.

Hal landed nearby on firmer ground to assist. He recorded that with 'no load and minimum petrol a run of a mile and a half was required to take off'.

inhabitants of the camp with the Transjordanian authorities. The Druze leaders gave an assurance that neither they nor their followers would come to Azrak and that the camp would not be used as a resort for armed men although a small number were allowed to remain as a guard for the camp. During the latter half of 1926 however it became apparent that the Druze leaders had not fulfilled these conditions and that the camp was being used by all the main leaders of the Druze revolt either as their permanent habitation or as a safe retreat from the fighting which was still being carried on against the French in the Druze country. The Druze leaders were asked for an explanation but made excuses so unsatisfactory that it was decided to enforce the neutrality of the camp by the despatch of a force to Azrak to eject all armed Druze and to prevent their return. A force consisting of three sections of No.2 Armoured Car Company Royal Air Force and three companies of the Transjordan Frontier Force under the command of Group Captain L.W.B. Rees VC acting in conjunction with air forces accordingly occupied Azrak on 17 April 1927. As soon as the news of the advance of this force reached Azrak the Druze chiefs, with a considerable number of their fighting men, departed into the Jebel Druze. On arrival of the British column at Azrak martial law was proclaimed: the camp was searched and men not allowed to be in the district were arrested. These were dealt with by Court Martial. A system of passes was established and by this means the camp was kept clear of all unauthorised persons and by 10 May the need for further military activity, except for small patrols, no longer existed....By 25 July all the Druzes had left Transjordan territory. The force at Azrak was then withdrawn. Thus an episode which in its early stages had threatened to develop most unfavourably was terminated without offensive action having to be taken. This result was due largely to the support in strength of the air forces and also to the employment of aircraft [of No.14 Squadron] to carry out reconnaissances for routes for the armoured cars and transport and to ensure that the ground ahead of the column was clear of a possible enemy.

The Azrak headquarters established for the Druze operation was transferred from Amman by air in just an hour by Vickers Victorias of No.216 Squadron flown up especially from Egypt. Hal flew into Azrak himself on several occasions.

With the serious business dealt with at Azrak, Hal shot duck on the marshes there. This was somewhat typical of RAF life in Transjordan in the 1920s. Every advantage was taken of being in this intriguing country of contrasts, with its different cultures, its magnificent archaeology, its sporting opportunities, and the often harsh beauty of the wadis softened by beautiful oases. Hal visited Petra twice, flying first to Ma'an, at that time the terminus of the Hidjaz metre-gauge railway, where there was a small hotel. (The railway, with its many miles of track below sea level, ran from Damascus to Medina through Saudi Arabia with a branch line to Haifa. It was built to connect Istanbul to Mecca but got no further than Medina because of the outbreak of the First World War.) From Ma'an

A Vickers Victoria troop carrier and transport, as used in the Druze operation in April 1927, in company with a Sopwith Snipe.

A Vickers Victoria interior. The aircraft is J7992.

Hal and his friends took the road for Musa where the police provided horses and an escort to ride through the narrow gorge to Petra.

When service transport was available, parties were sometimes made up to spend a weekend in Jerusalem. The road ran down the mountains of Moab past Es Salt, a settlement on the main highway from Amman to Jerusalem thought to have been built by the Macedonians during the reign of Alexander the Great, 'where each side was lined with blue lupins in spring', to Jericho in the Dead Sea valley. Hal's room at the King David hotel in Jerusalem overlooked the courtyard in front of the Church of the Holy Sepulchre. 'It was fascinating to watch all the different types of people visiting the church,' said Hal, 'but we missed seeing the Holy Fire arriving by runner from the north.' The Holy Fire is a miracle in which a blue light rises from the marble slab covering the stone bed believed to be that upon which Jesus' body was placed for burial and which is now in the Holy Sepulchre.

Social life at Amman was pretty good too. A few of the senior officers had their wives and families with them but in the main the men were single. Officers, sergeants and airmen had their own messes where dinners and dances were held but there were also opportunities for them all to socialise together. Sport was played at squadron and station level and within the working week time for participating was factored in.

The RAF Depot (Middle East), at Aboukir (near Alexandria) in Egypt, overhauled aircraft and engines. They also built propellers because it was found that locally-made airscrews lasted much better in the hot climate than those made in England. When the DH.9's Liberty engines were due for overhaul they were flown down to Aboukir and of course the crews

Concert parties were a staple diet of postings abroad. Social life in general could be good.

took full advantage of the occasion, enjoying a break by the sea while the engines were changed and aircraft serviced. Excursions by train into Cairo led them to 'a restaurant which included a floor show with the most incredibly activated belly dancers it is possible to imagine'. And a visit to a famous ice-cream shop founded in 1909 by the Swiss pastry chef and chocolate maker, Giacomo Groppi, was a must. Hal always took his film and cine film to the Kodak 16mm library for developing and processing, ready to show on his own projector to the men in the Amman canteen, together with those he had hired from the library. If he wasn't on the Aboukir flight himself one of his fellow officers chose the films. Each week there was a different two-hour showing.

Hal took on the role of test pilot, or at least of an evaluator, for a short while when a biplane Avro 561 Andover, of which only four were built, was allotted to him to fly and report as to its suitability for the desert. It had a single Rolls Royce Condor III engine of some 650 horsepower. There was only one set of flying controls and they were all manual. 'We worked out a method of changing pilots while in flight,' recorded Hal, 'and I did a number of long flights in the Andover and gave a fair report, but no more were ever built because the economy axe was beginning to fall.' The aircraft had been ordered by the RAF to replace DH.10s on the Cairo-Baghdad air route. It could be equipped for freight, twelve passengers or armed troops, or as an ambulance able to accommodate six stretcher cases. The pilot sat in an open cockpit below the leading edge of the upper wing. His navigator sat beside but below him and had access to the cabin.

Other diversions for Hal at Amman were of a more political nature, such as when he played a small part on a day which was in his eyes 'most unique' sometime in early 1927. He wrote:

> The Emir Abdullah of Jordan, who often entertained us to Turkish coffee in his palace at Amman under the watchful eye of his Circassian bodyguard from an area along the north eastern shore of the Black Sea, decided to call all his tribal chiefs to a feast to try to get them to bury the hatchet among themselves and there were many of them.

An Avro Andover. Hal evaluated the latter's suitability for the desert.

The company, once gathered, assembled on the floor of the old Roman amphitheatre in Amman. Other than Hal, non-Arab participants included various RAF officers including Group Captain Rees, the High Commissioner Field Marshal Lord Plumer and Major General Frederick Gerard Peake, known as Peake Pasha, creator of the Arab Legion. With the sheiks as well it proved to be a large gathering.

> We were seated cross legged on rich Persian carpets laid on the earth and, in accordance with Arab etiquette taking care not to show the sole of a foot to anyone, when a great hubbub was heard. We looked round to see eight Nubian slaves stripped to the waist carrying a huge wooden dish bearing a baby camel (which had been cooking all day) resting on a bed of rice and in a great pool of very hot gravy which splashed over the rim on to the naked shoulders of the slaves, making them howl. They put the great dish down in front of the Emir. Then drawing their daggers they plunged the knives into the camel's hump and cut the smoking meat down in strips before opening up the carcase to expose the intestines. The camel meat however was only for the important guests. The lesser sheiks received generous portions of sheep, most of which they took away tucked inside their clothing. Then

the ceremony started. The Emir with his right hand selected choice parts of the intestines for his honoured guests and then we were allowed to tackle the strips of meat already cut. It was the custom of course to use the right hand only. Tear off a portion of meat. Roll it into the rice and chew away. The meat was rather stringy and after a bit one's fingers almost stuck together. Rough cloths were brought round when we had eaten our fill to clean our hands on. Turkish Delight sorts of sweetmeats followed with thick sweet coffee.

Later in the year on 8 November Lord Plumer invested the Emir of Transjordan with the insignia of a Knight Commander of The Order of St Michael and St George (KCMG) which is awarded to an individual who renders extraordinary or important non-military service in a foreign country to Great Britain. A large investiture parade comprising the Arab Legion, the Transjordan Frontier Force and the Royal Air Force was held on Amman aerodrome with Hal proudly leading the RAF detachment on a march past.

The Emir's feast. Tribal chiefs arrive.

The Emir's feast. Sheiks and invited guests gather in Amman's amphitheatre.

Amman aerodrome. Hal (X) leading the RAF detachment in a march past on the occasion of the Emir of Transjordan's investiture with the KCMG.

On 7 April the following year (1928) the Crown Prince of Italy, Umberto of Savoia, visited Amman aerodrome as part of a visit to the Middle East (he was in Jerusalem on 1 April) and Hal again was involved in the ceremonial when the RAF provided a guard of honour and the

Amman 1928. Lord Plumer's car and his *major domo*. On this occasion Plumer was at Amman for the visit of the Crown Prince of Italy. He had also attended the Emir of Transjordan's investiture.

Transjordan Frontier Force gave a display. The Prince of Piedmont (as he was titled) was destined for a military career and became the commander in chief of the Northern Armies of Italy and then of the Southern, but in truth his was simply a ceremonial role as Mussolini was the actual commander. Umberto became the last king of Italy for just over a month in 1946.

Later in April a colossal cloud of locusts which had come up from Africa swept over Jordan, so densely concentrated that the sun was obscured. Hal had one of his aircraft in the air at the time and it landed at Amman covered with so many crushed locusts that it looked as if it was plastered with yellow mud! The local train could not get up the nearby hill owing to locust slime on the lines. 'It was amusing to watch the lizards jump on locusts on the earth, snap off wings and legs and leave the bodies for collection later while they collected more'. A military

The Crown Prince (the tall figure in the centre) with Italian officers from the cavalry, infantry, navy and air force with Hal on the right.

operation was launched to deal with the insects when they got to the stage of eating the crops. The locusts also interfered with the presentation of No.14 Squadron's sports prize giving by the Emir. As the squadron diary succinctly recorded the 'function was somewhat interfered with by low flying clouds of locusts'.

There may have been no need for the use of force in 1928, remarkable in that it was the first year since the squadron's formation that its aircraft were not fired upon, nor did they use their own weapons in anger, but it was essential that training continued to keep air and ground crews at the top of their game and the Lloyd Cup Competition was one way in which this could be done. The brainchild of Lord Lloyd, who was High Commissioner for Egypt and the Sudan in 1927, the competition was designed to test the reliability and efficiency of every RAF squadron in Middle East Command. No.14 Squadron participated in the first such competition from 23–26 April 1928 and Hal wrote a report for the powers that be once the competition had concluded and the squadron was back in Amman. It didn't make particularly happy reading.

First Day. Twelve DH9.As left at 0800 and all arrived at Abu Sueir for breakfast. Crews had to refuel their own aircraft and the drill was for the pilot to stand on top of the engine while the passenger opened the 4-gallon petrol tins with the special opener and handed the full tins to the pilot. Refuelling was timed by the judges. Leaving Abu Sueir, two machines' throttles jammed. This delayed take off. Twelve aircraft left at 1130 for Ramleh. One machine lagged astern near Kantara. It transpired afterwards that the pilot did not try his switches when the engine commenced to run badly. Had he done so the fault would have been discovered and a landing made at Kantara. Near Maddan station this machine landed on a salt pan. A 'T' was put out [in a signal square, used to communicate with pilots in the air if there was no radio, the landing 'T' indicating the wind direction with the tail of the T pointing downwind] and the remainder of the flight landed. The leader then took far too long in deciding whether the force-landed machine should continue. Meanwhile the remaining eight who had been circling round decided to land as fuel was running short. All twelve machines were on the salt pan which was so soft the wheels left deep ruts. It was at last decided to proceed to Ramleh. Eight planes took off but a ninth went on its nose after a tyre burst. The eight then landed again and stopped engines. Salvage work on the ninth commenced and it was made fit to take off. Starting up by hand was exhausting in the heat. One's mouth dried up by the strong salt air and water would not slake our thirsts. Water was near boiling in our wing tanks. Eventually eleven machines took off for Ramleh hoping to reach there by daylight. Eleven all landed OK without wing flares or ground lights which was a great piece of luck as we had no navigation lights and so the danger of air collision was extreme. We were all too exhausted to refuel that night and depressed because by the landings on the salt pan we had disqualified ourselves from the competition. We got six hours sleep that night and the next day it was hot (105°) when we refuelled.

Second Day. Over-revving engines on the first day had caused water leaks and one machine had to remain at Ramleh because there was no time to change cylinders. Each aircraft took in 100 gallons at Ramleh. The ten machines reached Heliopolis Cairo and later landed at Aboukir at about 1600. Two engines were found to need extensive repair however and as under the rules of the competition our crews had to do all repairs the men had to work all night changing cylinders and soldering other leaks. We did all we could to help but they were very tired next morning.

Third Day. Ten machines left at 0600 and only had to fly to Cairo and back to Aboukir. This was a rest day and we all felt much refreshed by our sea bathing.

Fourth Day. Ten left at 0700 for Heliopolis. We flew by compass and near Katatbara one fell out of formation and landed and after more troubles nine machines reached Heliopolis. Two unfortunately had to be left at Heliopolis owing to bad cylinder and water leaks thus cutting out all A Flight, leaving three of B and all four of C. After another spot of bother with C Flight six aircraft arrived back at Amman. I was very pleased that all *my* aircraft had come through the competition without trouble. This was mainly due to my not keeping aircraft in the flight after their flying times had expired. There were many lessons to be learnt by the competition and it was very well worthwhile.

There were indeed many lessons that had to be learned, for in terms of reliability and efficiency this was hardly a ringing endorsement of No.14 Squadron's capabilities. But Squadron Leader Hopcroft took Hal's report and set about rectifying the problems. The second competition was held in the November of 1928 with the squadron setting out on the 16th for Hinaidi and returning to Amman the following day. On the 18th it flew to Abu Sueir via Ramleh, returning on the 19th. Over the four days 1,600 miles was flown and none of the participating aircraft suffered any malfunction and none had to drop out. The squadron accordingly won the Lloyd Reliability Cup.

This came at the end of Hal's eventful posting in Transjordan and Palestine. He still had his eye firmly fixed on the future and throughout his time in the Middle East had been studying hard, as time permitted, in preparation for the RAF Staff College exam. 'A number of books had to be read,' Hal recalled.

> They dealt with history, the history of war, campaigns of the great captains, naval warfare and strategy and various air publications. I used *The Times* guaranteed book service to get the books and it took about three years to read the lot. The entrance exam was written and took three days. One was only allowed to sit after interview by one's Air Officer Commanding and an Air Ministry check up as to age, medical board and confidential reports over the years.

He took the exam in Baghdad before returning home and he passed. On 30 December 1928 he entered the college in Andover. Its brief was to train selected officers and prepare them for staff duties at the Air Ministry.

Chapter Eleven

Staff College and the Air Ministry

T he crest of the Staff College is the Hawk of Horus and the motto *Visu et Nisu* means *By Vision and Effort* – not as many of Hal's colleagues liked to pretend, *Vice is Nice*! On his course there were thirty students from the RAF, Navy, Army, Indian Army and Empire Air Forces and as passing meant gaining a year's seniority they were all determined to succeed. The year was divided into three terms and there was an expectation to make good use of holidays too. Hal with two fellow students went to Italy over the Easter of 1929 on a visit arranged by the Air Ministry and with a representative of the British Embassy in Rome they toured the Alfa Romeo and Isotta Fraschini works in Milan and the Savoia seaplane plant on Lake Maggiore. They were aware that there was a mock-up of the seaplane Italy was entering for the Schneider Cup race in the Savoia factory but were kept well away from any signs of it. 'A charming *Regia Aeronautica* officer, Commandante Maddalena, escorted us everywhere. He had landed a seaplane on the ice to rescue General Nobile whose airship had crashed attempting a polar fight,' reported Hal. Umberto Nobile designed and piloted the airship *Norge*, the first to fly across the polar ice cap from Europe to America and which may have been the first aircraft to reach the North Pole (the first claimed flight over the Pole by Richard E. Byrd and Floyd Bennett has since been discredited). Nobile also designed and flew a second polar airship, the *Italia*, a flight which ended in a crash and triggered Commandante Maddalena's rescue as part of an international effort.

Back in England 'we never had a spare moment in the college, what with lectures by staff, government speakers, scientists, industrialists and students (I lectured on air control in desert countries), syndicate work, air operations, appreciations, essays and conferences.' The syllabus was indeed demanding and very wide ranging and much of it was concerned

Buildings at the RAF Staff College, Andover

with military history, on land and sea as well as air. For example, Hal made copious notes on Stonewall Jackson and his campaigns, the Battle of Gettysburg, the strategy of the Russo-Japanese war 1904–1905, British history of the nineteenth century, principles of maritime strategy, air operations in Waziristan 1925, the Fleet Air Arm, the French Revolution, the Napoleonic wars, the Industrial Revolution, parliamentary reforms from 1832, the history of Ireland, Great Britain and world politics 1878–1911, self-governing colonies and their history, the Hertzog Policy in South Africa and so forth. A very mixed bag indeed and one wonders about the relevance of some of it. The course did eventually get down to the nub of things with air drill (theory), squadron formations, the air defence of Great Britain 1926–1927, notes on Army co-operation and the organisation and employment of aircraft working with the army, aircraft currently in RAF service and their performance, aircraft and personnel available in 1928 and the duties of a station commander.

Making good use of his allotted holiday time and enjoying relief from such intensive study – and Hal took it very seriously – during

The airport at Porto Littorio, Rome, into which Hal flew for his Italian visit
during Easter 1929.

the summer of his Staff College year Hal first of all spent time with
the Royal Navy on board HMS *Rodney* in the North Sea, then at the
Bristol engine works where he saw all stages in the manufacture of radial
aero engines. 'The engine test beds had a wonderful silencing device
whereby the sound was deflected by baffles so that only a loud hiss

Commandante Maddalena of the *Regia Aeronautica* who escorted Hal (to his left) and other members of the Staff College course during their visit to Italy.

resulted.' Next, at Cardington the R.101 airship was under construction in its huge hangar.

> When completed it was to start an air service to Egypt and India where mooring masts were being built as was a special hangar at Karachi. When we visited the station the framework was complete and the gas bags were being installed. We walked through the passenger accommodation. Everything had to be as light as

possible and so balsa wood was extensively used. But perhaps
the most extraordinary sight was the making of the 'gold beaters
skin', sheets from which the great gas bags were made.

According to some sources this skin was made from the genitalia of the
ox: others say it is the outer membrane of its intestine. Whichever is true,
at Cardington forty or so women, each with a barrel full of ox parts in
salt, made up a mosaic of them on a canvas screen. The method of making gas-tight joins in the skins was allegedly known only to a family from
Alsace who were employed by the Royal Aircraft Factory for many years.
Indeed the British had a monopoly on the technique until around 1912
when the Germans also adopted the material for the internal gas bags of
their Zeppelins although in the process they exhausted the available supply. The ox parts at Cardington came from the OXO Company in South
America.

The whole country was shocked by the R.101 disaster in 1930.
There had been various technical problems which the engineers said
were sufficient to delay the start but the Air Minister, Lord Thomson,
wouldn't hear of it. For political reasons the flight to India via Egypt
had to take place as arranged, his rationale being that there was only a
million-to-one chance that anything could go wrong. So the airship left
its mast at Cardington on a stormy Saturday night and set course for
France. Progress was slow and there was a progressive loss of height
until finally, near Beauvais, R.101 crashed into the ground at full power
as the captain tried to climb and save her. Lord Thomson was among
the dead. Three men in the tail escaped. 'I saw the headlines on the
Sunday morning and rushed to the office,' wrote Hal who by this time
was at the Air Ministry.

We were soon busy organising the funeral which took place at
Cardington. We arranged special trains to convey relatives to
the mass graveside. All the undertaking had been done by the
Bertram Mills family who were the government appointed
agents in the matter.

The disaster effectively marked the end of airship development in England. Not so in Germany though. At this time the Germans were operating the *Graf Zeppelin* which had completed a number of ground-breaking flights. In August 1931 she visited the London Air Park at Hanworth, very close to where London Heathrow was later built, and the following July she returned as part of a round-Britain tour and operated charter flights over London. Hal recorded all this on his new Bell and Howell cine camera. In November he also took his camera to Calshot on Southampton Water when the huge, twelve-engined Dornier DoX landed after a flight from Amsterdam. She was *en route* to the United States from Friedrichshafen, but it was to be a very prolonged flight for, after visiting Calshot, it was interrupted at Lisbon at the end of the month when a fire consumed most of the portside wing. The damage took six weeks to repair before the Dornier could continue on her way. She was beset with several more mishaps flying along the western coast of Africa and it wasn't until June 1931 that she reached the Cape Verde islands. From there she crossed the Atlantic to Brazil then flew north, finally reaching New York at the end of August, almost nine months after leaving Germany. She wasn't the sprightliest of aircraft. Her twelve 610 horsepower Curtiss Conqueror engines imparted a maximum speed of 131mph and a cruising speed of only 109mph with a range of just over 1,000 miles. Her service ceiling was 10,500 feet. It was the sheer size of the flying-boat which fascinated Hal although along with many other commentators of the time he couldn't see a commercial future for the type because of the cost and the limitations of her performance. They were right.

Other course visits with the Staff College took Hal to the Army tank ranges where, whilst travelling across country, he and his fellow students tried their hand at aiming what Hal records as a 6-pounder tank gun but which was probably a 2-pounder, the standard tank armament of the day. The former wasn't developed until the Second World War began. On another day they were at sea on an aircraft carrier watching experiments in deck landing by Fairey IIIDs with no arrester wires. Then there was a trip in an H-class submarine, *H43*. They dived off the Isle of Wight and 'as we watched the depth gauge go down there was a sudden bump. We had hit bottom. The captain ordered 'blow numbers one and two' or something like that until the depth gauge showed we were rising.' Back on dry land they went to television inventor John Logie Baird's studio in Frith Street, Soho and 'we saw ourselves on a small screen in a very flickering picture'.

There was a certain amount of flying (around forty-seven hours) during Hal's year at Andover on three types: he quotes them as being the Bristol Fighter, DH.61 and Avro 504N (known as the Avro Lynx after its engine). The Bristol Hal was, of course, familiar with but this was possibly his first encounter with the Avro and the de Havilland. Hal describes the latter as the DH.61 with a Cirrus engine. But the aircraft (a large biplane transport aircraft of which only ten were built for an Australian requirement) was powered variously by Jupiter, Jaguar or Hornet engines. The Cirrus III powered the DH.60M Moth and this was more likely to have been Hal's aircraft, given the context of the Staff College. Flying was designed to keep those on the course current and, in the main, involved practice approaches and landings, some cross-country navigating, slow

Amongst many other visits whilst at Staff College was one to the H-class submarine, *H43*.

Hal on the conning tower of *H43*.

flying in the Moth ('ground speed 30 mph'), aerobatics and formation flying. On 22 March 1929 his log book noted that he 'passed the Fairey long distance monoplane over Andover'. They were actually called Fairey Long Range Monoplanes, a pair of which were built. These were experimental single-engined, high-wing aircraft. Hal would have seen J9479 which first flew in November 1929. The second, K1991, flew in June 1930. On 12 June he flew to Gosport and 'watched an L Class submarine diving'. The L class was a derivative of the E Class which was the mainstay of the Royal Navy's submarine fleet during the First World War. The Ls served throughout the 1920s with the majority being scrapped in the 1930s but with three remaining as training boats during the Second World War.

The Staff College course ended with a Combined Operations exercise with the Army Staff College at Camberley and the Royal Naval Staff College at Greenwich. Lord Trenchard, Chief of the Air Staff, was the last lecturer and he spoke to each man individually about his next appointment and so it was he who told Hal his job would in Air Staff Organisation at the Air Ministry. Just before he went on leave for Christmas Hal was also told to put up two and a half stripes. He had been promoted to squadron leader.

Hal would spend almost three years at the DOSD, the Directorate and Organisation of Staff Duties, from February 1930 to January 1933. On his appointment he attended a levee at Buckingham Palace with hundreds of others, all in full dress. (Hal hired his from the London tailors Gieves Ltd..) A levee was a formal occasion, preceded by briefings and rehearsals in the procedure for being presented to the king and queen in the Great Throne Room. There were no refreshments and, of more importance to some of the old generals perhaps, there was no sign of any lavatories!

The DOSD was in Adastral House in Holborn. Officers serving at the Air Ministry received a London allowance to cover extra expenses. Standard dress was a dark suit, bowler hat and rolled umbrella. Uniform would of course be worn when visiting stations. Hal lived at the RAF Club in Piccadilly at first, then moved to digs at Earls Court. His chief was Air Vice Marshal Bowhill, 'a splendid man to work for'. Hal shared his duties with Wing Commander Reggie Marix 'with whom I shared an office and who was a most amusing companion and a great ladykiller'. AVM Bowhill had had a fascinating and varied career, starting as a midshipman in the Merchant Navy in 1896. By 1920 he was the Chief of Staff to Group Captain Robert Gordon for the Somaliland campaign against the Dervish forces of the Somali religious leader Mohammed Abdullah Hassan, usually known as the Mad Mullah. He went on to be Officer Commanding the RAF Depot at Aboukir in Egypt in 1925 and Senior Air Staff Officer at HQ RAF Iraq Command in 1928 at the time Hal was in the Middle East although Hal doesn't record whether he met him there.

By contrast Reggie Marix was a founder member of the Royal Naval Air Service and, in October 1914, during an attack on Zeppelin sheds at Düsseldorf became the first pilot to destroy an airship on the ground. In *Reggie: The Life of Air Vice Marshal RLG Marix CBE DSO* the author John Lea quotes Reggie's own account of this action.

What with one thing and another it was afternoon before we were airborne. I had a good trip and got to my destination without incident. But the shed was not where I expected to find it and my map had been wrongly marked. So I had to fly around a bit which excited some interest. I was at 3,000 feet and some AA opened up but well wide of the mark. I found the shed further away from the town than expected. I closed and as soon as I was sure of my target I put my nose down and dived with my engine still on. One would not normally do this as it puts an awful strain on the rotary Gnome as the revs go up. One usually switched off to come down but then it took a certain amount of time for the engine to pick up again. I wanted no loitering near the ground.

The Gnome stood up and when I was at about 500 feet I released the two bombs, one after the other, and began to pull out of the dive. I had kept my eyes fixed on the shed but I vividly remember the rapid points of fire as the ground machine guns opened up. I had been robbed of surprise by having to fly around looking for the shed. Having got into a climb I tried to turn away but to my momentary consternation found that I could not move the rudder. The rudder bar was quite solid and I was heading further into Germany. But I quickly appreciated that one can turn, although more slowly, on warp alone. This I did and set course for Antwerp. As I pulled out of my dive I looked over my shoulder and was rewarded with the sight of enormous sheets of flame pouring out of the shed. It was a magnificent sight.

Reggie was flying a Sopwith Tabloid, so named because of its diminutive size. Two years later he was seriously injured whilst test flying a Nieuport. At 200 feet one wing detached and the aircraft plummeted to the ground with Reggie trapped underneath. His injuries were such that he wouldn't fly operationally again. His right leg had to be amputated and the left was severely damaged. But he was of such character that he was determined to stay on in the RNAS and, from April 1918, in the RAF. By 1930 he had been promoted to wing commander. As John Lea says:

He was warm and responsive to people but at the same time self-disciplined. A party goer and giver when the setting was appropriate but dedicated to round the clock duty when his country needed him. He was a raconteur, pianist, hypnotist and writer of light hearted prose yet was never free of pain since the loss of his leg.

Such was this resolute, determined and complex character. There is little wonder Hal warmed to him and happily worked alongside him for three years. During those three years hours were 10am to 5pm Monday to Friday with an hour for lunch, but they inevitably often had to work for much longer. 'There was always too much paperwork,' complained Hal.

One had no sooner cleared one's 'in' tray than our clerk would come in with another arm full of files. Some files were nearly a foot thick with past history tied up with recent papers with up to date material. Action on the files was endlessly varied. Action on some took months to finalise, others were 'immediate' and had to be dealt with at once. A green file meant a question in Parliament. Then one had to drop everything and action the file. A red file contained secret matter.

One of the many projects he and Reggie worked on was the organisation of the 1931 Schneider Trophy seaplane race. This meant a lot of paperwork and visits to Calshot on Southampton Water where the seaplanes were to be based. The result was that Britain won her third successive trophy and thus secured the Schneider Trophy permanently. Hal wrote that Italian and American aircraft also competed. But his memory appears to have failed him for the Italians and Americans didn't compete on this occasion. The 1931 race was in fact originally to be between Britain, Italy, France and Germany but when the latter two countries withdrew it was down to the Supermarine and Macchi companies and their chief designers, Reginald Mitchell and Mario Castoldi. The Italians formed the *Reparto Alta Velocita* on Lake Garda in 1930 to put seven specially selected pilots through eighteen months of training. The designs of the seaplanes were astonishing. Castoldi's – the Macchi-Castoldi MC.72 – had two Fiat engines coupled in tandem to generate a total of 2,800hp which could be raised to 3,100hp for short periods. Each of the engines was 11 feet long and weighed over 2,000lbs. A major consideration was adequate cooling and radiators featured on the wings, fuselage, the front of the floats and the struts that supported the floats. The floats themselves doubled as fuel tanks. Five of these aircraft were planned but the first of them crashed after reaching a recorded speed of 375 mph. The Italians immediately petitioned for the race to be postponed but Britain refused and was left as sole entrant with Reginald Mitchell's Supermarine S.6B (there were two of the type). Even this was thrown into doubt for a while as Supermarine were in financial difficulty at the time and the Air Ministry refused to spend any more money on a racing event. The day was saved by a philanthropist, Lady Lucy Houston, who intervened by contributing £100,000.

On 13 September 1931 both British S.6Bs took off from Lee-on-Solent before an enormous audience of an estimated half a million people crowding the coast of Portsmouth and the Isle of Wight. The British team set a new world speed record of 380 mph and, as already stated, won the Schneider Trophy outright thanks to their third straight win, even if it was without opposition on the day. Both Hal and Reggie were judges, ensuring amongst other things that the aircraft kept strictly to the proscribed course around the Solent. At the end of September an S.6B recorded an average speed of 407.5 mph, the first time any aircraft had exceeded 400 mph.

For Hal there was an amusing postscript to all this over tickets to watch the race.

> The phone rang and a husky voice said 'I am Drogheda.' This made no sense to me so I asked for a repeat but still could not understand. The voice got more and more irate so I said 'just a minute'. I then changed my voice and asked who the caller was. The voice calmed and said it was Countess Cathleen of Drogheda. She asked for tickets and said her maid would collect.

> Later in the day a very gorgeous creature was announced and
> I got into such a spin that I gave her the wrong tickets!

Come August 1930 Hal was entitled to some leave and he spent it visiting
the Baltic states. He sailed from Hull in a small freighter carrying Bristol
Bulldog fighters for the Estonian Air Force and the ship sailed through
the Kiel Canal which 'was to me of special interest because every bridge
was of different design. The German engineers wanted to show what
they could do'. And Hal realised they could do a lot. It took 9,000 workers eight years to build the canal which was officially opened by Kaiser
Wilhelm II in June 1895. Between 1907 and 1914 its width was increased
to allow the passage of battleships which enabled them to travel from the
Baltic to the North Sea without having to circumnavigate Denmark. It
also shortened Hal's journey time and at Tallinn he stayed with an old
friend who introduced him to an Estonian Air Force mess where 'one
learnt the correct way to drink vodka. Drain the glass in one gulp and
then eat a small piece of toast spread with caviar'. The ship's next port
of call was Riga (Latvia) where he stayed with another RAF friend. This
time he was taken to inspect a lake where moorings were being laid for
three flying-boats to use some weeks later, a flight which Hal was organising at the Air Ministry. He left his ship at Riga and took a train for
Berlin via Lithuania and Poland and then on to the Hook of Holland.

> In those days before Hitler came to power the conditions in
> Germany were grim. Germans begged money for food from me
> in the Unter den Linden. But there were certain parallels here to
> the situation in Britain in 1930 where unemployment was high.
> Welsh miners roamed the streets begging for money and old
> friends who were out of work often came to my office asking if
> there was any opening for them in the RAF in any capacity.

The fact that Hal's base of operation at the DOSD was in the centre of
London didn't prevent him getting in some flying. This was either practice flying so that he could keep current or flights to RAF stations in

the southern half of England as part of his regular duties. Northolt was the airfield he flew from. In the main he used the Fairey IIIFs of No.24 (Communications) Squadron, an interesting squadron that operated eight different types of aircraft for liaison and communications duties. Apart from the IIIFs, Hal's log book records Bristol F.2bs, Avro Lynx and Gypsy and Tiger Moths. He also occasionally got his hands on a Westland Wapiti but these weren't No.24 Squadron aircraft, they were Wapitis Hal collected from the Westland factory at Yeovil and ferried up to the packing depot at Sealand near Chester. They were destined for India to be used in the army co-operation role. Returning to the Fairey IIIF there is a delightful story that Philip Jarrett relates in his book on the aircraft which is worth repeating here. The IIIF was curiously named, as other Fairey products all bore names, many of them alliterative like Fairy Fox, Fairey Flycatcher, Fairey Firefly etc. One of the gatemen at the Fairey factory, a Mr. Hearn, who always pronounced 'th' as 'f', is reputed to have said 'I see they all starts with a F like the Fairey Fawn, Fairey Fulmar and the Free-Eff!'

There were other things that Hal managed to escape from his Holborn office to do flying-wise, like 'inspecting certain routes of overhead power lines such as the Thames crossing and other river crossings'. On 1 August 1930 he flew from Northolt to Portsmouth via Halton and *en route* 'viewed overhead power lines from the air'; and on 27 February 1931 he flew up to RAF Digby in Lincolnshire for a 'survey of a route for overhead power cables'. On 30 December 1931 he was at Hornchurch 'to inspect overhead electric cables near the aerodrome', whilst on 19 August 1932 he was in the same area to 'to examine Thames crossing masts and to decide if red and white painting would be of value.' Three weeks later he noted that the 'cables were strung and visible'. Masts and cables of course constituted a danger to aircraft and had to be very visible and plotted accurately on charts.

Also of interest from this period of Hal's flying was when, on 4 June 1931, he took off in Fairey IIIF K2856 which had been fitted with 'Goodyear Air Wheels' but he noted that it 'was difficult to turn when taxying' with them.

Hal's time at the Air Ministry came to an end in December 1932. He had applied to return to squadron duty and in the New Year he was posted to the Central Flying School at Wittering for a refresher course on single-seater fighters. Whilst there Hal's new wife Nora and his new son John moved to her parents' flat in Harrogate. Nora, a designer of ladies corsets, and Hal had met at a private party somewhere in London and had married in Harrogate, from whence Nora came, on 9 October 1931 before moving in to a flat in St John's Wood. She had already been promised to another but Hal pursued her so assiduously (with untold numbers of bouquets of red carnations) that she finally gave in, broke off her engagement and consented to marry Hal instead. They had planned to honeymoon at Juan les Pins on the Cote d'Azur but the value of the pound fell, so they decided they couldn't afford to go and chose Fowey in Cornwall instead.

When they came back to London they went to see *Cavalcade* at the Theatre Royal in Drury Lane. Hal was very fond of the theatre and there are frequent references to what they saw over the years. 'It was a marvellous production by Noel Coward,' he later said, 'but sad in parts. We felt it was a forecast of what our lives might be.' And then along came John, the first of four sons, who chose to arrive on Nora's

Hal's wedding to Nora in Harrogate on 9 October 1931.

Hal in wedding uniform.

birthday – 25 September 1932 – in a nursing home in Welbeck Street. Hal visited after his day at the Air Ministry each evening. 'I compared notes with other fathers as we waited in the anteroom before being summoned to go in to see our wives and babies.'

It was ever thus.

Chapter Twelve

Demons – Biggin Hill

It was a great relief for Hal to be on an RAF station again after three years at the Air Ministry. The refresher course he had been assigned to lasted a month and he completed it on 13 February 1933. The aircraft used were Avro 504N trainers, Hawker Hart bombers and Bristol Bulldog fighters. The ubiquitous Avro was a First World War design, production of which didn't end until 1932, by which time almost 10,000 of all variants had been built. The lovely looking Hart was a Sidney Camm design of the early 1920s and the version used at Wittering was built specifically as a bomber-trainer. There were few Bulldogs on the station but Hal flew both a IIA version (with some revised detail of the original production Bulldog II) and the two seater TM trainer.

'During the course, the following had to be carried out to the entire satisfaction of the instructor who flew in the rear seat,' recalled Hal. 'Straight course keeping, all types of turns, aerobatics, forced landings with and without engine, inverted flying, spinning inverted, rolling off the top of a loop, slow rolls, barrel rolls and instrument flying. A daily flying report on each student was discussed with the Chief Flying Instructor.' The final test was with the CFI in the rear seat of a Bulldog TM and Hal passed out with an 'above the average' assessment which earned him his posting as Commanding Officer of No.23 (Fighter) Squadron at RAF Biggin Hill, relieving Squadron Leader Paxton DFC who moved on to the command of No.25 Squadron at Hawkinge. 'I greatly enjoyed the course,' said Hal, 'and found it a most valuable "brush up" especially in aerobatics which could not be carried out on the DH.9As of 14 Squadron.'

His posting to Biggin Hill opened up a whole new world of opportunity for Hal and the squadron he was to command became famous for the exhilarating displays of synchronised aerobatics at the Hendon

Air Display. The station had recently been rebuilt as a direct result of the Salisbury Report of 1923 which recommended expansion of the RAF and it was proposed that two squadrons should be established there, No.32 Squadron with Bristol Bulldogs being the other. Hence the provision of more accommodation for personnel and up to date workshops of the latest Air Ministry design. Additional land around the original Biggin Hill was bought on which to enlarge the old North Camp and messes, barrack blocks, married quarters and offices were built, all completed by September 1932, five months before Hal's arrival. He initially stayed in one of the flats in the Officers' Mess until a married quarter was ready and then Nora and baby John came down from Harrogate with all their goods and chattels.

The squadron was in the process of rearming with Hawker Demon two seater fighters with Rolls Royce Kestrel II.S engines. 'When I arrived the squadron was in the process of fetching twelve Demons from the Hawker works at Brooklands aerodrome. The first thing to do of course was to get all pilots proficient at handling the aircraft and after that to start intensive training by day and night.' The Demon was a development of the Hawker Hart which Hal had become acquainted with at Wittering and it had the same sleek looks. When the Hart, a bomber, entered service it was faster than any of the RAF's fighters, so it was logical that a fighter version of the Hart be developed; thus the Demon was born.

> It was then the fastest fighter we had in the RAF and was very nice to fly. I flew the same aeroplane (K2853) for over three years. Although the undercarriage was of the fixed oleo type and the tail skid was normal, wheel brakes were provided. This was something quite new and gave wonderful control on the ground. It dispensed with having men on the wingtip when taxiing. We also had the latest radio telephony, night flying and oxygen facilities. It had two Vickers with Constantinescu gear firing forward and an improved Scarff mounting for the rear gunner's Lewis guns. Rate of climb was about 12 minutes to 16,000 feet.

George Constantinescu was a Romanian who registered over 130 inventions, including hydraulic machine-gun synchronisation gear which allowed guns to shoot between the spinning blades of the propeller. The gear was first used operationally on DH.4s and rapidly became standard equipment. The Gloster Gladiator was the last British fighter to be equipped with it. The Scarff ring was a machine-gun mounting developed during the First World War by Warrant Officer F.W. Scarff of the Admiralty Air Department. It allowed an air gunner in an open cockpit to swivel and elevate his Lewis machine gun quickly and easily to fire in any direction.

In April 1933 Hal was warned to prepare for a demonstration of air drill at the Hendon Display on 24 June. The first such display had been held thirteen years earlier in 1920 and was designed not only to attract public attention but also to raise money for families struggling financially, having lost a husband or father during the First World War whilst serving in the RFC or RAF. (This idea ultimately became the RAF Benevolent Fund of today.) They continued to be held annually until 1937 (with the Royal International Air Tattoo their successor today). It was soon realised that the displays were an ideal way of showing the public the capabilities of the RAF whilst in the process providing good training for all those participating. The Hendon Air Displays became a much looked forward to event in the annual calendar and were in the 1920s actually part of the London scene. Not only that, they were a financial success. The display set pieces gave bombers and fighters the chance to show what they could do and the crowds were awestruck by individual and formation aerobatics performed by a whole succession of fighter and trainer aircraft. But it all had to come to an end in 1937, the Coronation Display for King George VI, as with war approaching preparations for that had to take precedence.

Back in 1921 the *RAF Record* said:

Five CFS Snipes did the most wonderful formation flying that ever happened. They looped, they rolled, they dived, all in wonderful formation. Not content with that, they did much upside-down flying, in line and in V-formation.

No.23 Squadron Demons. When Hal arrived to command the squadron they were in the process of converting to the type.

And when the weather was bad, *Aeroplane* could comment:

> Only a force, part of whose daily work is to keep accurate for-
> mation, to find their target with bomb and machine-gun, to
> snatch a message from a string, to loop and roll and dive with
> beautiful precision and to pursue and fight the enemy in the

Hal inherited some unlikely looking aircrew with No.23 Squadron at Biggin Hill!

air, could have done these things under the deplorable conditions of this year's display.

For 1933 Hal worked out a series of formation changes for his squadron's contribution and at the end of April practice began. This was going to be a high profile event and the press went to town with publicity for the display and Movietone News and other film companies came to Biggin Hill and filmed them. But display training had to be combined with air fighting exercises, night-flying co-operation with searchlights ('from 17,000 feet over London one could see the lights on the French coast on a clear night') and providing target formations for squadrons competing

The RAF Display at Hendon in 1933.

for the Sir Philip Sassoon trophy, an annual competition between the fighter squadrons of the Home Defence Force, Sir Philip Sassoon being the Under-Secretary of State for Air at the time. But from May onwards it was almost exclusively Hendon that Hal had in mind and he had his squadron in the air practicing day after day. Come 24 June the display was completed successfully 'although low cloud increased the amount of concentration required'. Some items fell foul of the poor weather, the biggest casualty being the finale, the set piece, an attack on a submarine base.

On 1 July the new aerodrome at Speke Liverpool was opened by the Secretary of State for Air, Charles Stewart Henry Vane-Tempest-Stewart, the 7th Marquess of Londonderry.

> The Liverpool Corporation went quite a splash over this and chartered a civil aircraft to fly the wives of the COs of units taking part up to Speke and home again. This was the first time Nora had left John but he was quite happy with Nannie. No.23 was based at Sealand near Chester for the event but we were all accommodated with our wives at the Midland Adelphi Hotel in Liverpool where after the opening we all attended the Lord Mayor's dinner with speeches by the Secretary of State. I repeated our air drill display (in better weather this time) and finished it by diving past in squadron formation at 210 mph.

A couple of weeks later the squadron was involved in the annual air exercises from which Fighter Command developed the tactics and procedures for the defence of England against air attack from the Continent. They were under R/T (radio telephony) control from the operations room at Biggin Hill, a procedure in its infancy. Just one day was lost because of 'negative weather when the duty pilot reported that even the birds were walking'.

In September 1933 the squadron flew to Sutton Bridge on The Wash for live firing 'with front and rear guns against targets on the ground and towed by aircraft. The noses of the ammunition were dipped in different coloured paint which showed when the targets were examined thus identifying the gunners. A new type of reflector sight was used for high firing against an illuminated sleeve target.' Squadron members competed for the Brooke-Popham Cup in which Hal came twelfth out of twenty-six participants. The cup had been presented by Sir Henry Brooke-Popham who, during the First World War, served in the Royal Flying Corps as a wing commander and in the new Royal Air Force after the war became the first Commandant of the Staff College at Andover. He later held high command in the Middle East, ultimately retiring from the RAF in 1942 as an air chief marshal.

On 7 February 1934, ever keen to get his hands on a new aeroplane, Hal flew a Hawker Fury on test, conducting high altitude firing and tracer trials off the south coast. In September of the previous year he had flown the Gloster SS.18 which became the Gauntlet, entering squadron service in 1935, and found it a delight to fly. Every so often his log book shows rather enigmatically such entries as '12th October. Gordon K2766. Experience on new type'. This was a twenty-minute solo flight in this two-seater aircraft. Then again on 21 March 1935: 'Westland Wallace K4014 with Sgt Ross. Air Experience.'

Mainly though it was the Demon that Hal flew and he recorded many hours on the type flying typical pre-war squadron sorties – formations,

No.3 Armament Training Camp, RAF Sutton Bridge, September 1933. No.23 Squadron deployed here for live firing.

interceptions, cross-countries, air firing, battle flight attacks, night-flying, R/T tests, air firing, practice bombing and so forth. Then on 23 June the routine was broken when the Air Ministry chose No.23 Squadron to go to Paris as a guest of the French government to take part in celebrations of the twenty-fifth anniversary of the first crossing of the English Channel by Louis Bleriot in 1909. They flew ten Demons from Manston to le Bourget whilst a troop carrier flew the ground crews and equipment. The squadron's officers had been invited to lunch with a French squadron at le Bourget and Hal was wise to what might happen.

> Knowing French hospitality and with an eye on RAF orders about drinking and flying I got Air Vice Marshal Joubert, our AOC who accompanied us, to ask that it be an aviators' lunch only as we had to fly that afternoon. But I am afraid the French did not play. It was a fabulous lunch and at one point I counted five glasses of wine beside me. However all was well. We all had time for a snooze in the sun to recover before taking off in formation to fly at 2,000 feet across Paris and do our air drill display at Buc near Versailles. Whilst leading my flight in to land at Buc a replica of the original Bleriot monoplane took off right across my line of approach. Our use of brakes to manoeuvre on the ground to avoid it brought cheers from the crowd.

This was the first time that an RAF squadron had performed at a French air display. There had been no time to work up a new demonstration for Buc, so the crews practised their Hendon formation on the way over to France. Peter Rudd in his book *The Red Eagles – A History of No.23 Squadron, Royal Air Force, 1915–1994* recalls that 'this was watched from his own personal aircraft by the AOC, Air Vice Marshal Sir Phillip Joubert.' Of the display at Buc Peter Rudd says 'it was received with frenzied applause and M. Bleriot was so overcome with emotion he had a heart attack but recovered in time to see the formation of Demons flying over his little monoplane'. Heart attack it wasn't but purely being overcome with emotion must have had its effect on Bleriot. He did die of a heart attack two years later in Paris.

Hal continues: 'we had tea with the President [M. Lebrun] and watched a display by the French Air Force before flying back to le Bourget.' However he didn't mention in his memoir that also there enjoying tea was the British Ambassador, the Air Ministers of Britain and France and most importantly of all the guest of honour, Louis Bleriot himself.

> Having seen the aeroplanes safely moored for the night we had a most hazardous high speed drive in French Air Force cars to Claridges Hotel near the Arc de Triomphe. A bath and change into mess kit found us ready to board more cars to take us out to the Pres Catalan restaurant in the Bois de Boulogne for a State banquet. The French of course do these things in superb style and what with wines, a delicious menu and an orchestra in the magnificent setting of what was the best restaurant in Paris it was indeed a night to remember. Uniforms of most foreign air forces alongside the glamorous and much bejewelled ladies reminded one of a stage presentation. My partner was the wife of the Italian Air Attaché who was also a sight for sore eyes. Sir Philip Joubert replied to the President's speech in his usual fluent French and we hit the hay at Claridges early on Sunday morning.

The squadron was scheduled to be on show to the public again on the Sunday but on the ground, not in the air. They were taken to the Longchamps racecourse and were cheered by the crowds throughout the day. That evening they were left to their own devices and, despite a surfeit of food and drink and late nights over the previous couple of days, many of the squadron's officers still managed to get to the *Folies Bergère*!

> As may be imagined it was a fantastic show and the girls revealed full measures of the female form divine. Afterwards Patrick Beatty, a relation of the famous Admiral, with others

went on to a night haunt where he demanded roast beef and Yorkshire pudding with a large whisky at 4am. He got it but it cost him five pounds.

The squadron were due to return to Biggin Hill from le Bourget on the Monday morning but were delayed by fog. When it cleared the French opened the doors of a hangar to reveal yet more food – tables of fruit and cakes with glasses of champagne.

> Again Joubert and I eyed each other but the champagne was very mild and we got away with one glass. As we boarded our Demons the French wives and girlfriends presented each of us with a bouquet of red and white carnations and blue cornflowers with red, white and blue streamers each accompanied by a loving kiss.

All Hal could manage for lunch on landing at Biggin Hill was a glass of orange juice! It was presumably their involvement in this French diversion that precluded their participation in the 1934 RAF Hendon display. And no doubt it was the Royal Review the following year which reduced the scope of the Hendon display considerably and No.23 Squadron doesn't appear to have taken part that year either although it had flown in formation at the first Biggin Hill Empire Air Day on 25 May.

*

Hal's memoir mainly relates to his RAF career but as we have seen he occasionally writes of other things. One such was when he and Nora spent part of his annual leave in August 1934 on a voyage from Gillingham on the Medway to the Hamble near Southampton with a Major Edwards, his wife and sister in a nine-ton yacht of ancient vintage. All went well until they got to Ramsgate where they found the main boom gooseneck had slipped (the forward end of a boom attaches to the mast just below the sail with a joint called the gooseneck) and they could hardly get into harbour. Then once alongside they found that the heads were completely blocked, so sending the ladies ashore the next day Edwards and Hal had the odorous task of clearing the obstruction. 'Something,' Hal said sniffily, 'he should have done before we left Gillingham.' Sailing from Ramsgate to Dover was a wet trip with a lot of spray coming on board. Hal had to leave the yacht at Dover and travel to Uxbridge to attend a conference at Air Defence of Great Britain Command, the precursor to Fighter, Bomber, Coastal and Training Commands which came into being in July 1936. Returning a day or so later he found that Major Edwards and his family had everything dried out but owing to their carelessness (Hal was obviously becoming disenchanted with them all) they missed the BBC morning shipping forecast before setting off for the Hamble. They sailed to Dungeness, towing the dinghy as it was too large to get on the deck, then ran into increasing wind and a head sea as they staggered around Dungeness with the help of the engine. Hal takes up the story.

> We made slow progress and after a bit water appeared slopping round the cabin. We decided to use the pump. The pump was on deck at the stern and to use it we had to wrap a bit of old towel round the piston and prime the cylinder with sea water before we could get suction. It was too rough to get on deck to pump so we had to lean out of the cockpit which was very tiring on the tummy muscles. Then the dinghy started to fill. It was now becoming a drag on the yacht and we were not making progress. The dinghy would become submerged, then with the pull of the yacht it would rise up, spill out a lot of water then fill again with spray and repeat the performance. At last Edwards agreed to abandon the dinghy which we did and then we made more progress: it was recovered later washed up on the shingle at Dungeness and reported to the receiver of wrecks. We decided to use the engine to get on but it refused to start. Dusk came on and Major Edwards collapsed from exhaustion on the settee.

The pumping occupied the ladies in turn and the movement of the boat made work on the engine impossible. We had to pump to prevent being waterlogged.

The seriousness of our situation began to dawn and Nora and I began to think of John and what would happen if we got into real trouble. We got near Beachy Head and into calmer water. I said I would sail her all night if I could be fed and given drink and this Nora supplied. At one point I thought of running the yacht ashore but then dawn came and the crew woke up. The wind changed and we got round Beachy Head and went into Newhaven all dead tired. We felt better after a rest but still not a hope of starting the engine. We found out later that the engine timing had slipped so no wonder it wouldn't start. The run from Newhaven onwards made up for everything. A following wind pushed up our speed to six knots as timed over the measured mile off Lee and we moored in time for a good bath and meal ashore.

*

On 6 July 1935 the newly-constructed RAF Mildenhall (it had only opened the year before in time to host the inaugural Great Britain to Australia air race) welcomed King George V, who came to the base to conduct the first ever Royal Review of the Royal Air Force. The RAF assembled over 356 of its combat aircraft from thirty-eight squadrons, lined up in rows together with crews across the Mildenhall grass airfield for His Majesty's personal inspection. 'I led 23 Squadron to and from Mildenhall each day prior to the review for the rehearsals,' reported Hal proudly. 'We created rather a sensation by landing 12 Demons all at the same time at Mildenhall where there was lots of space.' After the inspection at Mildenhall the king drove to nearby Duxford to watch the flypast by all the review's participating aircraft. 'Each squadron had to take off at the precise time ordered and keep station accurately.' Quite a feat of organisation and timing.

Also in 1935 the Air Ministry selected No.23 Squadron for a test of the Mobilisation Scheme for reserve personnel and vehicles to determine the speed at which the Packing Depot at RAF Sealand could dismantle Demons and prepare them for shipment, and also the time taken by squadron personnel to erect the same aeroplanes in the open on an aerodrome. The reservists were mostly London bus drivers who quite

The Royal Review, Mildenhall, 1935. Official Programme.

The Royal Review: the arrival of King George V.

The Royal Review: King George V inspecting aircraft.

enjoyed the change to RAF vehicles. After call up and collection of their kit at a mobilisation centre they picked up various types of transport from stores depots and brought them to Biggin Hill where Hal assembled a convoy which he led all the way to Sealand and back. The motorcyclists in the convoy had the authority to stop all traffic at junctions

The Royal Review: fighters taking off.

The Royal Review, Duxford. The saluting base for the mass flypast of all participating aircraft from Mildenhall.

and crossroads so as to let the whole convoy pass through without being split up. The Demons were flown separately to Sealand and dismantled in the Packing Depot hangars. Wings were detached, as was the fin, and the propeller was taken off but the engine wasn't removed. The fuselage was left with the undercarriage installed so it could be towed by lorry to a ship's side. The exercise revealed many technical shortcomings on the part of the Packing Depot, many of which had not been corrected when Demons were shortly afterwards packed for shipment to Malta during the Abyssinian crisis as Hal would soon discover at first hand. For on 1 September Squadron Leader G. Howard DFC took over from Hal as commander of No.23 Squadron. Howard's appointment only lasted until 17 September though by which time the squadron had lost all of its aircraft and most of its pilots. Peter Rudd again:

> The Demons were given major inspections and despatched to Sealand where they were crated and sent to the Middle East. No.41 Squadron suffered a similar fate. Two new squadrons, Nos.64 and 74, were formed with the Demons at Heliopolis and Malta to reinforce Middle East Command. By March 1936 No.23 Squadron had, according to the Form 540, lost all its officers and airmen pilots but the Biggin Hill station commander's car received a superb overhaul as the ground crews had no aircraft to service!

Chapter Thirteen

Demons – Hal Far

In the spring of 1935 Hal was told he was being posted as the RAF Instructor to the Indian Army Staff College at Quetta, near the Afghanistan border, but before he and Nora became too excited about the move the posting was postponed after a hugely destructive earthquake on 31 May which destroyed much of the city and killed an estimated 60,000 people. The postponement was converted to a cancellation when Hal was detailed to take a fighter squadron to Malta instead. He became OC No.74 Squadron, the Tigers, on 3 September 1935. But initially it was all very hush hush. It came about thus as Hal explains.

The station commander at Biggin Hill (Wing Commander Grenfell) rushed across from Wing HQ to my office in the hangar waving a signal from Air Defence of Great Britain Command. 'You are to report to the Chief of Air Staff by 0900 tomorrow Jim.' [Hal was known as Jim during his RAF career, but he has been called Hal throughout this narrative for reasons of consistency]. I wondered what I had done now. The secretary to the CAS received me and gave me *The Times* to read until the CAS himself, Sir Edward Ellington, was ready. When I saw him he said, 'Crowe, I want you to take a squadron of Demons to Malta for the air defence of the island. We don't want the Italians to think we are sending a squadron so you will have flights from three Demon units while their parents are still in the UK. Are there any points you want cleared up?' I asked about allowances and what was to be done about families in married quarters. The CAS at once dictated a minute to the finance branches but it took over a year for the matter to be cleared up satisfactorily.

When Italy declared war on Abyssinia in 1935 the British government thought that as a result of its efforts in trying to stop the fighting Italy might be bold enough to declare war on Britain and, if that were to happen, British forces in the Mediterranean, Middle East and Aden would prove to be understrength. Steps were taken to send reinforcements and as Malta lies so close to southern Italy it was thought it might be the first to be attacked. After very short notice ten officers, eighteen NCOs and seventy-nine airmen sailed in the HMT (Hired Military Transport) *Neuralia* from Southampton on 3 September 1935. The ship had detachments from the Royal Navy, Royal Marines, Royal Engineers and an anti-aircraft brigade on board as well. (Note that in 1935 'brigade', in terms of how it was made up in the Royal Artillery, really meant, rather confusingly, 'regiment'! The AA brigade travelling to Malta was probably the 4th AA Brigade which became 4th AA Regiment in 1938 when the accounting units of infantry, armour, cavalry and artillery were brought into line. The 4th AA Regiment later became the 4th Heavy AA Regiment and part of the Malta defences.)

The RAF men came from Nos.3, 25 and 32 Squadrons at Biggin Hill, No.56 Squadron at North Weald, No.65 Squadron at Hornchurch, an Auxiliary Air Force squadron known as 601 (County of London) at Hendon, the Balloon Centre at Lark Hill, the Air Armament School at RAF Eastchurch and men unattached to any unit from RAF Calshot, RAF Henlow and RAF Leuchars. Such was the short notice that the men were only inoculated and vaccinated after sailing. As the move was to be as secret as possible the unit was not given a squadron number but was known initially simply as Demon Flights. As the CAS had intimated, the parent units from which the men came were still in the UK and therefore had to all intents and purposes not moved. It wasn't until 14 November 1935 that Hal received a signal from the Air Ministry to say that the Demon Flights were henceforth to be known as No.74 (F) Squadron, 'backdated to the 3rd September'.

The *Neuralia* disembarked the men at the Grand Harbour in Malta on 11 September. The SS *Maihar*, which had sailed from Ellesmere Port with the aircraft ('which had been packed for shipment at Sealand under the scheme we had recently tested,' reported Hal) and all the other stores came into Marsa Scirocco Bay three days later, but the swell was too much for lighters to go alongside for unloading. The following day it was decided to bring her round to the Grand Harbour, the swell having subsided, and unloading began in the evening (it was a Sunday). The 200-ton floating crane from the dockyard was brought alongside to deal with the motor transport while crates, fuselages and other stores were put on to lighters by the ship's derricks. They were offloaded at the RAF wharf but this wasn't a very speedy procedure as only one hand-operated crane was available there. Nevertheless, by the end of the day ten crates containing wings and two Leyland lorries had been brought ashore. Hal rather wryly noted:

> Although the move was supposed to be secret I found cases on the wharf at Valetta consigned to 'OC 74 Squadron' before we had even been given a number! And an Italian tug with all the radio aerials imaginable was clearly reporting our movements to Rome.

The Demons were shipped with engines installed, undercarriage and centre section *in situ* and mainplanes and empennage in light crates as had been rehearsed at Sealand. It was done this way to facilitate their rapid putting together in Malta. A warrant officer engineer and three riggers had travelled in the *Maihar*, inspecting the aircraft twice daily during the voyage and then superintending the unloading. The No.74 Squadron Operations Record Book (ORB) records:

> All aircraft arrived undamaged. Great credit is due to the Packing Depot and the ship's owners and officers for the care taken in stowage and unloading. The only adjustment found necessary during the voyage was the tightening of the wing nuts on the metal straps securing the axles of the aircraft to the blocks fixed on the deck.

A 200-ton floating crane unloaded the motor transport at Valetta.

By the end of 16 September twelve aircraft had been landed and one was towed by Leyland lorry tail-first along the road to Hal Far before dusk. Work started again early the next morning and the remainder of the fuse-lages and the wing crates had made the journey by mid-afternoon with a stop for a re-grease of the Demons' wheels halfway. The road between Valetta and Hal Far had a good surface and the two Leylands on towing duty managed 7 or 8mph, taking about an hour for each journey. At cease of work on the 18th eight Demons had been rigged and the remaining four were waiting to be 'trued up'. By the 20th eleven aircraft were available with one needing a part from stores which had yet to be unpacked, but guns weren't fitted to every aircraft. The poor state of the armament equipment sent from England meant that it was a further week before all Demons had their fixed forward-firing .303 machine guns in place. 'Perhaps they should have been left *in situ* instead of being removed when packed for transit,' wondered the record book keeper. They were short of

Preparing the Demons for unloading at Valetta.

other items too thanks to faults in packing and many 'immediate' signals had to be sent to the UK for parts. The lack of spare engines and the poor chances of getting replacements in the near future initially limited flying to an average of half an hour per day per pilot.

*

Malta was known to irreverent British servicemen as the land of yells (of the *dghaiso* men in their colourful boats as they touted for passengers), bells (the church bells which rang everyday as they celebrated one feast day or another) and smells (of a densely inhabited island with less than adequate sanitation). The Maltese people were fervently pro-British and the armed forces played a huge part in their lives. Valletta harbour was home to the Mediterranean Fleet – battleships, cruisers, aircraft-carriers and destroyers – whilst Sliema Creek was used by

The Demon fuselages being lowered onto lighters at Valetta.

submarines and minesweepers. Malta dockyard was a major repair and refitting facility which meant ships didn't have to return to home ports for such work to be done.

The Army had substantial garrisons on Malta and the Fleet Air Arm (which in 1935 had been an organisational unit of the RAF since 1924 and did not come under the direct control of the Admiralty until mid-1939)

Towing the Demons to shore.

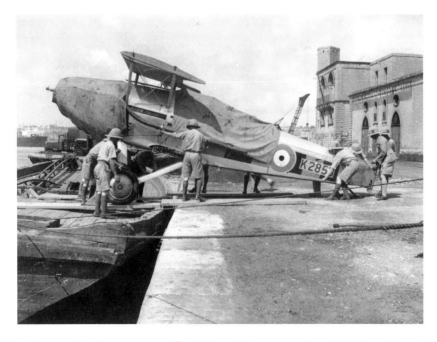

The Demon fuselages were offloaded and later towed to Hal Far eight miles away where they were reunited with their wings.

Towing a Demon fuselage to Hal Far.

and the RAF itself also had a significant presence. Hal Far originated as an airfield extension to the nearby Calafrana seaplane base but in April 1929 was upgraded to an RAF Station in its own right, although it continued to function as a shore base for carrier aircraft in the Mediterranean. On the same day as it was upgraded a Station Flight of Fairey IIIFs was formed and on 25 November Lieutenant Owen Cathcart-Jones took off from Hal Far in a Fairey Flycatcher and made the first landing of a fighter aircraft on an aircraft carrier at night. This was HMS *Courageous*, anchored in Valletta harbour.

With the increased Italian threat, Malta's importance as a base for air operations grew and aircraft carrier activity around Malta increased correspondingly with HM Ships *Eagle*, *Glorious*, *Courageous*, *Furious* and *Hermes* frequently docked at Valletta with their aircraft ashore at Hal Far – Blackburn Ripons and Baffins, Fairey IIIFs, Flycatchers and Seals, and Hawker Nimrods and Ospreys in the main. The increased use of the airfield meant a corresponding improvement in the support facilities such as married quarters for locally-based staff, barracks, NAAFI stores and more hangars. The Abyssinian Crisis led to all Fleet Air Arm aircraft

The Grand Harbour Valetta. Photo by the RAF Calafrana Photographic Section.

at Hal Far at the time flying onto HMS *Glorious* which sailed with the rest of the fleet to Alexandria and the eastern Mediterranean for safety, which is when No.74 (and No.22) Squadron arrived for the defence of the island.

Hal's old DOSD chum Reggie Marix was Station Commander at Hal Far and to celebrate Hal's arrival he organised a Demon cocktail party.

(Hal had double the reason to celebrate when he had mail from Nora to say that Michael, their second son, was 'on the way'.)

> It was to be something special so he invented a new form of intoxicant in the shape of crushed prickly pear, gin and vermouth and the whole coloured bright purple. It tasted horrible and the ladies, having grave suspicions about Reggie's intentions, refused to be tempted into drinking a tot or two.

But Reggie Marix could do more than come up with exotic cocktails. Whilst at Malta he invented an intercept calculator designed to enable British fighters to effectively come to grips with an air attack on the island. In his biography of Reggie, John Lea explains further:

> Based on a triangle of velocities concept it computed vectors for the defenders to intercept an incoming raid at the greatest possible distance from Malta, thus reducing the numbers of enemy likely to get through. In the days before radar and integrated, computerised fighter defence systems, this innovation marked a major step forward. Air HQ endorsed the technique. The Air Commodore who dealt with it was encouraged to find that the RAF in Malta had an officer who was inventive enough, and sufficiently aware of the dangers lurking up to the north, to come up with such a big contribution to the air defence of the island.

With war becoming an increasingly likely possibility Marix developed contingency plans to meet *any* form of attack on Malta. His work didn't go unrecognised and he was promoted to Group Captain on 1 January 1936. Hal took his friend and colleague for an air experience flight the following day in K2853. This was Hal's preferred aircraft, one which he had predominantly flown with No.23 Squadron and which had followed him out to Malta.

When No.74 settled down to operations, and it wasn't long before they did, they were always at two hours' notice which could be reduced to an hour or even fifteen minutes according to reports received.

RAF Hal Far. This photo was taken by RAF Calafrana's Photographic Section.

When at two hours, pilots enjoyed the relative comforts of Hal Far's permanent accommodation. Anything less and they stayed near the aircraft. At weekends and off-duty times, Valetta with its clubs and cinemas (Hal Far had its own cinema too) was not far away by car. The food was good and drinks extremely cheap. Games, bathing and trips to the island of Gozo also helped to pass the time.

For night flying the old line of paraffin flares at Hal Far was unsuitable so Hal borrowed a ten-inch signalling searchlight from the Navy and produced the necessary power from a generator on a Morris six-wheeler so as to make the outfit mobile. He screened the beam and was able to cut down the period of illumination of the field. The landing surface at Hal Far was earth (with grass growing in the spring), stony in places, and after rain could become flooded, as happened during November 1935 when heavy rains frequently put the airfield out of action. A diversionary landing ground was created on the Marsa polo grounds to make it fit for landings if necessary.

If a Demon had engine trouble or was shot down and was unable to reach land it would have had to ditch. To allow for this, inflatable Youngman dinghies were fitted in the top-planes. When the aircraft came down they would inflate automatically and be buoyant enough to hold the submerged aircraft around fifteen feet below the surface of the sea (hopefully for subsequent salvage) as the pilot sat in the dinghy awaiting rescue. To facilitate this strong cables attached the dinghy to the Demon but pilots were very wary of the arrangement because if the device which activated the dinghy's inflation sequence went off accidentally in the air there would be little chance of controlling the aircraft with the grave consequences that that implied. Permission was therefore sought and obtained to do away with the idea of salvaging the aircraft and the cables were consequently omitted and only a light line connected the dinghy to the fuselage to allow the pilot to haul it in.

'Training was about the same as with 23 Squadron but with more of a naval flavour of course,' wrote Hal. 'For example we did live firing at a

Youngman dinghies were installed in the top planes of Demons and would inflate automatically if the aircraft ditched.

target towed by an RAF tug (the *Andromeda*) and at sea markers, at fog buoys towed by a destroyer and did live bombing on Filfola, an uninhabited island.' (A fog buoy consisted of a cross of wood around four-feet long and three-feet wide, in the form of a crucifix. The cross arms were designed to prevent it from turning over when being towed. At the foot was a scoop of galvanized iron or steel which threw up a visible plume of water.) Other training included firing at air towed targets; night flying in co-operation with searchlights; battle climbs using oxygen; and flight and squadron low-flying attacks on destroyer flotillas, AA gun positions, forts, harbours and carriers and cruisers whenever they came to Malta for attention in the dockyard – all in conjunction with No.22 Squadron and their Vildebeests which were also based at Hal Far (and inevitably Hal did get to fly one of these Vickers aircraft).

No.74 also conducted affiliation training with No.202 (Flying-Boat) Squadron and their Supermarine Scapas. Ground training included

Hal (left), OC 74, and Squadron Leader Ledger, OC 22 Squadron, outside the mess at Hal Far.

A Vickers Vildebeest of No.22 Squadron at Hal Far with torpedo fitted. No.74 trained alongside No.22 Squadron in Malta.

lectures on Italian forces and recognition of their ships and aircraft, working on aircraft wearing gas respirators, and close liaison with the Navy and Army with trips in destroyers to watch exercises. 'Perhaps it would be of interest if I describe one of the exercises and attacks 74 Squadron carried out on naval vessels,' wrote Hal.

> We did many exercises with the 19th Destroyer Flotilla which was then commanded by Captain Philip Vian and one of his captains was Lord Louis Mountbatten. On this particular attack 74 achieved complete surprise, the result of which was for the Navy to demand increased anti-aircraft armament for destroyers. Eleven Demons were to attack the ships some miles off the eastern tip of Malta. After take-off we climbed to 12,000 feet, got above light clouds and into the sun. Soon we could see the nine destroyers at speed in line ahead. I ordered 'flight astern' and did a straight power glide at about one third revolutions.

With the sun directly astern the ships' lookouts would have to look directly into the blinding sunlight to see us. We were not sighted until I attacked the leading ship and then of course the whole flotilla took violent avoiding action. This made it easier for us to select targets but it also helped the ships to give each other covering fire.

Philip Vian was an exemplary officer who rose to be an Admiral of the Fleet, retiring in 1952 as Sir Philip Louis Vian GCB KBE DSO & Two Bars; he was Mentioned in Despatches five times. Much of Vian's wartime service was in the Mediterranean where he led naval support during the Allied invasions of Sicily and Italy before transferring to the Pacific as Commander Air Operations of the British Pacific Fleet. After the cessation of hostilities he served as a Fifth Sea Lord in charge of naval aviation. As for Mountbatten Hal would get to know him later in his career in India.

In the squadron ORB there are entries alluding to sound mirrors. On 12 December 1935, for example, 'an exercise was carried out with the sound mirror' and, on 8 May 1936, 'sound mirror exercise carried out at night'. Sound mirrors were long, curved concrete walls which focused the engine noise of approaching aircraft on to a bank of microphones. The signals from these could be analysed to give a speed and position of the aircraft. It was decided to build a chain of these mirrors at various locations in the United Kingdom and overseas, including five in Malta. The first was located at Maghtab and became known locally as the concrete ear. The training of troops to operate sound mirrors was undertaken by the Air Defence Experimental Establishment in England. For the system to be completely successful it had to be able to differentiate between friendly and enemy aircraft and so it was necessary to calibrate the system by obtaining the sound signatures of all types flown by the RAF. Any different sound signatures would be assumed to come from enemy aircraft. Trials using a Supermarine Scapa of No.202 Squadron found that the range of the mirror was twenty-one to thirty-seven miles, with an average of twenty-five miles. It was estimated that the mirror would provide a six-minute warning of an enemy aircraft approaching Malta at 250mph. The four other planned Malta sound mirrors never materialised as radar was being developed at the time and this showed greater promise in detecting incoming aircraft. The sound mirror idea was scrapped, that at Maghtab being decommissioned in 1937. It can still be seen near Valletta today.

A summary of the work done by the squadron under Hal's leadership in Malta makes for instructive reading:

Hours flown	*2,162*
Rounds fired by pilots	*25,400*
Rounds fired by air gunners	*15,400*
(Total rounds fired	*40,800)*
Practice bombs dropped	*1,266*
Average low-bombing error	*11 yards*
Average dive-bombing error	*25.5 yards*

The squadron suffered no accidents whilst on Malta. There was one forced landing in February 1936 when one of the NCO pilots experienced engine failure at 4,000 feet but he landed safely on a strip which had been prepared on a site for a new airfield at Ta Kali. The aircraft was dismantled in an hour and towed back to Hal Far undamaged. The failure was caused by a fractured lower camshaft drive housing and subsequently the engines of all the Demons were removed and the part renewed in the workshops at Calafrana. The work was phased but it did mean there were times when there were only three serviceable aircraft at Hal Far. Something else which required attention was the poor condition of the fabric on some of the aircraft, especially in the area pounded by the slipstream from the propeller.

*

The first of 74's Demons were camouflaged on 3 October 1935, the colours being made up from dopes available locally, and all the squadron's

The first camouflaged Demon.

... and a side view

aircraft had been painted by the middle of November. These were the first RAF aircraft to be camouflaged prior to the Second World War which meant that No.74 Squadron were at the forefront of this development for a while. The Royal Aircraft Establishment at Farnborough had been experimenting with different forms of camouflage for front-line aircraft. Various forms of camouflage had appeared on British and German aircraft in the First World War but had only been done on a squadron by squadron basis rather than by a directive from a central authority. The general principle was to paint the upper surfaces of the aircraft in various patterns and combinations of green, brown and grey in an attempt to make it blend in with the surroundings when viewed from above. But the practice fell out of favour with the RAF after the war and by the 1930s polished aluminium or a silver doped finish, often with colourful identification flashes, had become the norm for RAF fighters. Whether the arrival of Farnborough scientists at Hal Far at the same time as the Demon Flights was planned or coincidental cannot be confirmed, but it is known that their brief was to carry out large-scale tests on the camouflage of landing grounds, with clear skies and fine weather important factors in the choice of Malta. The details of the actual tests are elusive but we do know that 74's Demons were almost immediately painted in a camouflage scheme. The use of locally available material is consistent with the seemingly *ad hoc* nature of the undertaking. Photographs show squadron aircraft flying over the Maltese landscape. Differing positions of the RAF roundels on the upper-wing surfaces of some of the aircraft is either a relic of their earlier markings or an attempt to break the symmetry of their more usual positioning.

In mid-December 1935 a war test was conducted whereby aircraft were taxied to stone pens (revetments) built around the airfield perimeter. From the opening of the hangar doors to the taxiing of the last Demon into the pens took just twenty minutes. Armed sentries were posted and the aircraft were fitted with camouflaged cockpit covers and engine cowlings which would tie in with Farnborough's airfield camouflage tests since the open cockpits of aircraft parked round the dispersal area would have shown up clearly from the air even if the aircraft themselves were

The effectiveness of camouflage. No.74's Demons over Malta. Note the different positions of roundels on the upper-wing surfaces.

In revetments at Hal Far.

painted to blend in with the surroundings. Once the signal was given it took five minutes for a machine to get away from the pens, measured from the start of removing these covers.

There is an interesting postscript to all the efforts to make the aircraft based on the island invisible and indeed to make the island invisible a far as was possible. An exercise was held to see how effective the island could be hidden from any night intrusion by enemy aircraft. Arrangements were made by the authorities to switch off all the lights on Malta on one particular evening whilst an aircraft flew overhead to observe the effect. Because the armed services' communications equipment was deemed too important to switch off the radio station was exempt from the lighting ban. The glow from the valves in the transmitting station and the phosphorescence of the surf around the island were all that could be seen – apart from the headlights of Reggie Marix's car as he toured around checking that all the lights were extinguished!

The exercise had one curious by product as Stewart Perowne explains in his book, *Siege Within The Walls*.

> It was described in the London *Times* as a vital 'trial occulation of lights' which it was. But it gave birth to the term 'blackout' as generally used. The reason was that nearly all those concerned in its organisation were members of the Malta Amateur Dramatics Club and therefore naturally used the theatrical term for the sudden darkening of the stage. As thus established that night in Malta, 'blackout' became a current technical term.

*

By early March 1936 there were signs that the Abyssinian emergency was easing and in May the Italians declared peace. This was lucky for Hal because it meant he could get leave in mid-May to see his new son Michael who had been born on 23 April (St George's Day) in Harrogate. He was back on the squadron by mid-June, was promoted to Wing Commander on 1 July and posted to the Directorate of War Organisation

No.74 Squadron in formation over Malta.

No.74 Squadron in formation over Malta prior to camouflaging.

at the Air Ministry on the 19th. Orders had been received on 13 July for the Demons to be dismantled ready for packing prior to return to the UK and RAF Hornchurch under the command of Squadron Leader 'Brookie' Brookes in August.

Hal was given a passage home from Malta in HMS *Boreas*, a B-class destroyer which, with the rest of the 4th Flotilla, was leaving Sliema Creek.

We had a smooth run until approaching Spain when we got an immediate signal ordering the ships to go to various ports to look after British interests as the Spanish Civil War had broken out. It was impressive to watch the flotilla 'flash up' boilers for steaming at full speed and then all turn away together. *Boreas* was ordered to Gibraltar and as we rounded Europa Point we sighted three very ancient cruisers of the Spanish Navy at anchor off Algeciras and, closer in, a few torpedo boats. As we entered harbour our wake caused one of these craft to roll badly and we heard afterwards that at that moment the crew were busy cutting the Captain's throat! We went alongside a tanker at once and refuelled, thence to a buoy and a visit ashore. As we sat in the evening sunshine having sundowners several aircraft came over us and bombed the old battleships which replied with rather wild anti-aircraft fire. Several shells fell near the harbour but no one was hurt. Next morning I was returning from a before breakfast swim when we saw *Boreas* lighting up boilers. We dashed on board and found orders to sail at once. Our first port of call was Cadiz. As we were not certain which side was occupying Cadiz the Captain flew white ensigns from every mast on the ship and lined up the crew for entering harbour. As we approached we saw the 12-inch guns of the port defences swing round keeping us in their sights, but nothing happened. We anchored and the Captain went ashore. He returned with the mayor who told us that they didn't believe the white ensigns but the lining up of the crews convinced them that *Boreas* was indeed British in spite of her silhouette being like a Spanish destroyer. Next we went to Huelva and embarked the wives and families of the Rio Tinto mines' British personnel. One lady was due to give birth at almost any moment so she was given the Captain's day cabin and full speed was authorised for the run back to Gibraltar. We got alongside in time for the baby to be born on dry land. *Boreas* was then ordered to remain at Gib so I was transferred to HMS *Wild Swan* [a modified W-class destroyer which was sunk by air attack in June 1942] for passage to Portsmouth via Tangier.

Chapter Fourteen

The Directorate of War Organisation

During leave prior to taking up his appointment in the Directorate of War Organisation at the Air Ministry on 10 September 1936, Hal had to find accommodation either in London or close to a good transport link in the suburbs. He found such a house to rent in Byfleet close to the Southern Railway line which ran in to Waterloo. The journey took forty minutes and from there he had only to walk across Waterloo Bridge to Adastral House on Kingsway opposite Bush House. Adastral House remained the home of the Air Ministry throughout the Second World War after which it moved to Theobalds Road in Holborn. The Crowe family stayed in Byfleet until 1938.

> My tasks in War Organisation covered the formation of new units and calculating their requirements in aircraft, equipment and armament to suit a major war. A War Book had to be compiled detailing action to be taken by all and sundry on declaration of a Continental war. Weekly conferences were often depressing because deliveries of new aircraft and equipment kept getting more and more behind our programmes. Despite this, when General Mobilisation was ordered in 1939 it all went fairly smoothly.

To facilitate this a Mobilisation Committee, of which Hal was a part, met regularly to determine the force which could be considered as fit for mobilisation during the ensuing three months and also to carry out a general review of the country's preparedness for war during the same period. To put this into context we need first of all to briefly consider the state of the RAF during the 1930s in the period leading up to the Second World War when British re-armament began to grow in response to German re-armament. In July 1932 the Nazi party became the largest political force in Germany and in January of the following year Hitler was sworn in as Chancellor. Throughout 1934 and 1935 an Axis alliance was being formed against a background of increasing tension. The Japanese Government terminated its commitment to the Washington Naval Treaty, by which the governments of the United Kingdom, the United States, Japan, France and Italy limited the construction of capital ships for their navies. As we have seen, 1935 was the year of the Abyssinian crisis precipitated by Italy and was also the year Germany repudiated the Treaty of Versailles and declared its intention of re-arming.

It became increasingly clear that the RAF needed to be strengthened. In the 1920s war seemed remote and there was great optimism for continuing peace, so much so that the establishment and equipment of all three armed services was allowed to run down. Throughout the 1920s and early 1930s production of new aircraft was slow. Targets were set but never met. By the beginning of 1934 the RAF in the United Kingdom was ten squadrons short of its minimum objective of fifty-two. Furthermore aircraft that were being produced were frankly antiquated in their capability and were obsolete before they reached squadrons. As late as 1935 the principal new fighter was the biplane Gloster Gauntlet with a speed of just 230mph and the new bombers were the Hawker Hind and Handley Page Hendon with a load-carrying capacity of just 500lbs and 1,500lbs respectively. Aircraft and engine manufacturers were on the verge of bankruptcy and were often forced to diversify into non-aviation related production in order to survive. To maintain a nucleus of an aircraft industry the Air Ministry had to ration out all new work, as little as it was, among some sixteen aircraft companies.

In 1934 the government woke up to the reality of what was happening in Europe and Prime Minister Stanley Baldwin announced that it had been decided to establish parity of numbers with Germany in the air. Under this expansion scheme the Royal Air Force would have 111 front-line squadrons at home and overseas consisting of a total of 1,252 aircraft alongside sixteen Fleet Air Arm squadrons of 213 aircraft, an objective that was to have been achieved by March 1939. But this was essentially just a show of strength using existing types and little attention was paid to producing modern designs. Moreover progress with this scheme was slow because assumptions didn't allow for an eventual war and so a sense of urgency was lacking. Nor did crises such as Abyssinia prompt the making of specific war plans because in 1935 international disarmament was still the objective of British foreign policy. In short, successive re-armament programmes were not geared to preparation for war but rather for the reinforcement of peace by backing up diplomacy with a show of force to intimidate potential combatants.

The early stages of re-armament were aimed at deterrence by displaying first-line strength but without reserves. The situation was exacerbated by financial difficulties. There was no budget to cover increased military spending in 1934. In the following year re-armament spending did appear in the budget but it was inadequate and would never have covered the planned increase in aircraft numbers. By the time Hal arrived at the Air Ministry in September 1936 new information about Hitler's re-armament plans had come to light which again revealed the inadequacy of Britain's plans. Consequently what was known as Expansion Scheme F had been sanctioned by the Cabinet (Viscount Swinton was Secretary of State for Air at the time) six months before Hal got his feet under his desk. Under its provisions the Air Force was to acquire more than 8,000 aircraft over three years. To accommodate the huge numbers now being planned there had to be commensurate increases in industrial capacity but it all fell short of what was required. By the spring of 1938 only 4,500 out of the planned 8,000 aircraft had been delivered. And of the 4,500 aircraft not many were of new advanced types which manufacturers had belatedly been developing. Not one Spitfire, Wellington, Hampden, Beaufort, Defiant, Skua or Lysander was available to the RAF and the Blenheim, the Hurricane and the Whitley were only just coming into service.

Throughout 1936, 1937 and 1938 the international situation worsened with the occupation of the Rhineland, the annexation of Austria and the cession of the Sudetenland to Germany with the Luftwaffe continuing to grow in size all the while. The British government responded by giving the RAF the first claim on available resources. Finance was no longer considered a major obstacle and the mantra became not what the country could afford but what the manufacturers could build urgently. Revised Air Ministry proposals required 12,000 aircraft in two years. In April 1938 the Cabinet authorised plans for this with obvious further implications for production capacity. It soon became apparent that manufacturers would fail to keep up with their own forecasts as shortages of raw materials and labour appeared where they had been least expected. Remedies were looked for and the Air Ministry amalgamated the responsibilities for aircraft production, design and development in the newly-created office of the Air Member for Development and Production, the precursor to Lord Beaverbrook's Ministry of Aircraft Production. Air Marshal Sir Wilfrid Freeman was placed in charge and was given the job of choosing the aircraft with which to re-arm the RAF and thus was responsible for the ordering of Hurricanes, Spitfires, Mosquitos, Lancasters and Halifaxes. He also played a pivotal role in the development of the Rolls Royce Merlin-engined P-51 Mustang and the A-36 ground attack/dive bomber which evolved from it. The Mustang was designed in 1940 by North American Aviation in response to a requirement of the British Purchasing Commission which had been established by the British government to buy US planes that would help supplement domestic plane production. The Commission approached North American to build Curtiss P-40 fighters under license for the RAF but rather than build an old design of a rival company the company proposed a more modern fighter of their own and the prototype Mustang was rolled out in September 1940 within 102 days of the contract being signed. The role of the British Purchasing Commission had far reaching consequences for it was British money that forced US industry to move to a wartime production footing as by December 1940 British orders for aircraft had exceeded $1,200,000,000 with deliveries of 300–350 per month and rising.

A civilian Director General of Production was appointed to support Freeman and to mediate between the aircraft builders and the Air Ministry in the planning of production. This was Ernest Lemon, later

Sir Ernest, one of the most capable engineer managers of his generation. He was Vice-President of the London, Midland and Scottish railway and he later became known as the production engineer who modernised the LMS and equipped the RAF for war.

Returning to the autumn of 1938, as Hal was about the leave the Directorate a report was prepared saying that industry was failing in its production and deliveries largely through its inability to train skilled labour with all the necessary speed. Then came the Munich crisis when the real situation as regards Britain's defences became obvious to the British public who came to understand that Chamberlain's concessions to Hitler were in fact due to Britain's military weakness. What happened next is beyond the remit of this book as Hal had moved on. History records that there were continuing production problems which prevented the RAF from being fully strengthened in the short term but that it was nevertheless able to shield Britain from the threat of German invasion in 1940 with its brave defence of the country during the Battle of Britain.

*

It was against this background that the Mobilisation Committee worked and as the outbreak of war became more inevitable the tempo of its meetings increased. So too did the numbers of staff in the various departments within the Directorate although this didn't always happen easily, for formal requests for additional staff had to be made to the Treasury. For example on 17 May 1938, a Squadron Leader Reynolds wrote:

> The establishment of [the department known as] War Organisation 2 provides for a Wing Commander and a Staff Officer: the branch is responsible for War Organisation in relation to home defence including the preparation of administrative plans and the organisation of the Home Commands in time of war, supervision of schemes and exercises, formulating general mobilisation regulations and arranging for the

reception of reservists on mobilisation. The introduction of the latest expansion scheme has greatly complicated the work of the branch since the scheme does not merely represent a proportionate all round increase in personnel and equipment but also involves certain fundamental changes in the establishments of the squadrons and thus necessitates a drastic revision of existing War Organisation schemes. The organisation of War Training schemes to meet increased war requirements and wastage has now become a matter of considerable urgency, but it has only been possible for the present staff to deal with the fringe of this problem owing to pressure of other work. Furthermore, decisions which have recently been taken to enlarge the reserve forces of the Royal Air Force and also to introduce new categories of reservists will add considerably to the work of WO2 in regard to the detailed preparation of schemes for mobilising and embodying these forces in an emergency.

The whole question of war organisation is a matter of great importance and urgency and the Air Council are satisfied that an additional squadron leader is required to deal with questions arising out of the introduction of the latest expansion scheme, and another to deal with war training problems, thus leaving the present staff officer free to concentrate upon questions relating to the mobilisation and embodiment of reservists. There is no doubt that each of these officers will be fully employed in dealing with their respective problems for a considerable time to come, but the position will be reviewed at the end of 1939.

The letter gives a sense of the increasing pressure under which the Directorate of War Organisation was finding itself. Three weeks later, on 6 June, James Rae, Undersecretary of State to the Air Ministry at the Treasury replied:

I have laid before the Lords Commissioners of His Majesty's Treasury Mr Reynolds' letter date 17th May 1938 in connection

with additional posts for the Directorate of War Organisation
which have also been the subject of semi-official discussion. In
reply I am therefore to inform the Air Council that My Lords
sanction ... two additional posts for Squadron Leaders in the
WO2 section of the Deputy Directorate of War Organisation for
the work of revision of existing war organisation schemes in the
light of the further expansion of the Royal Air Force subject ...
to review in eighteen months' time.

Hal headed up War Organisation 2 (WO2) with Mr G.E. Caswell MC
as his wonderfully titled Higher Clerical Officer (HCO) supporting
him. As head of the department Hal's responsibilities evolved during
his time there to encompass the 'general co-ordination of war organisation in the U.K., satellite aerodromes, station bomb stores and vulnerable points.' Beneath Hal, the department was divided into three
sections. WO2(a) was under the charge of a squadron leader and its
responsibilities were the 'war organisation of Bomber, Fighter, Coastal
and Maintenance Commands and mobilisation exercises'. WO2(b) was
also under the command of a squadron leader and its brief was the 'war
organisation of Training Command and war training organisation'.
WO2(M) was in the hands of staff officers and looked after the mobilisation process overall with a senior staff officer keeping the War Book and
with responsibility for 'mobilisation pools, re-equipment programmes
as affecting mobilisation and mobilisable [sic] strength'. Finally Hal's
HCO assisted by a staff officer dealt with 'mobilisation regulations and
questions relating to all classes of the Reserve and Auxiliary forces'.
The HCO was, as its secretary, also responsible for organisation of the
Mobilisation Committee's meetings and its agendas and for the keeping
of the Committee's minutes. Shortly after Hal's departure the organisation of WO2 was further refined and added responsibilities included
balloon barrage, station defence equipment, RDF and DF stations,
security measures and salvage organisation.

    There were two other War Organisation departments. WO1 was
involved in the 'study and co-ordination of general problems of war

organisation, the supervision of war manuals, publication of wastage and consumption rates, and co-ordination of chemical defence measures', whilst WO3 looked at the 'co-ordination of mechanical transport policy and all aspects of maintenance in the field, the preparation of administrative plans and all field contingents in war plus the issue of field mobilisation instructions, preparation of movement tables and supervision of schemes and exercises'.

*

What was the makeup of the Mobilisation Committee? It was a large one and forty people, including civilians, often attended. It became so unwieldy that there were frequent appeals to all departments to nominate as few as practicable to attend. The committee was chaired by the head of the Directorate of War Organisation who during Hal's tenure was Air Commodore William Welsh, later promoted to Air Vice Marshal whilst still heading up the Directorate: he was later further promoted to Air Marshal and commanded British air operations during Operation TORCH. Sitting on the committee were heads of all the departments within the Directorate, the meaning of the acronyms of many of which have been lost in the mists of time – DPI, DDRM, DDPO, O2, DDWO, E5, E1, FO1, P3, etc. – plus representatives of senior rank from Bomber, Fighter, Coastal and Training Commands and No.11 (F) Group. The Group Captain i/c records was also there. The number of items on its agendas was many and varied and increased the more that war seemed inevitable whilst at the same time the Air Council now officially directed that attendance at meetings should be limited and the distribution of minutes restricted for security reasons.

Typical items to be found on lengthy Mobilisation Committee agendas included reviews of the aircraft available and squadron re-equipment programmes; reviews of aircraft equipment and weaponry; reviews of the position as regards personnel, including matters such as the replacement of casualties; reviews of motor transport; reports on the command organisation of the designated war stations in the UK; and reports on the state of ground organisation in the UK, this covering repair, salvage, routine inspection, supply of equipment, control of ammunition stocks, station bomb stores, air ammunition parks, stocks of aviation fuel at stations, signal organisation, defence measures of airfields, satellite aerodromes and the repair of aerodromes in the event of bombing.

All in all this was a hefty list of subjects and responsibilities. Some of the burden was taken off the Mobilisation Committee's shoulders by delegating sub-committees to cover some of the work and then reporting back. Hal sat on some such committees, such as sub-committee B in June 1937 to 'consider and make recommendations regarding the allocation of war stations of the medium and heavy bomber squadrons likely to be included in the mobilisable forces of the Western Plan up to the end of 1937, having regards to the organisation of the Groups of Bomber Command'. The Western Plan was the name given to the whole mobilisation process and was updated regularly according to reports received on aircraft, equipment and personnel levels. New phases of the Western Plan were adopted as previous targets were reached.

The final Mobilisation Committee meeting in which Hal participated before being posted to India was held on the 15 September 1938 and it is worth having an edited look at the items discussed and reported upon to give an understanding of not only the remit of the Committee but the state of preparedness of the RAF for war twelve months before hostilities began. This meeting concerned itself mainly with Bomber Command matters.

Bomber Command Units and War Stations.

3 Blenheim and 3 Battle squadrons added to mobilisable strength.

Aircraft Equipment of Mobilisable Squadrons.

Battles: shortages of power-driven pumps for blind-flying equipment: lack of parts for container-carried bombs.

Blenheims: shortage of turrets, carriers, some gun equipment and small bomb containers.

Whitleys: only 50% of aircraft complete with blind-flying equipment. Short of turrets.

Wellesleys: up to 12 aircraft constantly non-effective owing to modifications to blind-flying equipment.

Personnel Questions, Bomber Command Units

Less than 50% of the crews fit for operations. The 19-year age limit for airmen posted overseas to be clarified.

Disposal of Partly Trained Crews on Mobilisation

Agreed to use No.6 (Auxiliary) Group as a Reserve Training Group under Bomber Command

Personnel for Defence Duties

Air Staff attention drawn to inadequate provision in war establishments of personnel for general defence duties, guards etc. Army unable to help.

Supply of Bombs

Decided to issue stocks to stations whether or not equipped with station bomb stores.

Aircraft Equipment for Mobilisable Squadrons

Heating of Browning guns. Hurricanes only able to operate in temps above 10 degrees C equal to 15,000 feet in summer.

Bomb Trollies

Lack of trollies causing difficulty in handling 250lb bombs.

Barrage Balloons

Possible to operate barrage of 142 balloons within 7 days of order. From November 1938 balloons available should increase by 50 per month.

General Personnel Position

Pilots – after filling vacancies in operational units no margin left for training units, therefore no source of replacement for casualties.

Airmen – total required to fill war establishment of all units is 32,346.

The subsequent Mobilisation Committee meeting, in which Hal was not involved, heard of the increasingly significant equipment problems. The Hurricane Browning gun-heating problem was being addressed but there was a shortage of reflector sights, indeed a shortage of spares in general and a proposal was made that no new aircraft be accepted from Hawker's until the arrears of spares had been made up. For Spitfires there was a shortage of gun-sights and the airscrew was unsatisfactory although a new airscrew of interim design would be available by the end of January 1939. The Blenheim re-equipment programme was running behind schedule and Bristol-built airframes needed considerable modification anyway. There was a shortage of Mercury engines for Gladiators and of spares for the Harrow, considered particularly serious as there were only two squadrons in reserve behind three front-line squadrons of this type. As for the Whitley there were no 'blind-flying panels' and they were equipped with unmodified navigational equipment. It would be nine months before production of mid-upper turrets for the Wellington could begin. The type was restricted to flying locally owing to icing trouble and was limited to 210mph through 'tail trouble'. Hampdens were plagued by icing problems and were short of armament. And there was a shortage of Cheetah engines for Coastal Command Ansons.

*

What was the state of the RAF in terms of squadron strength when Hal departed from the Directorate? Phase V of the Western Plan covered the period June to September 1938 and by the end of this period the projected situation (as envisaged when the report was compiled on 25 March) was as follows, although this was dependent on the production and equipment problems that were ever present being resolved. Some of the squadrons were due to re-equip with more modern types, possibly during this phase, but for the purposes of the report the existing types on strength were listed.

Fighters   six Hurricane squadrons
                                  one Spitfire squadron

	six Gladiator squadrons
	ten Gauntlet squadrons
	three Fury squadrons
	eight Demon squadrons
Heavy Bombers	three Heyford squadrons
	seven Whitley squadrons
	five Harrow squadrons
Medium Bombers	thirteen Battle squadrons
	thirteen Blenheim squadrons
	five Wellesley squadrons
Light Bombers	ten Hind squadrons
Army Co-operation	three Hector squadrons
	one Lysander squadron
General Reconnaissance	five Anson squadrons
	two London squadrons
	two Singapore squadrons
	one Stranraer squadron
Torpedo Bomber	one Vildebeest squadron

Hal's duties at The Directorate meant he had to pay 'flying visits to various aerodromes [and some of these squadrons, usually in a Hart or Tiger Moth] where we also did bombing up trials on Blenheim, Battle and Harrow aircraft'.

*

From the mid-1930s there were many new aircraft to be experienced with much more sophisticated instruments than previously and so the RAF purchased Link Trainers from the USA. The first of these was installed in Bush House and all pilots at the Air Ministry had to do a course on it. Wrote Hal:

The trainer took the form of a miniature aeroplane, so mounted that it responded to every movement of a real aeroplane in flight.

The cockpit was fitted with a full set of flying instruments to guide the pupil on his imaginary flight. What he did was automatically recorded and traced by a crab-like device on a chart on the instructor's desk where there was another instrument panel. The instructor was in telephone touch with the pupil to give orders.

The principle of providing flying training in an aircraft without actually taking off was created by Edwin Link who developed his flight trainer in the basement of the family factory (which manufactured pianos and organs) between 1927 and 1929 in New York. The first model was patented in 1930 after Link realised there was a need for an instrument trainer (as opposed to a flight trainer) and he fitted cockpit instruments as standard equipment to his design. The importance of this style of training was soon recognised, notably by the US Army Air Corps. An improved version, which was able to rotate through 360 degrees, allowed for the fitting of a magnetic compass. Other instruments were operated either mechanically or pneumatically. Link Trainers pivoted on a universal joint and were mounted on an octagonal turntable which in turn was free to rotate in azimuth on a square base. Between the fuselage and the turntable were four supporting bellows which were inflated or deflated by a vacuum turbine, its valves being operated as the pupil moved the control column thereby realistically recreating most of the sensations of flying. Both calm and rough air conditions could be created by the instructor. The trainer could also initiate stall when the recorded airspeed fell below a predetermined figure and went into a realistic spin with the instruments performing as would be expected in such a situation. A cross-country `flight` of up to 200 miles was possible during which the instructor was able to confront the pupil with most of the difficulties that could occur in a real flight. The trainer was also equipped to provide instruction in the use of radio signal beams and the Lorenz landing system for blind landing in fog.

In its time the Link Trainer was at the forefront of flight technology, saving many lives and aircraft in the process, and it was of course the forerunner of the very sophisticated flight simulators of today. Many survive in museums, often in working order. No wonder Hal was intrigued when told he would be on the Link Trainer course in April and May 1938.

There were 16 lessons. There were twelve of half an hour each which covered flying straight and level, climbing, turns of all types, and rates of turn in calm and rough weather and getting into the Lorenz beam and Lorenz landings. [The Lorenz beam blind-landing system was an air radio navigation system in use from the late 1930s developed by the Standard Elektrik Lorenz Company. Prior to the Second World War the Germans deployed the Lorenz blind-landing aid at many airports in and outside Germany and equipped most of their bombers with the radio equipment needed to use it. The RAF continued using the system as late as 1955 under the name Standard Beam Approach.] The cross country test lasted one and a half hours with rough weather and icing up added. After a 180 mile course with turns I finished up two miles from the destination. This with three consecutive landings on Lorenz beam got me past the examination.

The trainer required careful handling. 'Air Vice Marshal McClaughry who was Director of Training was rather a 'ham handed' pilot and when doing one of his tests he got all mixed up,' wrote Hal mischievously. 'Some of us were watching the trace when suddenly the instructor said, 'Gentlemen, remove your hats. The Air Vice Marshal is now flying through the dome of St Paul's!'

*

Away from the Air Ministry Hal was invited to a City dinner held by the Salters, one of the great London livery companies with modern-day associations with chemistry and science.

It was a tails and miniatures occasion with a fabulous menu embracing a different wine with each course. An orchestra with songs by a baritone and soprano entertained the guests. Halfway through there was a break for retiring when bowls of rose water were brought round with napkins to refresh the diners. When the great two handled loving cup was passed round, while one was drinking the men on each side of one stood up in accordance with an ancient custom as a protection in case one got stabbed. As we departed at the end we were each presented with a truly amazing box of candies for our wives or sweethearts who had spent the evening alone. The toast 'wives and sweethearts, may they never meet' was not given!

Chapter Fifteen

India

On 22 May 1938 Nora gave birth to twin boys, Christopher and Richard. In July Hal was told he was being posted to India to command No.1 (Indian) Wing at Kohat on the North-West Frontier. As some India squadrons were due to receive the new twin-engined Blenheim bomber Hal had gone on a day-long conversion course at Upper Heyford on 1 September, flying six times that day, three with Squadron Leader Nesbitt in L1162 and three solo in L1166.

The prospect of the move to the sub-continent by sea with four young children and their nanny, Jessie Hinton, was a daunting one logistically. All vaccinations and inoculations had to be phased so that neither Nora nor Nannie (as she was known to the family) were laid low at the same time. John and Michael took the treatment well, but Christopher and Richard didn't. The vaccination upset them and they became very ill. Whilst on embarkation leave Hal went to Dublin to visit his parents with his first-born John. He was there when a grief stricken Nora rang to tell him the tragic news that Christopher had died. Richard improved later but the question arose as to whether or not he should be taken to India. The doctor advised that they could only take him at their own risk and as they were reluctant to leave him with Nora's parents in Harrogate it was decided not to split the family up. As it turned out the sea voyage worked wonders and Richard made a full recovery.

As Hal was readying himself for India the Munich Crisis was looming and war clouds were gathering over Europe. On the day he and Nora did their last bit of shopping prior to travelling, preparations for war were evident in London. Trenches were being dug in the parks and the lamp posts on Westminster Bridge were being cut down to provide field of fire for AA gunners defending the Houses of Parliament. By this time all their luggage had gone in advance to Southampton for loading on the HMT *Nevasa* but all sailings were held up in case war broke out. Hal remembered that 'days of great suspense followed until finally Mr Chamberlain flew to see Hitler and returned [on 30 September 1938] to say the historic words "peace for our time". Tension eased and we received our embarkation orders'.

*

This would be an appropriate point at which to mention an instructive and fascinating little book entitled *Notes for RAF Officers Proceeding to India for the First Time* issued 'for the information and guidance of all concerned. By Order of the Air Council. September 1921'. Hal would have been given a revised edition. It had been written by an officer who had spent many years in the sub-continent but it was considered that the advice it contained was still relevant in the late 1930s. 'The RAF officer arriving in India,' it begins, 'brings with him in his kit much that is unnecessary and in his mind too often the glowing picture of a land of

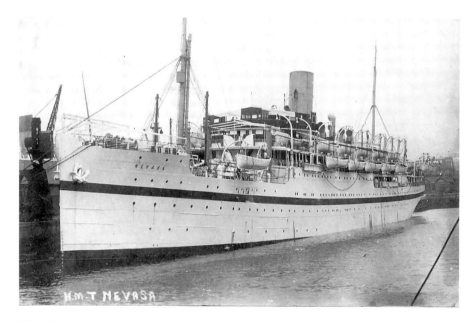

The HMT *Nevasa* on which Hal and his family sailed to Karachi. Photo courtesy of www.roll-of-honour.com.

unlimited sport and servants – both inexpensive – and of cheap living. The purpose of these inexhaustive notes is to give as far as possible a more modern picture.' The anonymous author then proceeds to do that.

Dealing with the climate first of all, and specifically hot weather when temperatures range from 100 to 120 degrees Fahrenheit [bearing in mind all of RAF India at this stage was located in the north of the country]: the occupants of bungalows sleep outside, either in the compound or on the roof, the bungalows themselves being left with every door and window open to facilitate cooling. Shortly after sunrise bungalows are shut up, every possible opening being closed. Only by shutting up, and shutting up early, can they be kept moderately cool during the hot weather day. At sunset they are opened up for ventilation and for the cooling process to begin again. It is the habit of residents in the Punjab during hot weather to go to bed late, rise with the dawn and spend the hot hours of the day sleeping under a punkah [fan] in the bungalow.

Few of the Punjab stations have electrical installations at present but most of them are expected to have them within a few years. The electric fan instead of the hand punkah pulled by the erratic coolie and the electric light instead of the dim, room heating, smelly and smoky lamp, do much to mitigate hot weather discomforts. ... The hot weather of the Punjab plains is almost impossible for children. A few ladies can stand it but generally speaking, from the end of April to the beginning of October, women and children are in the hills. It is a recognised principle that British ranks from Punjab 'plains' stations require a change to the hills in hot weather. ... The unit at Kohat moves to Parachinar – a hill fort near the Afghan border – to be under canvas for the hot weather.

Attention then focuses on the kit to bring to India.

The working dress in India is khaki drill and officers are advised to bring one well-cut suit of khaki drill – breeches and slacks – and have any other suits required copied from this pattern by the local Indian tailor. Field boots and gaiters are worn with the breeches. Shorts and stockings are not permitted. Blue mess kit for the cold weather is necessary: in hot weather white mess dress is worn. White mess kit will be wanted for the latter hot part of the voyage out. The white kit consists of [a] cavalry pattern short shell jacket with stand up collar which hooks across the neck, and shoulder straps of blue with badges of rank in gold braid: [a] soft shirt with two gold studs, white plain stand up collar and black tie, white waistcoat with four RAF buttons and white trousers with Oxford shoes *or* white overalls with Wellington boots. The latter is much to be preferred as the Wellingtons keep off the bites of mosquitoes and are a protection against snakes. ... White trousers to look smart require a certain amount of starch which means that after they have been sat down in once or twice in the hot weather they look as if they had been slept in. The head gear during the day is a khaki helmet with [the] RAF 'flash' on the left.

As for recreation:

Nothing in the way of equipment for games and sports should be left behind e.g. saddlery, guns, fishing rods, golf clubs and tennis racquets though, if not possessed, they can be bought in India.

Games played were polo, tennis, golf and racquets. Sport included hunting to hounds, pig-sticking on horseback or on foot, shooting and fishing.
Personal wellbeing and home comforts were also a concern:

Mosquito nets should be bought in India on arrival. It is not generally realised that bedding is required immediately on landing in India for the train journey. It is well therefore to bring out a valise containing two pairs of sheets, pillow or pillows and pillow cases and two or three blankets or rugs and a couple of towels. Other sheets, blankets and towels required later can be bought good and cheaper than in England. A camp bed is useful and should be brought out if possessed. Camp equipment is obtainable in India. Deck chairs brought out for the voyage should not be left on the ship – they will be useful in the station. A push bicycle is most useful and should not be left behind if possessed.

The author of these *Notes* was well aware that many officers would be accompanied by wives and children.

Married people are advised to bring out household things if they have them i.e. crockery, silver and plate, cutlery, curtains and rugs, a few favourite books and pictures. ... Furniture is not worth bringing out and generally not worth buying even in India. Most people hire their furniture in the bazaar. For clothing ladies are advised to bring out any warm clothes they have but not to buy any new. Naturally a stock of light clothing is wanted and more evening dresses are wanted in India than in England. Most odds and ends of ladies' toilet articles and haberdashery are easily obtainable in India. Ribbons and stockings are difficult and repay bringing out a stock of. Also outdoor shoes that do not show the dust. A sewing machine, if in possession, is most useful and should not be left behind.

The notes then delve into establishment and living expenses, outlining the cost of living in India. Mess and club bills are discussed:

Drinks are expensive and can easily be the heaviest item .... If they are made so, apart from the danger to personal health and efficiency, the officer will never get the best in life that India has to offer.'

However, an unmarried officer would be pleased to know that provided he kept a close eye on his mess bill his pay 'is sufficient to allow him to play polo, with the facilities given for the purchase of ponies by the RAF Polo Club in India and save enough for leave in Kashmir'. As for officers with wives with them they were urged 'not to agree to any rate of wages for servants until they have inquired what the local rates are' as 'they vary somewhat in different stations'. Furthermore 'it is impossible to live unless some economy is made in servants' wages and the mistress of the house does some housework herself.' Then came the matter of language.

> It cannot be too strongly impressed that to effect economy in managing a house and servants the sooner a working knowledge of Hindustani is gained the better. Both unmarried and married officers should learn the language. Newcomers have to deal with English speaking bearers at first. They are always more expensive and rarely as trustworthy as Hindustani speaking bearers [personal servants].

The RAF in India was invariably stationed with units of both the British and Indian Armies. There were also civilian officials of the government of India on the stations, so society was almost always entirely official. Pre-war the RAF was dependant on the Army for accommodation and much of their supplies. It was important therefore to maintain mutual good feeling. Thus 'it is the duty of every RAF officer to call on all Army messes as soon as possible after arrival.' The great social institution in India was of course the Club, which usually contained reading rooms, a library, bar, ballroom, a euphemism known as an ablution room, and dining room. Clubs stood in compounds with large gardens and tennis courts. 'Here the station meets in the afternoon and before dinner to play tennis, dance, read the papers etc.'

There was plenty of advice as to how to keep fit in India. For example 'cultivate a respect for the sun and wear a sun helmet out of doors from an hour after sunrise to an hour before sundown in hot weather.' Then 'after sweating from exercise put on a sweater [and] change and bathe as soon as possible', although cold baths were not recommended, a warm bath being much better for regulating body temperature. Getting down to the nitty gritty, 'keep the bowels open: constipation in hot weather is often accompanied by fever. The before breakfast habit after the morning cup of tea is much cultivated by residents in the tropics.' Then comes some what might be thought obvious advice, such as making sure kitchens are kept clean, food is uncontaminated by flies, water is boiled before drinking and hot meals are avoided in the middle of the day. Finally, there is a warning.

> Nowadays no servant will stay with a master who abuses him or beats him. Much real harm has been done in the past by youths coming out to India who regarded every Indian as someone to order about and shout at. The better class Indian is well mannered and sensitive to bad manners in Europeans. It costs as little to be polite as to be overbearing. Some study of Indian life and society will be well repaid.

*

As was/is the way with the RAF, there were regulations to cover every possible situation and when proceeding abroad the administrators went to town. Hal was required to read *General Notes for Royal Air Force Officers Proceeding Abroad* and *General Instructions for the Guidance of Officers and Officers' Families Proceeding Abroad*, both of which go into great detail about what paperwork is required, who is entitled to what, how one should go about getting what is required and so forth. All very useful but administratively top heavy. There were restrictions as to where wives and families were permitted to travel – not to Iraq, Sudan, or to a foreign country to which an officer was sent for language study for example. But provided the officer was over 30 and above the rank of flight lieutenant they could accompany him at public expense to Malta, Egypt, Singapore, India etc. but only if the officer 'made an immediate application on his receiving his posting on Form 1542 through the usual channels'. Passages would only be granted if 'the officer's marriage has been duly reported to and recorded in the Air Ministry'. It would take too much space to examine all the rules here, but as a sample this is what is required for 'Unaccompanied Baggage' to India.

The port of entry into India for RAF personnel is Karachi and destination labels for this port will always be issued whether the passenger is proceeding direct to Karachi or transhipping at Bombay. When Unaccompanied Baggage is sent, the packages should be given a number in the form of a fraction, the denominator representing the total number of packages and the numerator the particular number of each package. The packages should be numbered according to their degree of utility for immediate requirements during the voyage and after arrival at destination. Articles such as golf clubs and lawn tennis rackets must be labelled 'Not Wanted On Voyage' and left in the Baggage Pen at the ship's side. They will be collected and stored in the Gun Room.

How much baggage could be taken to India? As a wing commander Hal was entitled to take (in Imperial measurement) 20 cwt, Nora 15 and the children 10 each; but Nannie was only allowed 2. In total a remarkable 2 tons 17 cwt or 2,895 kilos! There was of course a sliding scale according to rank. An air marshal with a wife, two children and a 'European Female Servant' (as she was termed in the *Guidance*) was entitled to 5,410 kilos but a flight lieutenant with a family a mere 1,778 kilos. Individual crates were not permitted to be more than 305 kilos. Of course cabin baggage was in addition to all this. Despite these very generous allowances there were certain things you could definitely not take with you at public expense: 'Privately owned aeroplanes, motor-cars, motor-cycles and side-cars, chaises and similar vehicles' or 'horses, ponies, dogs, cats and birds.' You could arrange private shipment if you wished but that would invariably be on a different ship.

*

Hal's memoir amounts to his own version of *Notes for RAF Officers Proceeding to India*. For anyone posted to the North-West Frontier they faced an epic journey by steamer, train and road.

We sailed for India shortly after Mr. Chamberlain returned from Munich. All passengers were officers and men of the RAF and Army with their wives and families all bound for lengthy periods of service overseas. There were lots of entertainments and anxious moments when children climbed about, running risks of falling overboard. The duty officers often had to turn couples out of lifeboats after dark! Michael was especially wild, dashing all over the ship. Richard was brought on deck daily in his cot and placed in the shade with his sun proof canopy erected. We had a calm passage all the way to India.

Hal paints an evocative picture of pre-war travel to the sub-continent by sea. The first port of call was in Malta where passengers could disembark. From there they sailed to Port Said. 'The floating flexible gangway was brought alongside and we walked ashore to buy cheap topees at Simon Arzt', Hal's second visit to the store, the first being back in 1925 as recounted earlier. He continued:

We did not land at Suez but further on went alongside the wharf at Port Sudan where we made up a party to go for a trip in a glass bottomed launch to see the marvellous coloured fish and coral in the dead calm shallow water. We took John and Michael ashore at Aden in a native boat rowed by the blackest cut throats you could imagine and had a walk round. We sailed up the Persian Gulf to Basra. The RAF at Shaibah airfield near the port arranged a grand ball in the mess and laid on transport to bring their guests across the desert from the ship. Next day a sandstorm blew up and in spite of four tugs we could not get away from the quayside.

We disembarked at Karachi some thirty days out from the UK where John Oliver who I was relieving at Kohat met us with Abdul, a bearer, and fixed us up in a hotel. I had to clear all our kit through Customs and book our rail travel to Kohat. In our compartment were four bunks and armchairs and we slept the three boys, Nannie, Nora and myself with only a camp bed in addition. We had a wash room and WC leading off the compartment. We had brought from the UK old sheets to soak in water and place wherever the dust from the Sind desert started to come in. The windows had three coverings: a wooden slatted sun panel, fly gauze and a glass panel. All the window panels locked from the inside to keep out intruders. Abdul brought food and tea from the dining car at various stops.

Hal's interest in railways was piqued by the Indian broad-gauge system as opposed to the British standard gauge. And by the engines and rolling stock too.

We left Karachi at dusk but before the train left John and I inspected the massive Pacific locomotive with its oil firing roaring like a large blow lamp, its cowcatcher and searchlight (both very necessary where there are no fences beside the tracks) and a crew of three. The engine was spotless.

After two nights, two days and 1,800 miles of travel via Lahore and Rawalpindi, the Crowes arrived at Kohat, a town of about 29,000 inhabitants lying 1,700 feet above sea level.

No.1 (Indian) Wing had organised our reception to the last detail. When we arrived at our bungalow our eight servants were lined up to receive us. There was one butler, two bearers, one cook, one cook boy, one sweeper, one dhobi clothes washer and one gardener. As it was cold weather, log fires were alight and a meal was ready to serve with drinks from the mess nearby. Cooking was on charcoal on a crude brick device. We had electric light but ceiling fans were only fitted in summer. Sanitation was by 'thunder box' and was always cleared by the sweeper without delay. Baths were filled with water heated outside and conveyed in tins.

Our bungalow was just inside the barbed-wire apron fences surrounding the cantonment. If I was to be away an armed guard would sleep on the veranda to protect against kidnapping.

A British girl, Molly Ellis, had been kidnapped at Kohat sometime previously. She was eventually released unharmed but her mother was murdered. The murder rate in Kohat at the time was at least one per day throughout the year and it was inadvisable for white women to go into the bazaar alone. The Army units with families and the RAF officers with families lived in one cantonment while the airmen and their families lived in a small cantonment at the aerodrome. Each cantonment was surrounded by thick barbed-wire fences with blockhouses for machine-gun posts. All personnel had to be inside the barbed wire from dusk to dawn.

The road to Peshawar via the Kohat Pass was British territory and so long as travellers remained on the road they were safe, but if they strayed off it then they were in tribal territory and could be shot at without warning. Half way through the pass there was a tribal rifle factory. Using parts of old cars and so on and with the crudest tools imaginable the tribesmen would produce near perfect copies of the British .303 rifle although the barrel would wear out after about 25 rounds. Making the bolt for the rifle was the most difficult part and so if bolts could be stolen from the British it would help production. Consequently all service rifles had to be chained to the walls and after practice firing on the range all empty cases had to be collected and bullets collected from the sand in the butts.

European families had to go to the hills in March because part of the Kohat Military Hospital closed for the hot weather, to reopen in September. They went to Kashmir by road along the beautiful valley of the Jhelum River. The road ended below Gulmarg where Nora and the boys were going and for the remainder of the journey everyone had to ride on ponies. Nora hired a log hut at Gulmarg and from the veranda they could see the massive Nanga Parbat mountain of 26,600 feet, eternally snow covered. Log fires warmed the hut which did have electric light although it was unreliable. If visiting other huts at night a light was carried to scare away the leopards which roamed about locally, often killing the ponies in their pens.

You were not supposed to walk or play golf for the first week at Gulmarg so as to get acclimatised to the height of over 8,800 feet but I'm sure that advice wasn't always followed! I spent a short sick leave there after a bout of sand fly fever. The boys on the other hand never had a thing wrong with them but Nannie had to go to hospital with ear trouble and we had an Indian *ayah* [nursemaid] to look after them. The Indians love children and when Michael's pet bird escaped from its cage all work ceased while the whole staff chased and caught it.

Life was gay in Kohat and Peshawar in cold weather when families were back down from the hills. The clubs ran dances and entertainments. A golf course was much used. It was well manned by caddies and boys called *agiwallahs* to find one's ball. A cinema showed oldish films. In winter we sat in overcoats with rugs to watch films but in the hot weather the ceiling fans almost drowned the film's sound.

*

While Nora and the family were settling in Hal was finding out about No.1 (Indian) Wing of which he formally took command on 10 December 1938. He had been reading up about the situation in India and indeed about the RAF's presence there and their remit as far as the North-West Frontier (now part of Pakistan) was concerned. An official booklet, *Frontier Warfare—India (Army and Royal Air Force)*, was instructive.

The North-West Frontier was divided into three areas for the RAF, the northern area comprising the region to the north of the Khyber Pass up to the foothills of the Himalayas: the central area lying south west of the Khyber Pass, roughly between the rivers Kabul and Kurram, mountainous country criss-crossed by deep valleys and dried-up water courses: and the southern area to the south-west of Kohat from the Kurram

The Khyber Pass, North-West India.

River down towards Baluchistan. This was dominated by Waziristan, the stronghold of tribal resistance. There were at least two million tribesmen in this 27,000 square miles of territory – Mohmands, Afridis, Wazirs, Mahsuds and many lesser tribes, all referred to as Pathans and deeply committed to their Islamic faith. They all lived by a strict code of honour which extended to hospitality, even for a hated foe. They acknowledged no man as their master except in matters of religion. They were proud but cruel and fearless guerrilla fighters.

Convinced in 1915 of the need for military aircraft to assist Army operations in this troublesome part of India the then Viceroy, Charles Hardinge, 1st Baron Hardinge of Penshurst, asked for an RFC unit to be sent from England. A flight of the newly-forming No.31 Squadron was despatched and based at Nowshera, thirty miles east of Peshawar, becoming the first RFC unit to be resident in the sub-continent. 'A' Fight was joined by 'B' and 'C' Flights by July 1916 and throughout the rest of the

First World War flew reconnaissance and ranging missions for artillery as well as bombing and strafing sorties against tribesmen resisting the rule of the British Raj. No.31 was later joined by No.114 Squadron, both flying BE.2s. In 1918 when the peacetime establishments of the fledgling RAF were being planned it was decided that three squadrons based in Europe would transfer to India. These were Nos.20 and 48 Squadrons, flying Bristol F.2Bs and No.99 Squadron flying DH.9As. A fourth bomber squadron, No.97 flying DH.10s, followed shortly afterwards. All were based in the north-west of the country. Incidentally RAF squadrons were known locally as *Hawa Jahaz* (ships of the air).

At the same time as squadrons moved in, landing grounds for forward operations (often adjacent to existing army forts) were created. In support, various depots, aircraft parks and headquarters units were established. One of these was at Gilgit in the extreme north-east of the country, a town nestling among the 25,000-foot mountains of the Karakoram Range next to the border with China and important historically as it lay on the Silk Road. Only twin-engined aircraft were allowed to visit Gilgit and Vickers Victoria and Valentia troop carriers were therefore used. Even though the mountains bordering the Indus valley were higher than the ceiling of these aircraft, they were the only twins in India which could be landed on the small field. Hemmed in by mountains it was impossible to go round again if the first landing was misjudged.

The game of polo is supposed to have originated at Gilgit, so Hal heard.

> Certainly we saw a game being played which was very similar but much more dangerous. A sort of rag ball was used and the players galloped all over the place ... quite regardless. A Hunza band of noisy drums played during the game, presumably to encourage the players. Other things I noticed were Markhor mountain goats with their huge horns on the hillsides: and the locals who seemed to spend a lot of time in their long sleeved *chogras*, warming themselves over charcoal braziers at the shops and tea houses in the crisp mountain air. On one occasion when I visited we took stores and petrol from Peshawar and brought

A Vickers Victoria at Gilgit, one of the landing grounds established for forward operations.

back two missionaries who had been in China most of their lives and had travelled with yaks to Gilgit from Xinjiang Province hoping to reach India. They had never seen a railway train and were thrilled to see one at Peshawar.

On another occasion Hal visited Drosh, a charming place beside the Hindu Kush range, and brought two murderers heavily chained to their armed guards back to Peshawar.

*

The creation of landing grounds fifteen years or so before Hal's arrival in India was happening during a decade of widespread unrest in the region. In response, on 1 March 1924 the RAF Chief of the Air Staff, Sir Hugh Trenchard, issued a secret directive entitled *Employment of Aircraft on the North-West Frontier of India*. 'The problem of controlling the tribal territory ... has always needed special treatment by reason of the psychology, social organization and mode of life of the tribesmen and the nature of the country they inhabit', it said. And this was certainly true. Since the mid-nineteenth century the Wazirs, Mahsuds and other mountain tribes who lived on the North-West Frontier had harassed the British by stealing cattle, by looting and by the kidnapping and ransoming of British citizens. Incensed by Britain's two invasions of Afghanistan in

Another forward airstrip, this one at Drosh.

the mid and later 1800s in what has become known as The Great Game, the quest for domination of the area by Russia and the United Kingdom with the British invasions attempting to stop Russian expansion, tribesmen in Waziristan continued to challenge British forces after the Third Afghan War of 1919. British and Indian soldiers and the RAF had their hands full defending their convoys, forts and patrols and so the service devised a policy of air policing of the frontier as they were doing in Iraq. If the tribesmen staged a raid or attack, the bombers would be called in. The Hugh Trenchard directive recommended that action be immediate as 'hesitation or delay in dealing with uncivilized enemies is invariably interpreted as signs of weakness'. Furthermore 'in warfare against savage tribes who do not conform to codes of civilized warfare, aerial bombardment is not necessarily limited in its methods or objectives by rules agreed upon in international law.' In other words he was condoning indiscriminate bombing.

Notwithstanding this radical observation, air policing was developed under strict codes of practice. For example, aircraft were sent to drop bilingual leaflets (so called red notices) over a village where a hostile raiding party was known to have originated, the leaflets warning that unless a safe refuge to hostiles was denied by a specified date the village would be bombed. The leaflets recommended the removal of women and children by that date and even went so far as to suggest that the villagers should hand them over into the care of those who were about to bomb their homes, to be restored to them when they agreed to comply. The warnings were often accompanied by bombing demonstrations staged nearby.

Trenchard's directive recommended that on the specified date strikes be conducted immediately 'to ensure the greatest concentration of men and animals around the village'. The bombs used should therefore be 'man-killing' and machine guns were to be 'fired against any movement'. Selection of the right bomb size was important and the document advised that 20lb bombs 'will only make a small hole in the huts of tribesmen, 112lb bombs will be expected to blow off the roof, while 230lb and larger bombs should destroy large houses'. Furthermore incendiary bombs should be used for good effect against villages and crops. The directive

NOTICE

To:—

THE MADDA KHEL.

1. WHEREAS you have failed to comply with your agreement of June, 1938, and have committed many hostile acts, including several attacks on DATTA KHEL Post, and have interfered with communications on the TOCHI ROAD, Government has decided that you will be punished by air action.

2. You have already been punished recently by the bombing of the SHAWAL TANGI and by the destruction of your villages of TARMORA and NARAKKI and of the villages in the MASTOI.

3. Air action in the MASTOI area will continue and, in addition, 48 hours after the dropping of this notice, the whole of your country with the exception of two sanctuaries named below will be subjected to an air blockade and your villages and habitations not in the sanctuaries may be destroyed by bombing if Government think fit to do so,

4. This air action will continue until Government are satisfied of the good intentions of your tribe.

5. The two sanctuaries named above are :—

    (a) The SPIN KHAK RAGHZHA area between the east bank of the MAIDAN ALGAD and the south-west bank of the GURGURAI ALGAD from MAZARAME to the junction of the MAIDAN and GURGURAI ALGADS and thence the country half mile north and south of the BABAI TANGI and DUGA KHULLA from the junction of the MAIDAN and GURGURAI ALGADS to the junction of STARE DARBALAI KWAR and DUGA KHULLA.

    (b) All land draining into the SHAWAL TANGI from RAMA inclusive down to its junction with the KHINA ALGAD. All land draining into the KHINA ALGAD from KANRAI to its junction with the SHAWAL. All land draining into the south bank of the TOCHI between SANDEPAL ALGAD and CHARMINA, excluding DWA TOI.

6. You will not be attacked in either of these sanctuaries unless you allow the Faqir of IPI into them. If you allow him to enter air action against the sanctuary effected will be taken after due notice.

7. For 48 hours after the dropping of these notices, you will be allowed to move into the sanctuaries without molestation and aircraft will fly over your country to see that you are complying with this order. You are NOT allowed to leave MADDA KHEL territory or take shelter with any other WAZIR or MAHSUD tribe; if you do so you and those who shelter you outside your territory will be liable to punishment.

8. If you wish you may ask for an interview with the P. A. but air action will not be suspended for this purpose, and you are hereby warned that the P. A. will not interview your representatives unless they represent your tribe as a whole.

9. You are to take with you your families and animals. You are not to return, either by day or by night, until Government has told you that it is safe to do so.

10. You are again warned that anyone who shoots at aircraft at any time will be liable to be attacked at once from the air.

11. TAKE CARE. Do not touch any unexploded bombs. They are highly dangerous and may go off if handled. If you find any unexploded bombs you should report the fact.

By Order of Government.

23rd February, 1939.

(3 Muharram, 1358 Hijri.)

A red notice which gave notice that a village was to be bombed if it didn't cease harbouring 'raiding gangs'.

went as far as to predict what the effect on the villagers would be. 'The enemy will as the result of such measures feel insecure at all times: men must hide in caves ... cattle if not driven into caves must be grazed in small bunches at great labour ... tillage of fields must cease ... .' Once a group submitted to the demands, pilots would drop another set of leaflets announcing no further bombing and that it was safe to return to village life.

In the early years of the RAF in India the squadrons flew old, unreliable types. In 1922, out of seventy potentially available aircraft a mere seven were fit for operations. It was as usual all down to funding with the RAF in India coming under the Army budget and the money went to the foot soldiers. F.2Bs, DH.9As and DH.10s had been designed for use in European climates and were now operating in very different, hostile conditions. Maintenance suffered from an almost total lack of spares which led to cannibalisation of two or three aircraft to keep one flying. However, by the end of the decade new aircraft had arrived. Westland Wapitis replaced the DH.9As and Hawker Harts and Audaxes were the new light bombers and multi-purpose aircraft. The tribesmen had no aircraft to counter the British of course, but they did have captured .303 rifles and cartridges. So unless dive-bombing or strafing, the RAF stayed above 3,000 feet, well out of the range of the enemy's rifle fire. If reconnaissance required pilots to fly lower they were advised to make full use of their speed, fly an irregular course and use their weapons to keep down hostile fire. If a pilot was unlucky enough to be forced down over hostile territory he removed the bolt from the Lewis gun if he could and threw it overboard before he crashed. Every effort was to be made to burn the aircraft when he came down by firing a bullet or flare into the petrol tank. If escape was out of the question 'it will be wisest to surrender with good grace and a bold demeanour, preferably to the older and more important looking men among the crowd for the younger element is liable to be hot-headed and unpleasant'. All this sage advice was to be found in *Frontier Warfare—India (Army and Royal Air Force)*. The British offered a reward of 9,000 rupees (about £20) for the return of a downed airman and this usually resulted in fair treatment in captivity. But such hospitality couldn't always be relied upon and the RAF gave safe conduct letters to aircrew. These were nicknamed gooli chits, *gooli* being a Pathan word for ball. Rumour had it that tribesmen often castrated their captives and the chits promised a reward if the bearer were returned unharmed.

By the mid-1930s the RAF's air policing campaign had been success-fully implemented but in November 1936 conflict flared up again when a British court ruled against the marriage of a Muslim girl who had con-verted from Hinduism, a verdict which enraged Muslims who accused the government of interfering in a religious matter. 10,000 tribesmen blocked roads, overran outposts and ambushed convoys. The British retal-iated by sending two columns in to Waziristan's long, peaceful Khaisora Valley and suppressed agitation there by imposing fines and destroying the houses of the ringleaders, including that of the Fakir of Ipi, Mirza Ali Khan, a Sufi mystic who declared a jihad against the British. He led an ambush against the two British columns, trapping them and killing fourteen soldiers. RAF air-drops of ammunition and supplies saved the day and there followed a multi-year campaign by the British to capture Ali Khan. But he was canny. He knew that to confront the British Army directly with their advantage of airpower would be futile so his tribesmen employed the guerrilla tactics they were so adept at. Squadrons of the Royal Air Force and Indian Air Force (which had formed in 1932) tried many ways of combating the guerrillas, including scorched-earth retal-iation – the burning of standing crops with jerry-can petrol bombs, the killing of cattle with strafing attacks, bombing operations to prevent the watering of livestock and stop the ploughing or harvesting of crops – but without much success.

'The fakir shifted from village to village and group to group, each protecting him in turn, and he was never caught,' Hal remembered. 'Red notices were dropped and we commenced bombing but it was very diffi-cult to bomb the fakir's gun factory which was in a series of caves near the Persian border in the sides of a steep sided narrow valley.' By 1939 the fakir was operating from across the border in Afghanistan and with war imminent in Europe the RAF were leaving Waziristan and British colo-nial rule in India began to fade. Thereafter he instigated the occasional raid on a village or an attack on a garrison but otherwise things remained relatively peaceful until the end of British rule in 1947.

*

This then was the India of the North-West Frontier that Hal came to. He had two squadrons in No.1 (Indian) Wing, Nos.27 and 60, both equipped with Wapitis. When he took over, No.60 Squadron had one flight at Miranshah in Madda Khel tribal country. Miranshah was a typical outpost of the British Empire, very Kiplingesque in appearance. Set in a valley deep in tribal territory it was surrounded by the mountains of Waziristan and connected with Bannu, around forty miles away, by a single road along which a twice-weekly convoy protected by armoured cars brought supplies and mail. It was unsafe to walk outside its walls in daytime for fear of sharpshooting tribesmen. Its walls were wide enough to drive a car along and armoured gates allowed the aircraft to be wheeled to and from the aerodrome as required: they were never left outside the protection of the fort. A British political agent was resident at Miranshah who was responsible for dealing with tribal matters. The Tochi Scouts were headquartered in the fort and worked in close co-operation with No.1 Wing. They operated in North Waziristan as part of the Frontier Corps stationed in the tribal territories. The corps was created in 1907 by Lord Curzon, then Viceroy of British India, and was led by a British officer of the rank of lieutenant colonel. Today the Frontier Corps still exists, 80,000 strong under the command of the paramilitary forces of Pakistan.

In April 1939 the Madda Khel tribe came to heel and a peace *jirga* [council] was held by the political agent in Miranshah fort.

> The CO of the Tochi Scouts and I sat with the political agent facing a very fierce looking scowling crowd of chiefs with their black beards, blackened eyes, khaki turbans and dirty robes, bandoliers of cartridges, knives, daggers and guns all squatting on the earth. On the walls above our heads the Tochi Scouts were manning four machine guns ready to open fire if the party got rough.

But all went off peacefully, ruffled feathers were smoothed and peace returned to the area when it was promised that bombing would cease.

Hal tells a story which describes the sort of work a political agent, an officer of the imperial civil administration, a government official acting as an adviser to in this case local tribal leaders, could become involved with.

> We badly needed an airstrip close to Parachinar near the Afghan frontier. The only possible place for it was in a valley but unfortunately the tomb of a *pir* [a local saint] was in the way. To demolish it for the sake of infidel flying machines would have grossly offended local religious sensibilities and might have started another jihad or tribal war. So what could be done? A Pathan political officer had a plan. One evening he came to the tomb dressed as an ordinary tribesman. He stayed all night, saying his prayers and meditating. Next morning he left a generous offering and went away without a word. That night he was back again. This time the caretaker saw him at his prayers and heard him invoking the spirit of the holy *pir* for guidance. In the morning he again left a generous gift and left without a word. On the third night he again came to the tomb. By this time word of his pious behaviour had got around and numbers of the locals came to watch him at his devotions. He displayed great anxiety of spirit and after a good crowd had gathered he rose to leave. The people begged to be told the purpose of his devotions. At first reluctant he was eventually persuaded. He said: 'for many years the *pir* sahib has appeared to me while I slept. The *pir* sahib was troubled and in great pain but I could not tell why. So I came here to pray and seek the reason for the affliction of so holy a man. I know now why he sorrows but alas I cannot do anything to help.' The people eagerly enquired as to what disturbed the *pir*. 'The holy saint's bones do not rest well down here on the stony plain. He would like his mortal remains to lie on a high hill where he could overlook and protect his beloved

people.' 'Why, that's simple,' the people said. 'We will move his bones there.' And they did. After a decent interval we were able to build the airstrip.

Let us look briefly at some of the specifics of the operational activity of No.1 (Indian) Wing during Hal's tenure as commander. Some modern high frequency direction finding (HF/DF) equipment of a semi-portable type on loan from the Air Ministry was installed on the airfield boundary at Kohat shortly after his arrival, but it isn't recorded whether this loan became permanent after a successful trial. Meanwhile a Bombay Coast Defence Exercise in which No.27 Squadron had participated came to an end during which they had flown 100 hours working with the Royal Indian Navy. The squadron was back at Kohat by 18 December with the ground party following three days later but were very soon off again, this time to an Armament Training Camp in Karachi on the 30th. Early in the New Year No.60 Squadron was detached to Calcutta for nine days for an exercise. One of Hal's responsibilities was the air defence of this teeming city but it lay 2,000 miles away! In January 1939 he organised an exercise with the Army to test the defensive arrangements currently in place.

I flew my own Wapiti (K1394) to Calcutta ahead of 27 Squadron with a night stop in Delhi to visit Air HQ. I lived with the Army in Fort William on the Hooghly River and we conducted the exercise from there. Calcutta is the most overcrowded city one can imagine and the smells and sights cannot be described adequately in words. My cousin, Doctor Featherstonehaugh, practised in the city and did well out of the rich Bengalis. He entertained me at the superb Bengal Club. The exercise went as well as could be expected considering the few aircraft we had. I returned by train right across India to Peshawar. Quite a trip.

In February Hal assumed tactical control of air operations in Waziristan carried out from Miranshah where Nos.1 (IAF) and 5 Squadron were detached, a responsibility he had until April before handing over to Squadron Leader

Nichols, OC No.5 Squadron. At the end of the month aircraft from this busy forward operational airfield began an air blockade of the Madda Khel. Army co-operation squadrons provided daily support to convoys and troops which included supply drops to forces cut off by bad weather. Extremely bad flying conditions existed throughout Waziristan at this time with large snow falls, rain and low cloud. The blockade continued until April when the Madda Khel agreed the peace terms at the *jirga* already described.

Chaz Bowyer in his *RAF Operations 1918–1938* includes an evocative description of life at Miranshah.

> At the height of ... operations the constant movement of aircraft coming and going gave the place an atmosphere of near perpetual motion. Overheated engines bellowed in a non-stop chorus, blasting minor whirlwinds of rock dust and grit into the blistering sunlight and pasting a coat of sweat-streaked filth upon the long suffering ground crews toiling to refuel and re-arm each incoming machine. With eyes reduced to mere slits in masks of sand and sunburn the erks [RAF slang for ground crew, said to derive from 'erkraft', the cockney pronunciation of 'aircraft'] remained cheerful and ever ready to offer a word of encouragement to the stiff-legged aircrews as they climbed out of their aircraft for a brief respite between sorties.

After some re-allocation of bases which meant that at Kohat No.60 had left and No.28 had arrived, the RAF squadrons active in the North-West Frontier area by April 1939 were Nos.5, 11 and 39 at Risalpur, No.20 at Peshawar, Nos.27 and 28 at Kohat, No.31 at Lahore and No.60 at Ambala. But this would all be subject to change again within a few months.

On 23 June Hal was temporarily promoted to Acting Group Captain as he took command of No.1 (Indian) Group when Group Captain Glenny was on leave. He held this positon until 15 July when Glenny returned. Hal then set off on an expedition with a party of pilots and aircrew aboard Imperial Airways Short Empire flying boat G-AETX *Ceres* from Karachi to Alexandria to collect and fly Blenheims back to

RAF Ambala where there were already a few examples of the type flying with No.60 Squadron. With refuelling and night stops at Jiwani (Uttar Pradesh), Dibai (Uttar Pradesh), Bahrain, Basra, Lake Habbaniyah, the Sea of Galilee and on to Alexandria harbour, this was an ideal way to travel – that is short flights with trips ashore at each refuelling stop and a comfortable night's accommodation. 'One could walk about the flying boat and enjoy a cocktail looking at the scenery through the large port scuttles,' reported Hal. The flight back to Ambala in Blenheim I L4910 wasn't quite so luxurious. It took seven days with Sergeant Churchill as navigator, Sergeant Banks as fitter and LAC Eke as W/T operator and included refuelling and night stops at Habbaniya, Shaibah, Bahrain, Sharjah, Jiwani, Karachi and Jodhpur.

In October Group Captain Glenny delegated the day to day control of the Ahmadzai and Chamkanni proscriptions to Hal. Raiding gangs were making use of villages as bases throughout these territories and red notices were dropped warning that if they continued to harbour these 'bad characters' they would be bombed, and they were, with their agricultural activities being interrupted as a consequence. The gangs' target was likely to be the city of Bannu which was in continual danger of looting forays. No.28 Squadron performed the proscription during the day and Valentias of No.31 Squadron from Lahore at night, proscription which carried on until December. In Chamkanni, meanwhile, Afghan rebel leaders had taken refuge. At the end of the month Red Notices were again dropped and bombing soon followed. After eight days the Afghan leaders had been given up to the political agent and the bombing ceased.

Hal did quite a lot of flying as commander of No.1 (Indian) Wing – 159 hours in total visiting stations and landing grounds throughout his area of responsibility and occasionally further afield. Most of this was done on the Westland Wapitis of the two squadrons in the wing (this two-seat general-purpose single-engined biplane proved to be a good workhorse in the harsh conditions in which they operated), but there were other visiting types too, such as the occasional Hawker Audax, prototype Lysander K6128 on one occasion, a single flight as passenger in an Airspeed Envoy in which the AOC-in-C visited Kohat and a week of

Valentia flying just before he returned to the UK. On 2 January 1939 he led nine No.60 Squadron Wapitis over the local Proclamation Day parade at Kohat.

Hal's time on the sub-continent was brought prematurely to a halt by the situation in Europe. War there was declared in September 1939 and in India families returned from the hills. Things became quieter on the frontier and the RAF was leaving. Chaz Bowyer again:

> As the longstanding British presence began to be evacuated the tribesmen in the northern provinces were frankly bewildered, unable to fully understand why their traditional fighting opponent, the British Army, was now relinquishing territory it had occupied, bloodily defended, and had never been decisively defeated in for more than a hundred years. For the men of the RAF who had served in the Frontier ... it had been an unforgettable part of their lives. A period of real hardships, deprivation, separation from kith and kin for a majority, yet also years of true comradeship and united purpose which would never be surpassed.

Hal flew back to England and was thus forced to leave Nora, Nannie and the boys to return home by sea. They sailed from Bombay in February, docked at Marseille and crossed France by train. Hal took off from Karachi in a Handley Page Hannibal of Imperial Airways, a very old and slow four-engined biplane which took four days to reach Egypt with night stops. At Alexandria he transferred to a Lockheed Electra. They refuelled at Sollum in Libya, then Malta, Tunis, Marseille and Toulouse before fog forced them down at Bordeaux. Fog across the Channel in England kept them at Bordeaux for a couple of days until they finally landed at Heston airport on 8 January 1940. Hal reported to the Air Ministry the following day where he found that he had been promoted to Group Captain on New Year's Day and was posted to the Directorate of War Training and Tactics at the Air Ministry, a position he took up on 20 January, becoming Deputy Director in July.

Another chapter in his RAF career was about to open up.

Chapter Sixteen

Directorate of War Training and Tactics

T he United Kingdom had been at war with Germany for four months when Hal arrived home from India in January 1940. All service and police men and women may have been wearing uniform and carrying gas respirators and steel helmets but there was no sign of active operations, for this was the Phoney War. There were no attacks by the German Luftwaffe on the UK during this period and the RAF were dropping propaganda leaflets on Germany. The static balloon barrage over London and other cities designed to deter low-flying attacks if they came was much in evidence. Blackout screens had been fitted to windows together with strips of stout paper to reduce damage from glass broken by bombing. Air raid shelters, either in gardens or indoors, had been prepared by householders and there were also large public shelters. Meat and butter and petrol for private cars were only obtainable through ration books. London Underground fitted watertight doors to tunnels where the lines ran under the Thames to prevent flooding caused by bombs penetrating the river bed: without this precaution passengers on the stations could have been drowned.

Hal found that the Operational Training and Tactics Directorate – soon to be renamed the Directorate of War Training and Tactics – had been evacuated from Whitehall to an empty school near Harrow as part of the general dispersal scheme, but it was soon moved back into London. Having just been promoted to group captain Hal proudly wore four stripes on his sleeves and gold oak leaves on the peak of his cap. In deference to his new status he was billeted in a luxurious house at Stanmore belonging to Frederick Handley Page, the aircraft designer, but when Nora and the boys returned from India they moved to a rented house at Hatch End. 'Air Ministry Movements Branch kept me informed about the progress of the return of Nora and the family from Bombay to London via France,' recalled Hal.

I met them at Waterloo station in the blackout. There were no porters so I took an empty push truck which took all their luggage and managed to get it on a taxi. We stayed at a small hotel that night but the staff had gone home and all we could get was soup and cake and that grudgingly.

Once settled into Hatch End, Hal got home from the Air Ministry as often as he could but there were many occasions when he had to sleep in the office and he always kept a small case there with shaving and washing gear for that eventuality.

The department in which Hal worked was less than two years old, having been formed in March 1938 as a sub-section of the Directorate of Staff Duties, and was initially called the Air Tactics section, endorsed by Dowding himself who wrote to the Under Secretary of State in November of that year saying 'the formation of the Air Tactics section has been noted with interest. Every endeavour will be made to pass information of tactical value as speedily as possible to the Air Ministry for use by the Air Tactics section'. The premise behind the latter was spelled out in a paper of July 1938. Before its formation the Director of the Directorate of Staff Duties, aided by a wing commander and two squadron leaders, was charged with the service training of bomber and fighter squadrons, the organisation and supervision of tactical trials, air exercises and equipment and training in regard to night flying. In addition he had to deal with a mass of day to day work caused by such matters as crew policy, publicity, displays and reviews. He was also responsible, with a retired officer to assist him, for the work of the Air Fighting and Bombing Committees and for initiating and following up the action arising out of the recommendations of those committees. In addition he was responsible for the study of tactics, the constant review of tactical policy, the co-ordination of tactical development arising out of proposals made by the Commands and by the Committees, and the detailed study from the tactical point of view of the results of trials, exercises and experiments. The pressure on the Director was such that these subjects had to be necessarily shelved and, moreover, he could not devote the necessary attention to the Committee work.

Air Tactics was formed with the idea of relieving the Director of all this, at the same time providing a centre of information on tactical matters and disseminating that information to other departments. The staff of Air Tactics, as for the Directorate of Staff Duties before it, was also small, although it would expand as the war progressed, and the workload continued to be heavy. The wing commander in charge was given the brief of the development of tactical policy, the provision of advice on tactical matters to Commands, liaison with 'Plans (Ops)' as to the tactical aspect of plans under consideration and the study of plans with a view to providing Commands with tactical information in the light of projected operations – as well as preparing papers on tactical matters for the Admiralty, War Office and Air Ministry and revising the Manual of Air Tactics. Under him he had four squadron leaders responsible for matters of Air Tactics (Armaments), Air Tactics (Bombing), Air Tactics (Fighting) and Air Tactics (Intelligence). A retired officer looked after the organisation of the department. The Directorate's brief was wide ranging and in early 1940 and as Deputy Director Hal attended conferences at the Air Ministry and Command headquarters both in the UK and France.

One of the operational exercises I attended in France ended shortly before the Germans invaded the Low Countries. Flying from Hendon to Amiens (via le Bourget and St Quentin) one got a good view of the camouflage painting on the track at Brooklands and the floating obstructions in the Staines reservoirs to prevent seaplanes landing invading troops. The exercise was at Chauny to the south-east of Amiens and during it I visited General Gort's headquarters in the crypt of Arras cathedral. It was evident from this visit that if the Germans did not respect Belgian neutrality there would be little hope of stopping them overrunning northern France. I watched the rapidly changing situation in France on the large wall maps in the War Room and a pretty grim situation was unfolding. One of the last desperate measures to try to keep the British Army supplied was to use airliners. What a hope.

After the Dunkirk evacuation the daily conferences at the Air Ministry dealing with measures for the defence of England revealed how weak and unprepared the country really was. 'For example, there was only enough .303 ammunition for two minutes continuous firing. This was around the time when the Home Guard was forming and it was not unusual to see thirty men in mufti with arm bands drilling with only one rifle between them'.

Hal's memoir reflects life as lived by the British people after Dunkirk.

Churchill was broadcasting at this time speeches which gripped the nation and encouraged everyone to do their utmost to repel the invader if he came. We must fight on the beaches, in the fields, in the streets and so on. But the invader didn't come and the real reason he didn't was that the Germans had not at that stage prepared for it. After a while however air photographs showed concentrations of barges and other craft in French and Belgian ports. If the enemy had invaded then there would have been very heavy casualties and so the scheme to evacuate city children not only to the British countryside but by sea to the USA and Canada too was developed. We seriously considered sending our three boys but eventually decided not to split the family but to all stay together come what may.

But still there were no bomb attacks. When would they start? On a clear moonlit night at Hatch End we had gone to bed and opened our window. After midnight I woke up to hear the deep throbbing note of German aero engines, but could this be right because there had been no red warning? The aircraft went away and then the sirens' warbling note rent the night. Now, was this a warning of a big attack? Or a late alert for a single raider? Should we wake Nannie and the boys and bring them down to our make-shift shelter under the stairs? Then the All Clear went. After that, daylight raids started. At first when the sirens went banks and shops closed and sent their staffs to shelters but soon people got used to danger and carried on as usual. Then the Germans began night raids in earnest and thousands of Londoners took bedding to the tube stations each evening and spent the night trying to sleep on station platforms, stairs and passages, to emerge after dawn to see perhaps their houses and streets piles of rubble and often on fire.

That almost included the family home at Hatch End.

I was coming home one evening and had gone as usual by tube from the Air Ministry to Euston, stepping over bodies in the tube stations and then boarding my overcrowded overground train. It was packed solid and I was wedged in the corridor, steel helmet on my head (as per regulations) and so jammed I could not raise an arm. At Willesden the train stopped. There was a red alert. Then an attack. Incendiary bombs fell on the track at right angles to the train. We were not hit but wooden coaches on each side of us caught fire and burnt like torches. The run to Hatch End that night took over two hours instead of the normal forty-minute journey. As I walked home along a short cut, reflecting on the fact that no-one on the train had panicked, I fell into a bomb crater made that day. Nora had been shopping in Hatch End that morning leaving Nannie and the boys at the house. While at the shops a single bomber dropped a salvo of sixteen bombs in a line between Nora and the house but not hitting it.

Our boys didn't mind the air raids. I remember one evening when they had gone to bed a red alert was given and we brought them down to the shelter in the hall. They had their toys and books with mattresses to lie upon and when the All Clear went and they repaired to bed, John came and thanked us for a lovely evening! On another occasion incendiary bombs dropped beside the house. The clatter of the containers for these small bombs sounded like a load of pea sticks as they fell into the garden which was brilliantly lit by the salvo. Again the house was undamaged.

And shortly after this Nannie and her boyfriend were returning to the house after dark when a land mine came down beside the road and remained hanging from its parachute which had caught in a tree. They didn't wait around! It was defused by the Army next day.

Those who lived through it always remembered the 1940 summer as one of lovely weather. Nora and the boys used to lie in the sunshine, as did many others, watching the formations of Spitfires and Hurricanes climbing to intercept the enemy and returning later, often much reduced in numbers. While they were doing that Hal was immersing himself in the work of Air Tactics. To give some idea of what he involved himself with, as well as visiting Fighter, Bomber, Coastal and Training Commands to discuss tactics and training, Hal would, for example, go to Duxford to fly the RAF's latest fighters including the Defiant, Hurricane and Spitfire. Then the British Medical Association became interested in aircrew reactions in war and he had working lunches with the secretary to discuss the matter. Later in 1940 when the Germans intensified their night-bombing attacks Hal told his staff to mark with pins on a large map the places where bombs were dropped each night. From this it became clear that attacks were being made on *straight lines* across the North Sea. In other words radio beams were being used to guide the pilots straight to their targets. Later they found that this was indeed so and the beams were called *Knickebein*.

Hal also attended trials of various new weapons, among them the Torraplane. The standard tactics for aircraft attacking ships with torpedoes was to approach at wavetop height before dropping them and then manoeuvre out of range of the ship's guns as quickly as possible. A low approach was necessary, otherwise, if the torpedo was dropped from a greater height or when the aeroplane was diving, it was liable to 'porpoise' or even break up. So scientists developed the Torraplane. A standard naval torpedo was fitted with wings so that when released it would glide down towards the sea. When it reached a set height above the water a trailing antenna hit the sea, triggering off a device which shed the wings, thus dropping the torpedo into the water. Trials with dummy torpedoes were carried out in the Clyde with an old steamer as target. In the first attack on the ship the aircraft approached at about 2,000 feet and when at the correct distance away it released the Torraplane which glided down dead on course to intercept the vessel, shed the wings and dropped. 'It ran and we could see its wake as it passed astern of us,' reported Hal.

> The second attack was not so good, the torpedo going right off course. Then as we watched the third attack approaching we realised that something must have gone wrong with the bomb sight because the aircraft was getting too close to the ship to release the Torraplane. We thought the attack would be abandoned but no, the pilot flew on towards us and the weapon was released. It came down at us in a fast glide. There was nothing the ship's captain could do to avoid a possible accident. By great good luck it just skimmed over the funnels and carried away a tangle of wireless aerials before plunging into the sea close to the ship. A few feet lower and it would have crashed into the funnels and casualties among the spectators standing nearby could hardly have been avoided.

The project was subsequently abandoned.

Chapter Seventeen

Director of Allied Air Co-operation and Foreign Liaison

Following promotion to Air Commodore on 1 June 1941 Hal was posted to the Directorate of Intelligence as head of the department known as Allied Air Co-operation and Foreign Liaison, often referred to as DAFL. By this time the RAF had formed squadrons manned by Poles, Czechs, Free French, Norwegians, Dutch and Belgians who had escaped to England in the face of the Nazi onslaught in Europe. Within the Directorate there was a section responsible for each nationality, each with liaison officers who could speak the relevant language and who were kept busy dealing with the multifarious requests and problems arising, work which necessitated extreme tact and patience. As Director, Hal had an endless series of interviews and meetings with very senior figures of each nationality: on a lighter side he shared meals organised by them, primarily at the Dorchester and Claridges, designed to persuade him to take kindly to their wants and demands. Hal had a special entertainment allowance to enable him to return their hospitality, usually at one of his favourite restaurants, 'L'Ecu de France'.

The chain of command was, as far as Hal was concerned, a simple one. He was directly responsible to the Assistant Chief of the Air Staff (Intelligence) Air Vice Marshal Charles Medhurst, who himself was responsible to the CAS, Sir Charles Portal. Medhurst also had the two Directors of intelligence (Operations and Security), four Deputy Directors of Intelligence and Assistant Directors of Intelligence (Photography and Science) reporting to him. Hal had succeeded Air Commodore A.R. Boyle at DAFL and, at the risk of straying too far from our story of Hal's career, it must be recorded that Air Commodore Boyle was one more of many interesting individuals with stories to tell that Hal encountered during his career. It is not recorded how well he knew Boyle personally but he would undoubtedly have heard of the incident after the French surrender in June 1940 when Boyle was threatened with a gun by one of the great eccentrics of the time, Lieutenant Colonel A.D. Wintle MC. After the surrender Wintle demanded an aircraft to fly to France to persuade the French Air Force to fly their planes to Britain to continue the fight from British air bases. When his request was refused he pointed a gun at Air Commodore Boyle and threatened to shoot him. As a result Wintle was imprisoned in the Tower of London. A soldier detailed to escort him there lost the arrest warrant and Wintle obtained a new one and signed it himself. After a few days of settling into his pre-trial confinement he wrote, 'I was surprised to find that as a way of life, being a prisoner in the Tower of London had its points.' Wintle was charged with assaulting Air Commodore Boyle and with conduct contrary to good order and military discipline. It was alleged that when he had drawn a gun on Boyle he said 'people like you ought to be shot'. Wintle admitted saying this and produced a list of people he thought should also be shot in the interests of patriotism. As a result of the court case he received a formal reprimand for his actions.

Hal's secretary at the Directorate was another interesting individual but of a very different mould, Pearl Witherington, who had been on the staff of the British Embassy in Paris before the war and whose story is one of great courage as Hal later found out. Born and raised in France she was nevertheless a British subject. She escaped from occupied France with her mother and three sisters in December 1940 and eventually arrived in London where she found work with Hal at the Air Ministry. She was determined to fight back against the German occupation of France in the most practical way she could and in June 1943 she joined the Special Operations Executive (SOE), began a period of intense training and was given the code name Marie. She parachuted into occupied France three months later where she joined the leader of the 'Stationer' network, Maurice Southgate, and acted as his courier. Networks, of which there were many, had the job of gathering information about the enemy to relay to SOE headquarters in London. When

Southgate was arrested by the Gestapo in May 1944 she became the leader of the 'Wrestler' network and was given a new code name, Pauline. The network was so effective in the run up to and during D Day that the Germans put a bounty on her head. They eventually succeeded in breaking up her group but she reorganised and launched very successful and disruptive guerrilla attacks on German columns travelling to the battlefront, killing many and going on to sabotage the enemy's supply lines. After the war Pearl Witherington married and returned to Paris to live. She was awarded a military, as opposed to a civil, MBE [instead of gallantry awards all SOE personnel were given service awards], the CBE and the *Légion d'honneur*. Long after Hal's death, and after a sixty-year wait, she was finally awarded her parachute wings. She died aged 93 in France. Hal remembered her as an ideal secretary who, with his stenographer and small army of clerks in the Directorate, 'did a splendid service in a difficult job'.

*

It wasn't only with exiled personnel of European countries that Hal had to deal, but air attachés of Allied countries across the world – Russia, Greece, the USA, Sweden and Japan (before Pearl Harbor) for example. This also brought its own problems but of all these other countries, the Russians, who for reasons of security always met Hal in parties of three, were the most difficult.

One day my Chief – the Director of Intelligence – rang me on my green phone on which conversation was scrambled to prevent eavesdropping, telling me to fly to Scotland immediately to meet a Russian General Golikov and bring him to London. A special aircraft would be provided and in case weather was bad a special train would be at my disposal as well. I was to ensure there was no slip up because on his previous visit things went wrong and he had to travel by slow train all the way from Invergordon to London and was in a furious temper on arrival.

Filipp Ivanovich Golikov was a Soviet military commander who is best known for not passing on to Stalin intelligence about German invasion plans in June 1941, either because he did not believe them or because Stalin made it very clear he did not want to hear them. He was in charge of the Soviet Main Intelligence Directorate (GRU) (1940–41), personally leading Soviet military missions in the United Kingdom and United States.

> Pearl phoned Nora while I flew in a [de Havilland] Flamingo of the King's Flight to Scotland. We landed at RAF Evanton on the Cromarty Firth and waited for news. Later I got a signal saying that owing to weather the Catalina flying boat carrying the General could not leave Archangel but should get away the next day. I released the Flamingo crew and went to the station to inspect the special train should we need it and with the District Manager and the guard tested the vodka in the dining car as well! When the Catalina finally arrived and had been secured to her moorings I received the General. He was a small, tubby, chain smoking little man, completely hairless with a bright red face. The weather was kind so we flew him to Hendon in the Flamingo where he joined the Soviet Ambassador. All had gone without a hitch.

In May 1942 the Soviet Foreign Minister Vyacheslav Molotov flew secretly to Tealing near Dundee in a converted Tupolev TB-7 bomber where he was met by Anthony Eden from the Foreign Office. From there they took a train to London to discuss with the British government the possibility of opening a second front against Germany. Prior to this visit, at the end of April a small Russian delegation had arrived at Tealing in a TB-7 on a test run and to discuss details of Molotov's proposed visit. Hal arranged for a Flamingo of the King's Flight to fly up to Scotland to collect the delegation.

> On the way back to London disaster overtook them. I had just arrived home from the Air Ministry when the Duty Officer rang

to tell me the Flamingo had crashed near York. I dashed back to Whitehall and learnt that all had been killed in the crash which was near Linton on Ouse. My first action was to tell the Soviet Embassy. I and a Staff Officer took the duty car and had to pick up one of my Russian interpreters from his Kensington flat. Not easy in the blackout but we made it. We three then drove to the Soviet Embassy where we found a riotous party going on with wives and children of the staff singing and dancing all over the place. I said I had serious news and at once Admiral Kharlamov whom I knew collected the attachés and we went to the conference room. I gave the news which shook them very considerably and offered immediate road transport to York which they accepted. It was soon clear they thought we had arranged the crash and so I was careful to point out that ten had been killed in all and why should we sacrifice six of our people for the sake of liquidating four of theirs? When they had left for Yorkshire I phoned the CO at Linton and got him to arrange something red to cover the Russian corpses. The red curtains in the sick bay were just the thing.

The whole affair then got to Prime Ministerial level and relations got steadily more difficult until a cylinder from one of the engines of the Flamingo was found in a hen coop near the crash site. This proved that the accident was due to the detached engine part with the resulting fire and vibration causing one main-plane to break up. The Russians were convinced at last.

The bodies were brought back to London and lay in state at the Soviet Embassy. The coffins were lined up in the hall covered in red flags with large red ensigns with inscriptions hung above them. Photographs of each man were fixed at the ends of the coffins and the whole scene filmed for Stalin to see later. Hal and other RAF officers spent time standing with swords drawn guarding the dead. The Russians demanded three bands at the funeral and a complete stop on all press reporting. They got them. A string orchestra played during the lying in state and a brass band played outside the Embassy as the coffins were brought out to the carriages. Another band played at Golders Green crematorium.

The subsequent accident report described the sequence of events. The Flamingo had refuelled at East Fortune on the way south from Tealing and it was during the final leg from East Fortune to Hendon that the accident occurred. The aircraft had taken off at 1625 in good weather with very little cloud. While over North Yorkshire flying at around 2,000 feet the starboard engine failed and then caught fire. Before any landing could be made the fire burnt through the starboard wing and caused the engine to break away, striking the tail of the aircraft in the process. Wreckage was scattered over an area of around three miles. It is probable that the pilot was attempting to get to RAF Linton on Ouse. A highly detailed examination of the wreckage was carried out with members of the Russian military present: they were also present at a Court of Enquiry and reported back to the Russian Government. No evidence of sabotage was found.

Hal's next contact with the Russians was when they sent Captain Feodrovi, 'a charming and skilled test pilot', across to England to fly the RAF's latest aircraft types. It was hoped that by allowing him to do this a test pilot the RAF had sent to Moscow would receive reciprocal treatment. But in spite of prolonged negotiations he was never given the chance of even seeing the latest Soviet aircraft, let alone flying one.

*

Hal didn't spend all his time on Russian matters of course. There were many other duties such as accompanying the King of Greece for a night at a bomber station. The King of Norway and King Peter of Yugoslavia also had to be taken on visits to operational units and there were important national ceremonial and commemorative occasions for which he had to attend services at St Paul's and Westminster Cathedral. But beyond this, and by far the greater part of his time was taken up with it, there was the day to day administration of his department to oversee, reports on the RAF squadrons manned by airmen from German-occupied Europe and the visiting of such squadrons. Quarterly reports on Allied air forces were drawn up and distributed to the AOCs of all UK-based RAF Commands and a few abroad. That prepared during the last few months of Hal's tenure at the Directorate made much of the fact that morale amongst the Allied air forces was generally high. Interestingly the report opens with a comprehensive description of the Combined Operation against Dieppe on 19 August 1942 in which eleven Allied fighter squadrons took part with five drawn from the Northolt Polish Wing, two Czech squadrons flying from Redhill, two Norwegian squadrons operating with the North Weald Wing, a French squadron flying with the Hornchurch Wing and a Belgian with the Kenley Wing. The report then moves on to discuss in some detail the status and recent operations of the various Allied air forces – the French fighter and coastal patrol squadrons, the Polish Bomber, Fighter and Coastal Command squadrons, the Royal Dutch Naval Air Service and Royal Dutch Army Aviation, Czech Fighter and Coastal Command squadrons, the two Norwegian Fighter and one Coastal Command squadrons, the one Belgian fighter squadron, and the one Greek fighter squadron and one general reconnaissance squadron flying with Middle East Command. There was a problem with the Yugoslavs though. 'No Yugoslav personnel have been used on active service since the dispute over the Yugoslav High Command.'

The above serves to demonstrate the complexity of work at the Directorate and the amount of information that was processed month by month. But it was information kept very close to the Air Ministry's chest for there was a specific instruction that under no circumstances were documents the Directorate produced to be copied. Furthermore the quarterly reports 'may not be shown to any member of an Allied Air Force.'

Chapter Eighteen

To India Again

In July 1942 the government of India asked for RAF officers with knowledge of the country to be sent out to them and Hal was amongst those posted to the Air Staff in Delhi. He was appointed Deputy Air Officer Administration (DAOA) HQ Air Forces in India from 27 August 1942. It was an interesting appointment which professionally Hal anticipated keenly but it was far from easy leaving Nora and the boys at Hatch End as in wartime there was no billet for families abroad of course. Hal and Nora's farewell at Euston station viewed sixty years later could be interpreted as being melodramatic – 'we said farewell exactly as in Noel Coward's play *Cavalcade*: each turned away and did not look back and then I went to board my sleeping car on the night express for Glasgow. It could have been the last time we would ever see each other' – but it was far from melodrama. It was as emotional as would be expected. They were to be apart for a long time. Hal survived the war and just over three years later the family was re-united, as they had parted, on a railway station, this time at Malton in Yorkshire.

Hal was instructed to join the SS *Carthage*, part of convoy WS22 assembling off Greenock, having sailed from Liverpool the day before. It was bound for West Africa. Carrying in excess of 42,000 troops and an unknown tonnage of stores, the convoy was an impressive sight, a fleet of grey-painted liners belonging to P&O, Orient, Blue Star and Shaw Savile amongst others at anchor inside the anti-submarine boom, with the commodore flying his pennant in the SS *California*. The *Carthage* was an armed merchant cruiser converted from a P&O liner in 1939, armed with eight 6-inch and two 3-inch guns and batteries of modern anti-air-craft guns manned by the Maritime Royal Artillery. She, together with the light cruiser *Aurora* and the destroyers *Partridge* and *Quiberon* with an additional local Freetown escort from 6 September of the destroyers

Antelope and *Pindos* until the convoy arrived at that port on the 9th, were charged with its protection. Hal was given VIP treatment, being allocated the captain's suite when at sea and his night cabin abaft the bridge when in port. Hal's privileged position meant that he ate well too – 'it was wonderful to have lots of meat and butter on board after the rationing ashore' – and had the run of the ship, including the operations room and bridge. The captain had been brought out of retirement and, having lived between the wars in West Africa was full of stories about black mamba snakes, huge spiders and witchcraft. 'He explained that the ship would be the rearguard to the convoy for whose safety we must be prepared to sacrifice ourselves,' recorded Hal. 'Nothing was to be thrown overboard as it would help submarines in their searches. No lights or smoking on deck after dark were allowed.' And then, rather less eloquently, 'sentries had orders to bash in the face of anyone seen smoking, irrespective of rank.'

Hal was understandably fascinated with the ship and the convoy which sailed on 29 August, passing through the boom defences of Greenock at dusk.

> We passed into the Atlantic through 'bomb alley' north of Ireland where very many ships were sunk and with more sea room all ships took station as detailed in our sealed orders which also laid down the zigzag routine to be followed – zigzag courses and times of change were calculated so as to confuse the U boats but which of course really prolonged the voyage. In our case our speed worked out at about 3 knots as the convoy had to cruise at the speed of the slowest ship to avoid stragglers. We wore life jackets day and night, sleeping in our clothes. All lifeboats were kept slung out ready for lowering. At dawn the first morning at sea *Aurora* fired at an unidentified four-engined aircraft thought to be a Focke Wulf but it disappeared in cloud. If it was a German we wondered how soon its report would produce a pack of U boats.
>
> As we got further out in the Atlantic we ran into a full gale but we were lucky because the wind and seas were astern of us and

increased our ground speed. The waves became tremendous, the captain estimating they were about 40 feet in height. It was a thrilling sight to see the huge grey liners pitching deep in the surging seas with clouds of spray over their sterns while their decks were crowded with troops. Our destroyer escort got a severe dusting. But we were slowly getting further south and the sea temperature was becoming warmer, an important point if we were sunk.

I was in the operations room when an emergency signal from the Admiralty came in. Decoded, it told us a concentration of U boats was in our area. In case of attack from astern the Commodore concentrated destroyers to the rear of the convoy. Two destroyers obviously got 'pings' on their asdic because they dropped a pattern of depth charges not far from us. There had been a sinking in our area, for next day we picked up survivors from two lifeboats.

The convoy anchored in the huge natural harbour of Freetown, Sierra Leone, and Hal went ashore to look around before transferring to the Blue Star Line's SS *Highland Princess* for the short run with the SS *Highland Brigade* to Lagos on 15 September, escorted by HMS *Boreas* (on which Hal had sailed home from Malta seven years earlier), the rest of the convoy sailing on to Capetown. It was crowded on board *Highland Princess* and Hal shared a cabin with four other air commodores, all old friends who were going to appointments in the Middle East and India. The ship called at Takoradi in Ghana to land troops and he took the opportunity to inspect the base there from where aircraft were flown across Africa to Khartoum and Cairo to reinforce squadrons operating in the Middle and Far East. The whole story of air ferry routes across Africa is worthy of a book in itself but suffice it to say here that these routes developed over a number of years before the war to meet the requirements of civil operators. A Trans-Africa route had been pioneered by the British along which Imperial Airways maintained a regular transport service between Lagos and Khartoum. Coastal bases had been constructed at Bathurst in Gambia, Freetown in Sierra Leone and at Takoradi and Accra on the Gold Coast. Across central Africa airfields had been built in jungle and desert at Kano and Maiduguri in Nigeria, Fort Lamy in French Equatorial Africa and El Geneina, El Fasher and El Obeid in Sudan. After war was declared and by the spring of 1941, British communication with Egypt by sea and air via the Mediterranean was virtually closed thanks to the German incursion into southern Europe and north Africa, but the existence of the Trans-Africa air route enabled the British to avoid shipping aircraft by sea around the Cape of Good Hope to Egypt as an alternative. Instead they could be flown across the waist of Africa. Takoradi was developed to accept crated fighters and bombers from Britain by ship: here they were re-assembled, tested and flown to Cairo. Transport aircraft were also based at Takoradi to collect ferry pilots after they had delivered their aircraft and bring them back.

In a similar way a South Atlantic air ferry route had been established between the USA and west Africa in July 1941 and was used by Pan American Airways and its subsidiaries, but after Pearl Harbor the US Army Air Corps Ferrying Command used the route to deliver Lend-Lease aircraft to British forces in the Western Desert, Lagos being one of the hubs from which aircraft as well as personnel and cargo were flown via Khartoum to Cairo and beyond.

On 22 September, just over three weeks since leaving Greenock, Hal took off as a passenger from Lagos in a Lockheed Hudson with six others on board, bound for Khartoum which they reached thirteen flying hours later via Maiduguri and El Geneina, flying over rain forest then savannah country, bare land with scattered trees and termite mounds. Ever curious, a day in Khartoum gave Hal a chance to see Omdurman where General Gordon had been murdered. The next stage of the journey on the following day was to Cairo, via Wadi Halfa, landing at Heliopolis. In Cairo Hal dined with Air Marshal Tedder who by that stage of the war was Air Officer Commanding in Chief, RAF Middle East Command. Hal had known Tedder since his days at the Staff College course in 1928 where he was an instructor. Tedder arranged for Hal to be flown up to visit the squadrons at the Burg-el-Arab landing ground near Alexandria where he was re-united briefly with several of the pilots who had served under him at Kohat.

Knowing Tedder as he did and having caught up with him in Cairo, Hal watched the former's career with interest throughout the rest of the war. After RAF Middle East Command he was appointed AOC-in-C Mediterranean Allied Air Forces and was closely involved in the planning of the Allied invasion of Sicily and Italy. When Operation OVERLORD was being planned he became Deputy Supreme Commander at Supreme Headquarters Allied Expeditionary Force under General Eisenhower under whom he had previously served in the Mediterranean. After the war he became Chief of the Air Staff.

For his part, having met Hal again, Tedder wanted to keep him with him in the Middle East but Delhi couldn't spare him and Hal continued on his journey. His log book reveals a detailed onward itinerary.

September 28

Empire Flying Boat	Pilot Captain James	30 pax	River Nile Cairo to Dead Sea	2h 10m
			Dead Sea to Habbaniyah	3h 20m
			Habbaniyah to Basra	2h 20m

September 29

Empire Flying Boat	Pilot Captain James	30 pax	Basra to Bahrain	3h 5m
			Bahrain to Dibai	2h 0m
			Dibai to Jiwani	3h 0m
			Jiwani to Karachi	2h 10m

September 29

Lockheed Hudson VI	Pilot ? Wood	2 pax	Karachi to Delhi	4h 0m

•

Air Headquarters India was in the South Block of the Secretariat in New Delhi with some of its departments in hutments in the grounds. In pre-war peacetime, the Viceroy of India and his Vicereine with their staff and government officials with their staffs all moved by train for the hot summer months to the hill station at Simla. But in wartime this move didn't happen, which meant that all government had to work through the stifling heat of the summer and that included HQ Air Forces. From his office windows in South Block Hal enjoyed a fine view towards the Viceroy's Palace and over the imposing circular Council Chamber with Old Delhi and the Jama Masjid mosque in the distance. Officers of Air HQ staff were luxuriously accommodated in a palace lent by the Maharajah of Bhavnagar.

Each bedroom had its own bathroom and opened out on to a walled garden used for sleeping outdoors in hot weather. The extensive garden round the palace was well maintained and was full of colourful birds and a family or two of mongoose which kept the snakes down. The road outside led to Old Delhi and trains of bullock carts, usually with the drivers asleep, creaked along day and night. At night jackals charged about only stopping to forage in the garbage. Official cars were strictly limited so we all bought bicycles to reach our offices and the shops in Connaught Place [the Lutyens' designed headquarters of the British Raj]. We kept in flying practice at Delhi Airport on aircraft of the HQ Communications Flight and on days off visited the many interesting old buildings, such as the Red Fort.

Unfortunately Hal contracted malaria twice whilst he was in Delhi and had ten days in Simla on each occasion to convalesce. The Flight Lieutenant Medical Officer at Air HQ was a Harley Street doctor and he took the greatest interest in Hal's case.

Hal was made an acting air vice marshal from 16 November 1943 for the period that he was holding his Air Staff appointment in Delhi to reflect the nature of the post. (He reverted to air commodore on 8 April 1944, some six months prior to the final posting of his RAF career.) Part of Hal's Delhi brief was to attend the Commander-in-Chief India's daily conference with officials from each branch of the Civil and Service administration and Hal very soon realised that no subject was too small or too large to merit Field Marshal Sir Archibald Wavell's consideration.

*

As well as RAF units based in India, Air HQ had those of the Indian Air Force (IAF) to deal with. In his memoir Hal comments briefly on one of the problems encountered at its formation.

When the IAF first formed men who volunteered were from different religions with all the attendant special requirements that that implied. These would have been impossible to cater for in small units like squadrons so, for example, it was stipulated that by joining up they must all agree to consume the same food which, uniquely, was agreed. Of the Army, Navy and Air Force, the IAF was the only service to achieve this.

It is worth pausing here to consider the founding of the Indian Air Force. Flying had begun in India in 1910 and during the First World War several Indians joined the RFC. From 1919 until 1933 the defence of India was entrusted, as we have seen, to a few squadrons of the RAF on the North-West Frontier. Then on 1 April 1927 the Committee of the Chief of the General Staff in India, General Sir Andrew Skeen, sitting in Simla and formed of well-known Indian public affairs figures including Nehru and Jinnah, recommended that an indigenous Indian Air Force be formed and in the early stages at least its pilots be trained at RAF Cranwell. This was at a time when the Commonwealth and Empire overall could boast so little in terms of airpower, many Commonwealth countries only having token air forces.

It took five years for the IAF to be authorised under an Act of the Legislative Assembly. Meanwhile the first six Indian cadets had left for Cranwell in 1930 and began their training. Whilst they were doing so there were flurries of signals between the Indian government and the Air Ministry in London with one faction in India urging the inclusion of the new air arm within the organisation of the Indian Army. But this was successfully opposed and the Indian Air Force Act was duly passed. The beginnings were modest with just one flight of three aircraft at Karachi commanded by Squadron Leader (later Air Vice Marshal) Cecil Bouchier, the flight being trained as an army co-operation unit. From 1933 until 1937 A Flight concentrated their efforts on training until it was eventually sent with its, by now, four Wapitis to the North-West Frontier to take its share of responsibility for this fractious region. A second flight, B Flight, was formed and sent to the Frontier too and by the end of the year C Flight came into being, all three flights forming No.1 Squadron, all pilots Cranwell trained. Apart from flying on the Frontier, detachments were also sent to southern India to co-operate with newly constituted artillery batteries. But when war was declared in 1939 the RAF was withdrawn almost entirely from the North-West Frontier and the policing of it was handed over in its entirety to the IAF. At the same time the IAF Volunteer Reserve, which stood up around a nucleus of a small number of regular RAF and IAF personnel, formed five coastal defence flights (CDFs) at India's largest ports, operating in a similar way to the Auxiliary Air Force in the UK. Aircrew were recruited from the ports and after training were posted to the flights stationed in their own cities. A small number of British business and professional men were also recruited, trained and included in the flights. The IAFVR's brief was defence of India's 3,000 miles of coastline abutting the Indian Ocean and the Bay of Bengal, flying reconnaissance patrols and escorting convoys. Their aircraft were Wapitis and a few Hawker Audaxes. In 1941 these old aircraft were swapped by some of the CDFs for a few Bristol Blenheims, Armstrong Whitworth Atalanta transports, DH.89 Dragon Rapides and a single DH. 86 (known affectionately as The Monster). Meanwhile RAF flying instructors were assigned to flying clubs in India to instruct IAF Volunteer Reserve cadets on Tiger Moths. In August 1941 No.1 Squadron began conversion to the Westland Lysander and the IAFVR was inducted into the regular IAF.

The CDFs were wound up at the end of 1942, shortly after Hal's arrival in India. They may have been small units flying old aircraft but they could still be effective and each of the flights had stories to tell worthy of any unit of a regular air force and once the CDFs were disbanded Hal began to hear some of them. A good example surrounds the exploits of Scotsman David Small of the Cochin CDF who was tasked with forming a new flight at Vizagapatam. The flight's numbers were small – two pilots including an observer, twelve airmen and two Wapitis which had flown on the Frontier in the early 1930s then spent a couple of years at a training school and were now to be employed in the unforgiving work of reconnaissance patrols over the sea. On 6 April 1942 one of the Wapitis took off, piloted by Pilot Officer Barker, a young Indian from Agra, with his CO, Small, in the back seat as navigator. They had flown twenty miles out to sea when Small saw gun flashes off to the north-east and directed Barker to fly towards them. Flying at 8,000 feet they found a Japanese naval force consisting of a battleship, an aircraft carrier, a cruiser and two destroyers attacking a merchant vessel and shadowed it, helpless, for an hour. During that time Japanese naval fighters were in the air but unaccountably didn't see the Wapiti. Vizagapatam was in no position to intervene but when darkness fell Small was determined to strike back in some way. He and Barker bombed up their Wapiti determined to at least damage a Japanese ship. They searched seaward in the dark to the limit of the aircraft's endurance but had to return when they failed to locate the fleet. The old aeroplane had flown fifteen hours between dawn and midnight.

There were casualties elsewhere amongst the CDF and stories of good luck and survival. The Calcutta CDF was one of the fortunate ones with a few Blenheims. In March 1942 one was flying 100 miles out over the Bay of Bengal when the crew became suspicious of a dhow, They descended to 50 feet to investigate , circled round it then, just as they were about to make off, the starboard engine failed. There was no time to recover at that height and no time to jettison the bombs they were carrying but they were lucky to make a smooth landing on the sea and also lucky that the Blenheim floated for half an hour. The three man crew – English wing commander, Indian squadron leader and Indian sergeant air gunner, stood on the wing until the aircraft sank. At this point they inflated the dinghy but it inflated so fast that it burst, so they had no option but to swim for it towards the dhow which they had been investigating. It took half an hour's steady crawl to reach it but it seemed the dhow's crew were as suspicious of the airmen as they had been of them. It was fortunate that Squadron Leader Hem Chaudheri could speak Bengali and he persuaded the dhow's crew that they were safe to take on board. An amusing post script to this story was that a fisherman on the dhow explained that when he first saw their aircraft he couldn't make up his mind whether it was a Ju88, a Japanese bomber, or an RAF aircraft. He then went on to describe in detail to Chaudheri the tactics of a Luftwaffe dive-bomber squadron. He had been a deckhand on a ship which had been dive-bombed off Piraeus, Malta and Crete so a single Blenheim was small beer to him.

*

Through his position as DAOA Hal soon became acquainted with the exploits of the fledgling Indian Air Force and he had a profound respect for what they achieved.

> The men were as keen as mustard. If an aeroplane went unserviceable it was a point of honour for the mechanics to work at it without stopping provided the spares were available.

But as keen as they might be, the IAF was only a tiny force and the RAF in India was very seriously understrength. The situation needs to be described so as to understand the fact that India was in a sense under siege and that Hal was thrust into what was really an administrative and organisational nightmare.

Chapter Nineteen

The Indian Problem

In Britain, one of the recommendations of the 1938 Chatfield Committee on the defence of India was the re-equipment of RAF squadrons based there, although as reflected in the previous chapter it did not address the almost non-existent growth of the IAF itself other than propose the creation of the IAF Volunteer Reserve and the manning of the Coastal Defence Flights. When Hal arrived at Air HQ he was very quickly caught up in the desperate need for aircraft and equipment and the National Archives hold a revealing record of 'Secret Cypher' messages that passed back and forth between the Air Ministry in London and Air HQ in New Delhi with Middle East Command also involved. As Hal intimated in his memoir, Wavell was insistent that he be apprised of every last detail. In the year prior to Hal's arrival and during his tenure as DAOA, shortages, requirements, amended schedules of delivery and aircraft losses *en route* to India were the subject of a constant, almost daily, flow of signals. At senior level these signals sometimes didn't hold back on expressing frustration, dismay, pessimism or even incredulity that demands couldn't be met even when couched in a formality of manner that Staff College taught that such signals should be written.

Involved senior RAF personnel in India and Middle East at this time were as follows: the AOC-in-C India Command was Air Marshal Sir Richard Peirse who in November 1943 became Allied Air Commander-in-Chief South-East Asia. Hal had quite a lot to say about Sir Richard whose RAF career was brought to a somewhat abrupt end in 1944 when he embarked on an affair with the wife of his close friend, General Sir Claude Auchinleck. He and she were sent back to England by Mountbatten when he got to hear of it. The Deputy AOC-in-C India Command was Air Marshal Sir John Baldwin and AOC Air Forces in Ceylon was Air Vice Marshal Alan Lees. Air Marshal Arthur Tedder was

AOC-in-C RAF Middle East Command. In London the Chief of the
Air Staff (CAS) was Air Chief Marshal Charles Portal, later 1st Viscount
Portal of Hungerford.

So, just what was the situation in India in the spring of 1942? (Cyphers
are unedited and are shown as sent.)

> From Air Ministry Whitehall to AHQ India repeated to HQ
> RAF Middle East.
> 30/3 [1942]
> Personal for Peirse (R) Tedder from CAS
>
> We cannot fully reconcile the aircraft position as you describe it
> in your AOC.56 28/3 with Wavell's 7300/C 27/3 and the infor-
> mation at our disposal.
>
> **Fighters**. In India and Burma excluding Ceylon you have 5, 17,
> 67, 135, 146, 155 and 258 [squadrons] – Total 7. This excludes
> 136 which you appear to be operating in Ceylon as third squad-
> ron. Of these, two squadrons are equipped with modern types
> – 5 squadron Mohawks, 135 squadron Hurricanes. This leaves
> balance of 5 squadrons to be equipped with modern types.
> 7300/C 27/3 shows total of 97 Hurricanes being erected in
> India, 96 ferried or due from M.E. These aircraft should enable
> you to replace wastage at 100% in 5 and 135 sqdns and pro-
> vide aircraft for further 4 sqdns. By end April you should have
> in India and Burma 6 fighter squadrons behind which 40 addi-
> tional Hurricanes should then have arrived at Karachi. By the
> end of May you should receive Nos.79, 605 and 615 squadrons
> complete with aircraft.
>
> **Bombers**. In India and Burma excluding Ceylon you have the
> following Bomber squadrons. 4 (IAF), 60, 113, 84, 221, the last
> two being established at 24 IE [initial establishment] are equiv-
> alent to 3 at 16 IE total 48. None of these has modern aircraft.
> Para 12 of Part 2 of 7302/C of 27/3 shows total of 80 light and

medium bombers established to be operationally available by 25th April. This is sufficient to equip 5 squadrons which can be maintained out of monthly flow of 30 Blenheims ex Middle East. 20 Wellingtons should have reached you by end of April so that one squadron should be equipped for this type.

General Reconnaissance Landplanes. Present monthly flow of 16 Hudsons is maximum we can send. We consider priority must be given to formation of one sqdn Calcutta area one Ceylon and one southern India. Flow should be directed to this end.

Tedder is already straining his resources to the utmost and I do not see how knowledge of his order of battle could affect your demand or increase the supply of aircraft from this source. If you tell Tedder what you most need he will continue to do his best for you.

You no doubt realise that we rely on your weekly state of aircraft returns to keep us informed of your aircraft position and we cannot properly assess your needs unless we have this information. We have received no return from India, Burma or Ceylon since 6 March and signals asking for this information remain unanswered. Must ask you to get your staff to render this return promptly and as accurately as possible. Statements of aircraft operational or serviceable are of little value as they do not give complete picture. If information not available from units best estimate of position should be made by your staff from the information they have of aircraft casualties and movements. Otherwise we have to make our own estimates which may be misleading.

From foregoing it appears at this end that you are receiving an appreciable supply of aircraft but that they are not finding their way into the front line quickly. Neither I nor Tedder can supply any more at present but if there is anything either of us can do to reduce the period between aircraft and date of first line serviceability please tell us urgently.

What Peirse and Wavell were ideally looking for was sixty-four squadrons of aircraft – eighteen fighter, four fighter-reconnaissance, four bomber reconnaissance, eleven light bomber, four medium bomber, two heavy bomber, six torpedo-bomber, four bomber-transport, four general reconnaissance flying-boat and seven general reconnaissance landplane. What they actually had come 1 August 1942 was thirty-five squadrons – seven fighter, four fighter-reconnaissance, four bomber-reconnaissance, five light bomber, two medium bomber, two heavy bomber, six torpedo-bomber, two bomber-transport and three general reconnaissance landplane.

The USAAF were also operating in south-east Asia – an area they termed the China-Burma-India (CBI) Theater– in which US forces were overseen by General Joseph 'Vinegar Joe' Stilwell, the Deputy Allied Commander in China. US (or joint Allied) units in the CBI included the 1st American Volunteer Group, the Flying Tigers. In early 1942 Lieutenant General Lewis Brereton was named Deputy Air Commander, under Air Marshal Peirse, of ABDAIR, a component of ABDACOM (American-British-Dutch-Australian Command). Based in Java he only remained in post until 23 February because of differences of opinion with Peirse and criticism from Wavell. By 5 March he was in New Delhi where he took command of, and began to organise, the new USAAF Tenth Air Force.

From Troopers London to Armindia 31/3 [i.e. from Portal to Wavell].

General Stillwell's orders are that he is to move his air forces into China as soon as practicable for operations against the Japanese flank and against Japan proper. Until this can be done he is authorised to operate his air force in support of you. To achieve this Gen Brereton commanding the US Army Air Forces in India now has his headquarters alongside yours. Brereton therefore has the necessary authority to use his heavy bombers and his ability to do so depends on their readiness for operations. You should satisfy yourself on this by asking Gen Brereton direct.

There should now be 14 Fortresses in India and three *en route*. It is intended to send 33 more. It appears that Gen Arnold [the USAAF's Commanding General] appreciates the urgency of India's need and is giving it priority over his other commitments of supplying aircraft to Australia and of the four heavy bomber groups destined to come to this country … the detailed programme of deliveries will be passed on to Peirse. The American fighters in India other than the Mohawks are all intended for the American Volunteer Group and we do not think we can interfere with their movement.

Portal's mention of 'Hap' Arnold's appreciation of the RAF's needs was underlined a few days later when, on 6 April 1942, Wavell wrote to Louis Johnson, the United States representative in New Delhi.

When we met on Saturday you asked me my most immediate need and I replied 'aircraft'. The Japanese attacks now in progress against Colombo and our shipping and India generally emphasise the vital urgency of this requirement. It is not too much to say that our whole position in India during the next few months depends on whether we can receive an adequate supply of aircraft. The figures I give you below do not in any way represent our ultimate requirements but are the numbers of aircraft for which I estimate that we can find crews if we can receive them during or before June, the earlier the better of course.

Fighters – 120 P-40s

Bombers – 120 B-25s

General Reconnaissance – 80 Hudsons

Bomber Transport – 40 DC-3s

If you could do anything to obtain us these aircraft as an urgent and vital requirement I shall be most grateful.

The Air Ministry's view was that this was 'probably all hooey since American production must already have been fully allotted between the United Kingdom and the United States'. The almost desperate tone of some of Wavell's communications with London prompted Portal to try and reassure him that all possible was being done. On the day Wavell wrote to Louis Johnson, CAS sent this honest appraisal to Wavell:

> The extreme importance of strengthening the air forces in India is fully recognised by all concerned here and we realise the heavy handicap which inferiority in the air imposes on all your operations and upon the security of India generally. Nevertheless we feel bound in fairness to you and to other Commanders in Chief at Home and Abroad to place before you a broader picture of the air situation as we see it in relation to our available resources. [These are] limited and so is our rate of expansion. We now have a total of 245 operational squadrons which we hope to raise to 338 by September 1942. This expansion depends on punctuality of execution of aircraft production programmes both here and in America and may not be realised. Demands from all theatres are soaring. Middle East now have 42 fully operational squadrons and require 88. Australia demands 75 squadrons and New Zealand 50. Moreover there are many areas such as Gibraltar, West Africa and South Africa which badly need some air forces and have almost none. Clearly we can only look at these demands in relation to the strategic importance of the various areas. Supreme importance of British Isles needs no emphasis. We cannot afford to reduce present fighter and coastal forces though we are constantly and heavily milking them for Tedder and you. Our present bomber force which is our sole means of hitting Germany is only 41 squadrons and is contracting largely as a result of withdrawals for overseas. Importance of Middle East lies in fact that loss of Iraq and Persia means total collapse of all war effort east of the Cape and opens the back door to Russia. Our estimate of enemy land based air strength against Near East,

India and Burma on 1st May is 400–500 aircraft. We have to look at your proposals also in light of movement and supply and maintenance factors. To build you up to an organisation capable of maintaining 66 [sic] squadrons would require in men alone about two average convoys leaving nothing for army or for air in Middle East for two months. Moreover to maintain total of fighter squadrons demanded by India and Middle East would absorb almost whole output of British fighter aircraft after fulfilling promises to Russia.

Our immediate object is to give you 100 fighters a month and we realise that this will necessitate your exercising most rigid economy. Every conceivable method of reducing wastage will have to be used, including deception, protection, strongest possible ground defence of aerodromes and above all fullest development of organisation and operational control will be needed to obtain maximum operational results for losses incurred. It is in these directions that we should ask you to look and to ask our help. Merely to multiply demands which our resources and shipping space simply do not enable us to meet can only lead to profitless embarrassment here and disappointment in India. We will continue to do our very best for you.

This was copied to SASO (Senior Air Staff Officer) and to Air Vice Marshal Alfred Collier, the Air Officer Administration to whom Hal was about to become Deputy, who would be responsible for 'fullest development of organisation and operational control'.

On the same date again, 6 April, C-in-C Ceylon, Vice Admiral Sir Geoffrey Layton, signalled Wavell. The previous day an air attack by carrier-based aircraft of the Imperial Japanese Navy had been made on Colombo, Ceylon's capital. A few days later they attacked the naval base at Trincomalee too. The targets were British warships, harbour installations and air bases and in broad terms the objective was to force the British Eastern Fleet to leave Asian waters. At Trincomalee the destroyer HMAS *Vampire* and the corvette HMS *Hollyhock* were sunk. The RAF lost eight aircraft and the FAA one in return for eleven Japanese destroyed.

Seven hundred people on the ships and on the base lost their lives. HMS *Hermes* was undergoing repairs but with warning of the attack she sailed but didn't get very far as a Japanese reconnaissance aircraft spotted her south-east of Trincomalee and seventy Japanese bombers attacked and she sank with the loss of 307 men. Layton reported:

> As far as can be ascertained enemy force composition unknown but containing possibly three battleships [and] four aircraft carriers is somewhere between Ceylon and Addu Atoll. Enemy will probably locate our Eastern Fleet sometime today and with his preponderance of aircraft and their superior quality have considerable advantage. Catalina reconnaissance although much reduced is still being maintained but even if enemy force is located it is doubtful whether it will be in range of Blenheims here. The immediate provision of long distance striking force aircraft of the Fortress type may relieve the present situation and is essential for the future security of Ceylon.

Wavell responded with 'small force of American heavy bombers are without trained gun crews and cannot operate by day. No others available. We have already represented to Chiefs of Staff urgent need heavy bombers in telegram which is being repeated to you.'

Vice Admiral Layton updated Wavell on 9 April.

> It is now quite clear that the Eastern Fleet will not be able to afford any appreciable protection to Ceylon or the eastern coast of India for some considerable time. It follows therefore that Ceylon requires much more powerful air forces than now exist. FAA aircraft are proving more of an embarrassment than a help when landed as they cannot operate by day in the presence of Japanese fighters and only tend to congest aerodromes. After today's operations our striking force consists of only three serviceable Blenheims. These aircraft are of little use

against warships and are extremely vulnerable to [Japanese] navy fighters.

At Trincomalee there are now 6 serviceable Hurricanes and in the Colombo area 16 which is 39 below our serviceable strength of a week ago. I regard with grave concern the fact that the enemy is free to resume his attacks at any moment. I regard it as essential that our 3 Hurricane squadrons should be made up to strength immediately. Ample reserve aircraft should be held at convenient aerodromes in Southern India ready to fly to Ceylon to make good wastage immediately it occurs. I suggest 100% would be appropriate.

No wonder Churchill said when hostilities had ended 'the most dangerous moment of the war, and the one which caused me the greatest alarm, was when the Japanese Fleet was heading for Ceylon and the naval base there. The capture of Ceylon, the consequent control of the Indian Ocean, and the possibility at the same time of a German conquest of Egypt would have closed the ring and the future would have been black.'

The Chiefs of Staff did respond to Wavell's continuing entreaties by ordering the transfer of thirty Hurricanes, twenty Blenheims and a Beaufort torpedo-bomber squadron with all ground personnel and necessary equipment from Middle East Command with the least possible delay. Tedder did his best to comply and sent Hurricanes and Blenheims as well as the Beauforts and was left waiting for replacements from the UK. The Air Ministry were also trying to find Catalinas to bolster the current force but No.222 Group who operated them were less than impressed.

Recent experience has shown that the Catalina is too vulnerable and covers too small an area in daylight to be effective for reconnaissance in such a large area as Indian Ocean. Suggest need for provision [of] Mosquito type aircraft for this role.

The Air Ministry scraped together eighteen Catalinas of which fourteen were serviceable and four were operated by the Dutch. But when they would arrive was not certain. As for the Mosquito the Air Ministry insisted '[it] is suffering from teething trouble inevitable in new types and tropicalisation will be a lengthy process. Mosquito is inadequate substitute for Catalina owing poor navigation facilities ...'

*

There was another theatre of war adjacent to India where the situation was dire: Burma. In February 1942, after the Japanese invasion of that country, General Sir Harold Alexander had been sent to India as GOC-in-C of British Forces in Burma. He was unable to hold Rangoon which was abandoned to the Japanese in early March. Thereafter Alexander increasingly left much of the tactical conduct of the campaign to William Slim, Commander of Burma Corps who, faced with overwhelming odds, Alexander ordered to retreat to India, at the same time contacting Wavell. Wavell in turn immediately appraised London of the situation.

From Armindia to Troopers.

12th April 1942.

For Chiefs of Staff from General Wavell.

Hutton [Alexander's Chief of Staff] has arrived with letter from Alexander on situation in Burma which he supplemented verbally. Morale of troops including many British units reported very poor owing to weak strengths, complete enemy command of air and no prospects of reinforcement or relief. I can at present do very little to help him. Of eight Hurricanes sent Burma lately after one successful action one only is now serviceable. Of remainder three are total losses largely owing to inexperience of pilots and difficulty of conditions. I have sent six Blenheims which have not yet been in action but can obviously accomplish little in face of enemy fighter strength. I have only total of 40 Hurricanes and Mohawks for defence of Calcutta and NE India with no reserves and simply cannot afford to fritter these away. There remains no warning system in Burma and aircraft can only operate from airfields in China, refuelling in Burma. In these conditions Hurricanes with their short endurance can accomplish little and are bound to have heavy rate of wastage. I have only one squadron of Blenheims and ten Wellingtons at present serviceable in India. I have no PRU [Photographic Reconnaissance Unit] and no machines to give Alexander reconnaissance he needs. Until middle of May when I hope to send brigade by Imphal-Kalewa route, reinforcements can only be sent by air and I have at present total of seven DC-2s available which also have to carry stores and other personnel urgently required. Am endeavouring to secure civil planes. Americans have no transport aircraft at present. Sorry to give depressing picture but you should know it. Alexander has good commanders who will do their best but I fear that force is no longer very reliable.

Allied troops were evacuated from Burma in May 1942. Air Chief Marshal Peirse later reflected on this moment.

When our forces came out of Burma the Air Force was in a parlous state. We had about fourteen battle weary squadrons, most of them sadly depleted. [Furthermore] batches of Air Force personnel, disorganised and unequipped, had contrived to escape to India after our defeat in Malaya and the Dutch East Indies. Apart from the Burma squadrons there was only the handful of obsolete service aircraft and converted airliners that had composed the former Air Forces in India. A small and out of date maintenance organisation existed in the North West many hundreds of miles from the scene of operations in Bengal. India was threatened in the North East, North West and in the South and our limited resources had to be stretched to meet any contingency.

On 19 April 1942 Wavell received a Secret Cypher from Winston Churchill who began by updating information on the supply of aircraft to India. 'Naturally we have been working continually at your problem,' he said.

> According to our reckoning you have at the moment in India and
> Ceylon about 230 fighters and 80 bombers. There are already
> on the way to you further reinforcements to follow – about 200
> fighters and 60 bombers. We have persuaded the Americans to
> send about 46 heavy and medium bombers.

Winston suggested that by the end of April Wavell would have 310
fighters and 160 bombers at his disposal, by the end of May 410 fighters and 235 bombers and by the end of June 490 and 295 respectively.
'I am assured that this is really all that can be done for you in this
period,' the Prime Minister wrote. He went on to describe what steps
were being taken to build up Allied naval force in the Indian Ocean and
thereby secure Ceylon.

> But all this gathering of a naval force will be futile if Ceylon, par-
> ticularly Colombo, is lost in the meanwhile. We must therefore
> consider the defence of Colombo by flak and aircraft as an object
> more urgent and not less important than the defence of Calcutta.
> As to the long Indian coastline between Calcutta and Ceylon it
> is not possible in the near future to provide air forces to either
> repel landings or to afford an umbrella for naval movements.

Then comes a direct question.

> Do you really think it is likely the Japanese would consider it
> worthwhile to send four or five divisions roaming about the
> Madras Presidency? What could they do comparable to the
> results obtainable by the capture of Ceylon or by pressing up
> north in China and finishing off Chiang Kai Shek. My thought
> therefore is that your treatment of the problem must be selective
> and that the naval base at Colombo and the link with China via

Calcutta have pre-eminence. Now that you know what air forces will be on the way you will no doubt be able to decide whether anything can be done for him [Chiang Kai Shek]. I must point out that the collapse of China would liberate at least 15 and perhaps 20 Japanese divisions and that therefore a major invasion of India would indeed become a possibility.

And thereby we come to the other pressing problem facing Wavell. Hal alluded to this when he wrote:

The United States Army Air Force carried out a fabulous airlift of supplies from north east India to Kunming in China. This meant flying 'over the hump' as the pilots called the Himalayan mountains, usually in shocking weather with a high rate of crashes, but the supplies were vital for the Chinese.

These supply flights were in support of both the Chinese war effort of Chiang Kai Shek and units of the USAAF based in China. The Second Sino-Japanese War was being fought, primarily between the Republic of China and the Empire of Japan. It began in 1937 and lasted until 1945. In 1942 America, with Allied assistance, began to aid China via airlift after the Allied defeat in Burma had closed the Burma Road. This presented immense challenges as there were no airfields in the China-Burma-India Theatre at which the large numbers of transport aircraft required could be based. Nor were there reliable charts, radio navigation aids or accurate weather forecasting. Despite this, between 1942 and 1945, almost 700,000 tons of materiel and fuel was delivered.

When the Sino-Japanese War began the China Nationalist air force had over 200 combat aircraft. From 1937 to the beginning of 1941 the Soviet Union had served as the primary supplier but many early Chinese aircraft also came from the American Curtiss Aeroplane and Motor Company. The entry of the USA into the war with Japan at the end of 1941 and the receipt of Lend-Lease aircraft from the United States (China was added to the list of Lend-Lease beneficiary nations in

April 1941). meant America replaced the USSR as the largest supplier. By the end of 1941 there were over 350 operational aircraft available, including the P-40Bs of Claire Lee Chennault's Flying Tigers. Modern American aircraft began to replace obsolete types from March 1942 with Republic P-43A Lancers. Training on this type was initially undertaken at Kunming in China's Yunnan Province but after a series of fatal crashes Chinese Lancer pilots were flown to India for training. From February 1943, preparing for the transition to more new American aircraft, the Chinese transferred *all* primary training on combat types to Lahore and other cities, using Boeing Stearman PT-17 Kaydets. Training for photo-reconnaissance continued in China. In March 1945 cadets completing primary training in India were sent to America to train further. Hal recalled:

> Chiang Kai Shek asked India to provide facilities for flying training. We lent the Chinese an airfield at Lahore and I often flew there to iron out their problems.

There, he was able to observe at first hand Chinese methods.

> Chinese discipline was strict and punishments differed from our way of thinking. For example, if a pilot made an error of airmanship he would be ordered to stand to attention in full flying kit in the scorching sun with one arm held straight up for periods varying according to the offence. He was watched from the control tower and if he allowed his arm to droop he had to start the period all over again.

On the other side of the coin:

> The Chinese officers loved to give parties in Delhi which I and others from HQ had to attend. These were a bit of a strain because the host would suddenly shout 'bottoms up' and everyone had to drain their glasses only to find them refilled at once.

The Chinese wives were attractive with their faultless carriage, hairdo and make up, their slit skirts and Anna May Wong figures [she was the first Chinese-American film star].

After the war Hal received the Chinese Order of the Cloud and Banner for his services to Chiang Kai Shek's cause. He was in exalted company as Claire Lee Chennault and Dwight D. Eisenhower were amongst the other recipients of this award.

*

In 1943 the *Journal of the Air Forces, India Command Edition*, published a piece by Honor Tracy entitled *The Chinese Few*.

> Looking for the Chinese Air Force is like looking for sixpence in a field of clover. There are millions of Chinese who have never seen an aircraft with the white sun on blue ground flying over their heads. They do not know what it means to hear their own fighters take off to engage the enemy. It could not be otherwise in so gigantic a country as China with its 6,000 miles of seaboard. It is however a little rash of the Nip [sic] pilots to claim the whole Asiatic sky as part of the Japanese Empire. Especially as at one time they received orders to avoid encounters with United Nations' aircraft of any sort.

This reference to the United Nations is in respect of the 1942 United Nations Declaration made by the Allies in response to the ineffective and largely non-representational League of Nations of 1920. Its text was drafted by Roosevelt and Churchill at the White House and on New Year's Day 1942 they, together with Russian diplomat Maxim Litvinov and politician Soong Tseven of the Republic of China, signed the document which later came to be known as the United Nations Declaration. Twenty-two other countries added their signatures the next day and this marked the first use of the term United Nations. During the war United

Nations became the official term for the Allies and to join countries had to sign the Declaration and declare war on the Axis. The UN proper was founded in 1945.

Yet the Chinese Air Force is remarkably small judged by any standards. The Chinese are a nation of peasants and merchants and western civilisation came to them late. The horror of modern warfare burst upon them suddenly and their resources, technical and industrial, were sadly inadequate. There was little money, few raw materials and, above all, no organised production, whereby losses could be made good. As aircraft were shot down in the beginning of the war, so gaps were made in the defence of China. There was no hope of replacement.

Even before the war however Chiang Kai Shek and his wife saw the danger ahead and realised the importance of aerial power. Madam Chiang Kai Shek took over the Air Ministry in 1936 to find the most disgraceful muddles going on everywhere. Madam Chiang and her colleagues soon cleared out the muddlers and began to build a force which should be small but good.

When the Japanese did invade there was no Battle of China as there was a Battle of Britain. Against overwhelming odds the Chinese could only carry out the same type of guerrilla operations as their army had been forced to do. A single bomber might suddenly dive down out of the blue and drop bombs on the Japanese naval craft moored along the Yangtse river at Shanghai: or a dozen Japanese bombers might be destroyed on the ground early one morning before breakfast: or as the Japanese came up to blitz an open town perhaps a couple of Chinese fighters would take them on and sell their lives as dearly as they could. In 1937 the Chinese brought down without loss to themselves six of the crack Kisaratsu squadron near Hangchow. How tiny are the resources of these valiant people may be seen from the fact that they still regard this as their greatest and most brilliant victory in the air.

As time went on and the Japanese outrages against defence-less people mounted up the Chinese grew more and more angry and more and more air minded. People gave money to buy air-craft. The tribesmen of Turkestan where no Japanese forces had ever been seen gave ten aircraft to the Chinese government: rich Chinese in America gave 6 million dollars: Chinese news-papermen launched the 'plane from each district' campaign. The whole nation reacted in the most spontaneous way from Mongolia to Yunnan. At the same time they developed a mod-est but effective 'guerrilla industry' known as *Kung Ho* or *Work Together*. Spreading production over huge areas was to some extent the answer to intensive bombing of industrial cities. They were able in this way to supply the smaller needs of the air force, such as spare parts, fabrics and certain types of instruments but China still must rely on foreign help for engines and artillery. For this reason the loss of the Burma Road came as a terrible blow, so terrible that people wondered how China would con-tinue resistance at all.

Three and a half year's training is necessary in the Chinese Air Force before a commission is granted. A Sergeant pilot is trained in a little less time than that. Officers and Sergeants alike are taken from the pick of Chinese youth and constantly have to pass examinations of all kinds. It was the American Colonel Jouett who first laid down the system for use in Chinese fly-ing schools eight years ago. The American Colonel Chennault, the famous aviator, also trained hundreds of boys along with his Volunteer Group.

The Chinese Air Force is still a frail, ramshackle affair with here a touch of Heath Robinson and there a dash of the Marx Brothers. What is important is that it has somehow destroyed over two thousand planes since the 'China Incident' began and it is gaining in power and experience every day.

Every little help that we can give the Chinese is a necessary act of self-defence.

Chapter Twenty

Deputy Air Officer Administration

T his then was the situation in India when Hal arrived, with the threat from the Japanese foremost in everyone's mind but with scarcely enough in the way of aircraft and equipment to provide a sustained aerial defence. Hal's responsibilities meant that he flew the length and breadth of this vast country visiting stations and commands, speaking to military personnel and civil servants and incidentally meeting the Indian people. He was to stay in India until the end of the war and his retirement from the RAF but in those almost three years he was party to, or dealt with the implications of, some very significant events.

> I had to visit Ceylon several times. It is a most lovely island. After calling at units in southern India [Bhopal, Begumpet, Bangalore and Cochin] I was a guest of the AOC, an old friend, at his picture book residence in Colombo.

This was in January 1943 and Hal had piloted himself and half a dozen military passengers from Delhi in a Lockheed 12 Electra. The old friend was Air Vice Marshal Alan Lees who in 1942 was Air Officer Commanding No.222 (General Reconnaissance) Group. Lees had preceded Hal by some years as Officer Commanding No.1 (Indian Wing) in 1932.

Hal as ever had an eye for things beyond the military.

> I started a tour of the island in a Dutch crewed Catalina [of 321 Squadron]. We took off from the racecourse airstrip right in the middle of Colombo and alighted on a lake at Koggala in the south of the island. How I wished I had had a colour camera to snap the local catamaran sailing boats going through the surf as the fishermen took them out from the shore! The lake

was surrounded by gigantic palm trees and was large enough for operating a squadron of flying boats. The mess on the lakeside was made up to be as like an English pub as possible. Catalinas based there did long flights to and from Australia, refuelling at the Cocos Islands. They had an endurance of 24 hours.

In fact they had more if they were stripped of all non-essential equipment and auxiliary fuel tanks were installed. A wartime emergency service linking Perth in Western Australia with Ceylon using Catalinas began in June 1943 and it remains to this day the world's longest duration scheduled airline service with the longest crossing taking thirty-two hours from Perth to Koggala Lake. After the outbreak of war a military flying-boat base was established at Koggala and when the Japanese occupied the Malay Peninsula in 1942 and the joint Qantas Empire Airways/Imperial Airways flight from London to Sydney lost Singapore as a refuelling point an alternative route was established through the base. Catalinas and Sunderlands of Nos.202, 204, 205 and 230 Squadrons operated from here, the sheltered waters of which were ideal for a heavily-laden flying-boat to take off from as opposed to the open sea.

After Koggala we alighted on the sea at RAF China Bay beside Trincomalee, the fleet base where we inspected the damage done by the Japanese on the 9th April 1942. Lunch with the Dutch squadron after a session on Bols was a typical meal with far too much to eat. On our direct course back to Colombo we landed at RAF Sigirya. We had to circle a few times to allow leopards to be driven off the runway. The huts for the unit based there had been sited in error on a route used by elephants on migration. The elephants were not going to be put off track by a few huts: in fact one had walked through the ablutions hut the night before and removed the roof on its back. The Transport Officer at Sigirya was worried as I inspected the airfield and its facilities because a large cobra had got itself wound round the back axle of one of his trucks and was being difficult to move. However, he found a car to take me on to Kandy close by. Kandy is a most beautiful place and is near the Royal Botanic Gardens at Peredinya where every type of Ceylonese palm tree and plant is grown. I saw a Mali [i.e. a member of the Mali Hindu caste] carrying without effort the trunk of a sizeable tree ... it was balsa wood. Extensive tree plantations cover the hills around Kandy. Tea picking is done by women who work like lightning tossing the leaves into deep baskets carried on their backs. The planters live in luxurious bungalows on the estates near the 'factories' where the tea is processed before sale.

Hal was really taken with Ceylon as his memoir continues to show:

Lots of interesting things can be seen on the road leading down from Kandy to Colombo such as a tree bare of leaves covered with flying foxes [fruit bats] all hanging upside down sleeping during the day and looking like a mass of old umbrellas: colourful coffee beans on bushes; rubber trees in ordered rows carefully tended with the milky latex liquid draining into little bowls: cinnamon trees and roots from which ginger is obtained. Elephants are usual sights on the road and in the evening carry home a young tree for supper. The 'sensitive plant' is fun to watch. When a fly touches its tiny tentacles they immediately retract capturing the insect for absorbing. The Moon Flower is also a quick mover. It grows as a sort of clematis on a wall and at dusk the large white blossoms open out and so rapidly that you can watch them grow. They die at dawn. Beautiful coloured birds by day and clouds of fireflies at night light the bushes and can be seen flashing as they fly.

It's paradoxical in one sense to see that Hal was able to put aside the pressures of his work and appreciate the better things in life. But this was only a temporary diversion, as all 'diversions' were on the sub-continent at this time, with the ever present Japanese threat overshadowing everything.

The return to AIR HQ Delhi was in the Electra but by a slightly different route – Colombo, Madras, Bangalore again, Begumpet, Bombay, Poona, Bhopal and Delhi. At Madras he was 'dealing with port facilities for future operations'. Additional berths for shipping were being built there. Bangalore was regularly on Hal's itinerary as it was where the Hindustan Aircraft factory was located, having been established there in 1940 with American help and with the British buying a one-third stake in the company, the decision to do so being primarily motivated by the opportunity to boost military supply in Asia. Air Marshal John Higgins became a director of the company after retiring as AOC-in-C of the Air Forces in India in August 1940. In 1943 the factory was handed over to the USAAF but still under Hindustan Aircraft management. It expanded rapidly and became the centre for major overhaul and repair of every type of American aircraft operated in India. When returned to Indian control at the end of the war the factory had become one of the largest such organisations in the region. At Bhopal Hal visited His Highness the Nawab of Bhopal who was shortly to be made an Honorary Air Commodore of the Royal Air Force.

By the time Hal began his flying around India he had amassed over 3,000 hours in his log book and he was adding more aircraft types to his already impressive list. A quick look for the period that he was DAOA reveals that his flying was intermittent but interesting. In early March 1943 it took him on one of many visits to the India Flying Club at Lahore where, as we have seen, pilots of the Chinese Nationalist Air Force undertook primary training. This was in a Percival Vega Gull of No.24 Squadron Communications Flight – they also had the Lockheed Electra on strength which Hal flew. A week later he was back at Lahore, this time piloting a de Havilland Leopard Moth and then flew on to No.1 (Indian) Service Flying Training School at RAF Ambala, 170 air miles away, which had been established to train Indian pilots. He was back again at Ambala in a Hawker Audax at the end of the month. In June 1943 Air Marshal Sir John Baldwin accompanied Hal to Lahore, then on to the RAF Aircrew Reception Centre and No.21 Care and Maintenance Party at Quetta where a new Command and Staff College was being built to replace that destroyed by the disastrous 1935 earthquake. New runways were also being constructed on the airfield. In the autumn Hal managed to get his hands on a Lockheed Lodestar for one of his Lahore visits, the aircraft appearing to belong to BOAC.

At the end of the year on 2 December he was one of six passengers in a B-25 Mitchell on their way to Comilla in Bengal, there swapping the Mitchell for an Anson for a flight to Chittagong which he reached on the 4th. At the time of Hal's visit Comilla was HQ Bengal Command but was very soon to be HQ Third Tactical Air Force which was undoubtedly the reason for Hal's visit. Third TAF formed on 19 December 1943, a few months after the establishment of South-East Asia Command, to provide close air support to Fourteenth Army. It was initially called Tactical Air Force (Burma) but was swiftly renamed as Third TAF on 28 December.

Chittagong was on the front line during the Burma campaign, being a critical base for all three services of the Allies. It had been attacked by the Japanese during the spring of 1942 to such an extent that British forces had to withdraw to Comilla and the city was temporarily evacuated. During the retreat the dock facilities at Chittagong were destroyed to deny them to the Japanese, but as Chittagong became the base for the British offensives into the Arakan region later in December 1942 they were themselves denied their use thanks to that decision. As a result of the early success of the 1942 offensive some RAF squadron flights had been moved forward to hastily-constructed airstrips. One of these at Ramu, codenamed Reindeer I and carved out of a muddy paddy field [from *padi*, the Malay for rice plant], Hal visited a year later on 4 December 1943 by which time it had become rather more established. He went on to Cox's Bazar, from where the first advance of the 1942 Arakan campaign had started and was now an advanced fighter airfield. 'Interesting to see that all huts with sliding doors and furniture were made from varying sizes of bamboo,' wrote the ever observant Hal. 'Local Burmese looked like Chinese,' he concluded. On the 7th his C-47 Dakota flew a full load of passengers from Comilla to Agartala, the city used as a supply point to advancing Allied forces on the ground. Unfortunately Hal doesn't record who these passengers were. Then on the 8th he was making the first of many visits to Imphal where the soon to be fought Battle of Imphal (from March until July 1944) was a turning point in the campaign with the defeat of the Japanese who had been attempting an invasion of India. Hal was there 'when the Japs were in the surrounding hills and amused themselves by shooting up the airfield strip at intervals'. He finally returned with a full load of passengers to Delhi on 11 December. Once again he doesn't record who these passengers were.

The situation in India was fast moving strategically, operationally and for Hal individually. By 1 January 1944 he was signing himself as Air Vice Marshal H.G. Crowe, DAOA, Air Command HQ, South-East Asia, RAF India. He had been promoted to acting air vice marshal on 16 November, no doubt to reflect the importance of the work he was doing, although this was rescinded on 8 April 1944 and he remained an air commodore for the remainder of his RAF career.

*

There is no better overview of air operations in India than one written by Sir Richard Peirse himself and he did just that covering the year 1943, the first full year of Hal's work as DAOA, which he submitted as Allied Air Commander in Chief, Air Command South-East Asia on 22 March 1944. It is an extremely comprehensive document and we can only consider it in very précised form here.

Sir Richard begins with 'For the Air Forces in India 1943 heralded the true passing from defensive to offensive operations'. This had not been possible previously due to the lack of forward landing grounds and the restricted radius of action of the aircraft available. (Construction of airfields (as opposed to forward landing grounds) was behind schedule. To overcome the problem *padi* strips in the forward areas were speedily prepared 'entirely due to the drive and enthusiasm of the Army and RAF officers who were put in charge of the work'. Peirse is talking of Burma here, which was the focus of almost all attention at the time and where 'Bengal Command covered a front of approximately 600 miles and with the small forces available the magnitude of the task facing the

Command can be appreciated'. The advent of increasing numbers of fighters and bombers of the USAAF during the last three months of 1942 and into 1943 eased the situation. Operationally, in the first half of 1943 the destruction of Japanese communications was the job of RAF and USAAF bombers with attacks on railway marshalling yards, dumps, railways, rivers, roads and bridges, barracks, store houses and transport concentrations. Because there was little enemy opposition the RAF's fighters, normally escorting, could be used offensively and Hurricanes equipped with long-range tanks also attacked communications targets, sometimes 250 miles behind the lines.

Operations in Southern India and Ceylon were directed at the protection of shipping and patrolling convoy routes and shipping lanes. Meanwhile on the North-West Frontier, under the aegis of No.223 Group, reconnaissance flights by the Indian Air Force were in connection with the rounding up of Maddakhel tribesmen. Elsewhere Hurricanes were beginning to be used in support of the Tochi Scouts. The tribe and the scouts were well known to Hal from his previous time in India of course and the Frontier would again become the focus of his attention in October 1944. In his report Sir Richard notes that

> modern high speed aircraft have been used on the Frontier for the first time, their increased firepower having an encouraging effect on our own troops and acting as a deterrent on hostile tribesmen. Hurricanes have carried out over 150 sorties, principally in direct support of the Army but also for photographic and road reconnaissance, for bombing and machine gunning areas which for political reasons have been proscribed and for dropping mail and supplies to isolated outposts. Vengeances have not yet been employed but their aircrews have been able to gain knowledge of Frontier conditions. It has been decided that their role will be limited to the attacking of clearly defined targets such as villages in proscribed areas. The Frontier generally has been quiet despite the activities of the Fakir of Ipi in Waziristan. There is no doubt that the recent successes of the

United Nations have had a chastening effect on the tribesmen. Frontier operations are now an Indian Air Force commitment and the area has served as a useful training ground for Nos.1, 3, 4 and 7 Squadrons. Intelligence and photographic facilities have been developed, the Kohat runway extended and other reorganisation undertaken with a view to modernising what has hitherto been one of the few surviving Royal Air Force anachronisms.

What a telling phrase! From June 1943 the monsoon began to make its annual impact on life and on operations throughout India and this remained the case until early October. The time was used for the important work of training 'and for the development of the resources of the Command'. Aircraft supply which had been so critical during 1942 was at last improving radically.

The number of aircraft held under my command has risen from 2,453 in June 1943 to 3,699 in November 1943. This is not only an enormous increase in numbers but obsolescent types are being replaced by more modern types … . The most important of our aircraft reinforcements has been the extensive modernisation of our fighter strength. Hurricanes have risen from 667 to 1,038. The number of Spitfires has risen from 13 to 153 and this has had a most decisive effect on the course of operations … . From the day that the Spitfires first arrived in the forward area they destroyed all three high flying reconnaissance aircraft that were sent over by the enemy who has not attempted a reconnaissance or a raid on the area where the Spitfires have been located since that time. So important was the success of the Spitfires that I sent a personal signal to the Chief of the Air Staff requesting him as far as possible to increase the Spitfire flow.

Sir Richard enumerates other aircraft under his command in 1943. The number of Vengeances had risen to 572 and 'the accuracy of bombing achieved by this type of aircraft has proved its value. It is a most useful direct support weapon particularly against the type of target presented by the enemy in the forward area'. Two Halifaxes and two Lancasters had arrived and these were being evaluated 'under the conditions prevalent in this theatre of war'. Liberators increased from twenty to sixty-nine but it was unlikely that the number of B-25 Mitchells used for pho-to-reconnaissance would increase although the Mosquito being used for long-range photo reconnaissance 'would if their number were to increase prove an admirable weapon for long range offensive reconnaissance and attacks on enemy communications'. There were only twelve in theatre. The Beaufighter (sixty-three by the year's end) had also proved invaluable in the same role as well as being used as a night fighter. 'The obsolescent DC-2 and DC-3 is being replaced by the C-47 Dakota,' reported Sir Richard, 'the total number of which has risen from 29 to 100.' Eighty-two Ansons were being used as training and communications aircraft whilst the number of Harvards for both the IAF and RAF had doubled to 298. Other aircraft listed as being on strength in November 1943 were 65 P-36 Mohawks, 229 Blenheims, 41 Lysanders, 4 Austers, 160 Wellingtons, 117 Hudsons, 61 Catalinas and 377 Miscellaneous [sic]. Of these aircraft 43 per cent were with 49 fully-trained squadrons while the remainder were with maintenance or storage units and either immediately available as replacements or in varying stages of repair.

Reading all of this in the context of the previous year's constant appeals to London for more aircraft by Wavell is instructive, for the Air Ministry had obviously eventually been able to respond more positively to his demands although the number of squadrons Peirse was able to field by the end of 1943 still fell short of the sixty-four that Wavell had been asking for.

Added to the increase in RAF resources was the strengthening of the USAAF presence in India.

Headquarters of the 10th USAAF have been located at Delhi and have maintained complete liaison with Air Headquarters. Bengal Command and Eastern Army Command have remained side by side and kept in constant contact with USAAF senior

Staff Officers in Eastern India. There has been a good co-ordination of air operations between the two forces. In general the 10th USAAF attacked distant objectives over Burma by day: RAF medium and heavy bombers operated by night: and RAF fighters and light bombers attacked all objectives within 260 miles of the forward airfields by day.

By the end of 1943 the Tenth US Army Air Force could muster 58 B-24 Liberators, 58 B-25 Mitchells, 30 A-36 Invaders, 22 P-51 Mustangs, 80 P-40 Warhawks and 17 P-38 Lightnings in theatre.

Of course all these aircraft needed fully functioning airfields to operate from. In March 1942 there were only sixteen such airfields with all-weather runways and twenty 'fair weather strips'. By November 1943, 285 airfields had been completed throughout the sub-continent with a further fifteen under construction. The massive programme had cost around £50 million – a huge sum. And the Air Ministry and Government of India didn't always get their money's worth. There had been a shortage of construction equipment and supervisory staff. Work carried out by civilian contractors had been shoddy and corruption had appeared to be endemic in some areas. Everywhere delays had been occasioned by poor communications and inadequate control. But despite all this, thanks to the commitment of a core of military and civilian engineers, problems had been overcome and the programme delivered.

*

It's time now to introduce Admiral Lord Louis Mountbatten to Hal's story. In August 1943 he was appointed Supreme Allied Commander South-East Asia (SACSEA) of the newly created South-East Asia Command (SEAC), arriving in India in October. SEAC covered India, Burma (Myanmar), Ceylon (Sri Lanka), Siam (Thailand), the Malay peninsula and Sumatra. Mountbatten was in overall command of all Allied forces within this area. At first his headquarters was in New Delhi but in April 1944 it moved to Kandy, nearer to the centre of his command but still retaining a small staff in New Delhi in what was called Rear HQ SEAC. At the same time Sir Richard Peirse's India Command was transferred to that of South-East Asia with the title of Air Command, South-East Asia (ACSEA) and with responsibility for Eastern Air Command (post-war known as the Far East Air Force) and No.222 Group. Commensurate with this a subordinate formation known as Base Air Forces South-East Asia (BAFSEA) was formed with its HQ in the buildings in Delhi just vacated by ACSEA and with full control over Nos.223, 225,226 and 227 Groups. BAFSEA was placed under the command of Hal's old friend, recently promoted Air Marshal Alan Lees, although he appears to have been succeeded by Air Marshal Leslie Hollinghurst after only a couple of months, moving on to be Air Officer Administration at Headquarters Air Command South-East Asia in Kandy. It is fair to say that Command arrangements in SEAC were always complicated.

The responsibilities of Mountbatten's position as SACSEA were never clearly defined but he adopted the approach that he was not simply co-ordinator of the forces under his command but an active participant. When he arrived in India there were persistent problems facing the Allies such as the fact that malaria and other tropical diseases were rife. Mountbatten immediately set in motion a process to bring malaria under control and he boosted morale by visiting the front-line troops. He held regular meetings with his senior commanders so that he was fully apprised of the current situation in all theatres although the waters were muddied somewhat by the fact that British and American objectives were different. While Britain wanted to liberate Burma and reclaim Malaya and Singapore from the Japanese, the Americans were primarily interested in Burma as a supply route to China. This did inevitably lead to clashes between Mountbatten and his American deputy, Lieutenant General Stilwell, but quite remark-ably, despite this, Anglo-US co-operation actually improved, most notably between the air forces of the two countries. Mountbatten relied upon his commanders – Air Marshal Sir Guy Garrod and then Air Chief Marshal Sir Keith Park – to brief him as regards the RAF and IAF. And he was convinced that combined operations, especially those involving the Navy, were the key to Allied success in Burma. London, however, concentrated on winning the war in Europe, the consequence of which was that, despite the improvements that had been made as reported by ACM Peirse, SEAC continued to be short of materiel to the extent that planned operations had to be cancelled or scaled down.

Despite this there was success. In February 1944 the Japanese attacked the Arakan region of Burma in an effort to weaken Allied forces before a larger attack on Imphal farther north. The Allies succeeded in thwarting Japanese intentions in both cases and a land route to China was opened which relieved air supply over The Hump. With the Japanese in retreat Mountbatten turned a defensive campaign into an offensive one and the Allies pushed on into Burma, taking Mandalay in March 1945 and Rangoon in April. Ultimately, after Hiroshima and Nagasaki, Japan surrendered on 15 August and with Mountbatten present to receive it, the formal signing of the surrender instrument was held in Singapore on 12 September.

At SACSEA, an 'Order of the Day' was prepared by Lord Louis for the information of all personnel. It began:

I have today received the surrender of the Supreme Commander of the Japanese forces you have been fighting and I have accepted this surrender on behalf of all of you. I wish you all to know the gratitude and pride that I feel towards every man and woman in this Command today. You beat the Japanese soldier in battle, inflicting six times the amount of deaths that he was able to inflict on you, and you chased him out of Burma.

Hal was party to Mountbatten's philosophy and ways of thinking.

When Lord Mountbatten came out from England to form South-East Asia Command one of his first actions was to use every means of raising morale. He did this by visiting units and telling men about the new equipment, landing craft and reinforcements we would receive. Some of his staff he had brought from England. He knew them from his work in the Combined

Operations set up. He infused quite a naval atmosphere at his headquarters. His handpicked WRNS had a separate mess which we arranged, with their living quarters surrounded by barbed wire. They were very smart in their white tropical uniforms. They were drilled each morning by a Gunnery Lieutenant.

I dined with Lord Mountbatten several times. He was a great film fan and after dinner we sat on the roof of his mess watching the latest productions from Hollywood brought in by the Americans. Films were also shown to other ranks in the Irwin Stadium [The stadium had been built in 1933 as a gift for Delhi from the Maharaja of Bhavnagar.] We all thought he made a mistake to bring his friend Noel Coward out to entertain the troops. Coward's performance was far too sophisticated and did not go down at all well. I remember one episode which was unfortunate to say the least. He was giving a song with his tame pianist at the piano when he saw two officers looking at a piece of paper and not at him. He was furious and walked out. Luckily there was a band present and they saved the party becoming ugly. Afterwards in the mess the two officers showed him the piece of paper. It was a photo of himself. Wonder how he felt then?

Hal regularly met Mountbatten's commanders, including the then Lieutenant General William Slim, commander of XV Corps when Hal first arrived in India, followed from October 1943 by command of Fourteenth Army. Slim was quite amused by a story he often told to those who cared to listen – and Hal did!

He was on a road in Arakan and had left his car behind. Suddenly a huge American bulldozer came along and Slim stopped it. 'Can you give me a lift? I'm General Slim.' The big Negro driver shouted back 'hop up General. I'm general salvage'.

*

We can't always rely on Hal's memoir or log books to tell us places he visited and why and records elsewhere are hard to come by that would do so. He presumably didn't always fly – although it would obviously have been advantageous to do so because of distances involved – and if he did he didn't always pilot the aircraft and would perhaps not have been so assiduous in recording such flights as he would have been otherwise. He does however make some oblique references to one or two other destinations. For example Karachi came under his remit, for there 'assembly and repair of RAF aircraft and the erection of USAAF planes' was undertaken. Presumably this was RAF Mauripur just outside the city which opened in 1942 as a transit airfield, or RAF Drigh Road which was a maintenance base. Huge numbers of aircraft staged through both during the war. Hal also mentions Palel 'as another advanced fighter airstrip with Japs around'. This would presumably have been during the Battle of Imphal with Palel being one of only two all-weather airfields vital to the Allied defenders. And Calcutta. 'I was at the Bengal Club with my cousin Dr Featherstonehaugh the Secretary when the Japs bombed Alipore docks. This was interesting to me in view of the exercise I had arranged when at Kohat several years before. Not much damage was done. A few bombers were brought down on their way home.' The rapid progress of the Japanese through South-East Asia in early 1942 meant that Calcutta was just within range of Japanese bombers and throughout 1942 and 1943 they did their best to disrupt the operations of the port.

On 14 April 1944 Bombay suffered a catastrophic explosion, not at the hands of the enemy but by an exploding ammunition ship. '[There was] destruction in the docks area after an ammunition ship had caught fire and could not be towed out to sea before it blew up wrecking a large basin with many ships alongside,' Hal said. This was a tragic episode which exercised the minds of many. Was it sabotage? The freighter SS *Fort Stikine* in the Victoria Dock carrying a mixed cargo of cotton bales, gold and ammunition was destroyed in two blasts, scattering debris, sinking surrounding ships and setting fire to the area, killing hundreds of people. A fire had been found burning in No.2 hold but the crew, dockside fire teams and fireboats were unable to extinguish it and couldn't find the source anyway because of the dense smoke. By mid-afternoon the order was given to abandon ship. Shortly afterwards came the explosion, splitting the ship in two and breaking windows over ten miles away. Showers of burning material set fire to two square miles of the city adjacent to the docks. Eleven other ships were sunk or were sinking in both the Victoria and neighbouring Prince's Dock. Emergency personnel on the site suffered heavy losses. At least sixty-six firemen died as attempts to fight the fire were disrupted when a second explosion three quarters of an hour later sent burning cotton bales on to more docked ships, the dockyard and slum areas outside the harbour. It took three days to bring the fire under control and it was seven months before the docks could be used again. Figures are disputed but the official death toll was 740 with 1,800 people injured. Many families lost everything. Thousands became destitute: 6,000 firms were affected and 50,000 people lost their jobs. Compensation was subsequently paid to citizens who made a claim to the Indian government for loss or damage to property.

Gold bars are still occasionally found during dredging operations in the twenty first century and are supposedly returned to the British government. The inconclusive enquiry into the explosion identified the cotton bales as probably being the seat of the fire.

Chapter Twenty-one

No.223 Group

Hal was appointed Air Officer Commanding No.223 Group at Peshawar on 5 October 1944, flying from Delhi in a Lockheed Hudson to take up his duties on the 30th, taking over from Group Captain Horner. Given the predisposition of the RAF to not always make such obvious decisions this seems to have been a very sensible appointment considering Hal's previous experience on the North-West Frontier.

Prior to India No.223 Group had something of a convoluted history. It had initially been formed in August 1941 at Singapore, moving almost immediately to Kuala Lumpur. From January 1942 it was at Palembang controlling air operations over Sumatra but was then redesignated No.225 Group. On 1 May 1942 it was reformed from No.1 (Indian) Group as No.223 Group at Peshawar to control units operating along the North-West Frontier. The area for which Hal was now responsible included Kashmir, the North-West Frontier Province, Baluchistan down to Jiwani and Karachi on the Arabian Sea and also the Punjab. In close consultation with Sir George Cunningham, the Governor of the North-West Frontier Province at Peshawar (or during the summer months at his residence at the Nathia Gali hill station), Hal occasionally conducted air operations against the Frontier tribes although in truth during the war most of the Frontier remained largely calm. This is borne out when looking through the records as it seems 223 Group was largely left alone by Air Command South-East Asia and it rarely features in the Command's beautifully kept Operations Record Books, the emphasis understandably being on Burma and the war against the Japanese there and the rest of south-east Asia. The relative calm of the Frontier enabled a majority of troops and air assets to be deployed to the more needful theatres although occasional periods of trouble did mean the necessary retention of a military presence in the region. During Hal's time, a British committee under Lieutenant General Sir Francis Tuker was looking at future policy for the Frontier and recommended a withdrawal of *all* regular forces from tribal territory into cantonments along the border. From these the tribes could be watched. But that didn't happen during Hal's tenure.

Shortly before Hal's arrival there was a tragic reminder that security had to be taken very seriously. A Squadron Leader Hancock from No.223 Group and a Squadron Leader Bath and Flying Officer Steeper-Owens from No.151 OTU were murdered as they cycled along The Mall in Peshawar.

> Two shots were fired as a result of which F/O Steeper-Owens was killed instantaneously. S/Ldr Hancock died in hospital very shortly afterwards. S/Ldr Bath was twice stabbed by a sharp edged weapon and sustained a fatal abdominal wound. He staggered about 60–70 yards down The Mall, collapsed and succumbed to the injury. All three officers died without being able to give any information to the persons who first arrived on the spot. The motive for this triple murder is not yet known but it is understood from the Civil Police Department that there is reason to believe that the arrest of the murderer is expected at an early date.

It took a little longer than that for it was 27 November before

> police enquiries revealed that the individual responsible was one Mohammed Amir. This person recently ran amok in the Sadar Bazaar and in broad daylight stabbed two Hindus and two Sikhs. He was released from jail two months ago after serving a sentence of eight years rigorous imprisonment for stabbing a cashier in Mall Road. A short, locally made .303 rifle has been recovered and identified as the weapon used by the murderer. Mohammed Amir has confessed his guilt.

This was no politically or tribally motivated crime but the action of a person with mental health problems and underlined the point that attack doesn't always come from an expected quarter. At his trial the following May Mohammed Amir was condemned to death.

*

Amongst the squadrons, bases and units under Hal's command were No.84 Squadron RAF at Samungli (Quetta) flying Mosquitos; No.8 Squadron (IAF) at the same airfield flying Spitfires; No.151 Operational Training Unit at Peshawar operating Mohawks, Hurricanes and Harvards to train fighter and ground attack pilots; No.344 Maintenance Unit at various sites through the region; No.1 Officers and Cadets Training School Lower Topa; No.1 School of Air Force Technical Training at Ambala, No.7 School at Quetta and No.8 School at Saharanpur for the training of IAF ground crews; No.1 (Indian) Service Flying Training School at RAF Ambala; and the Base HQ, Aircraft Depot and School of Flying Control at Karachi as well as the flying-boat base at nearby Korangi Creek. All of these are now Pakistan Air Force or Army establishments. Peshawar itself is home to the PAF's Northern Air Command. In his memoir Hal adds 'training in parachute jumping from American Dakotas took place at RAF Chaklala near Rawalpindi'.

He also lists the 'RAF section of the Chinese EFTS at Walton (Lahore)' which we have already described, the overseeing of which was Hal's responsibility as DAOA. A film held by Colonial Film in their archive and which was produced by a British Armed Forces film unit, shows officer cadets of the Chinese Nationalist Air Force undergoing pilot training at the Northern India Flying Club at Lahore, nowadays known as the Lahore Flying Club. The film's narrative is as follows:

This film documents efforts by Allied air forces to train and support the Chinese Air Force which had suffered heavily at the hands of Japanese air forces (particularly those of the Imperial Japanese Navy). Captain Wong, Chief Engineering

Officer, arrives to inspect a parade of Chinese Nationalist Air Force cadets. Cadets on parade. The hangar of the Northern India Flying Club. Aircraft being serviced: the aircraft are Boeing Stearman PT-17 biplanes (also known as Kaydets) in Chinese Nationalist markings. Pilots run to their aircraft. Pilots approaching a long line of parked aircraft. Aircraft in flight and aerial views of the airfield. Clothing is issued. A staff car stops just in front of camera: it is marked with both a Royal Air Force roundel and a white Chinese Air Force sun emblem. Cadets jump off the back of a lorry and form up. A truck full of cadets passes camera and drives through an entrance arch towards the school. The arch is adorned with a variety of Chinese writing. The cadets are shown a large tableau representing a map of China; a large (apparently Japanese) bomb stands erect in the centre of the map and is inscribed 'WAKE UP!' Clothing parade: cadets are issued with clothing supplied by the RAF. Close-up of a cadet signing for the issue of his cap badge. A cadet boards an aircraft with his instructor in the front cockpit. Two mechanics start a Kaydet's engine and it taxis away. The aircraft takes off.

Hal wasted no time in visiting as many of these units as he could. With aircraft of No.223 Group's Communications Flight at his disposal, by the end of the year he had visited Kohat, Miranshah, Gujrat, Chaklala, Basal, Lahore, Fatehjang, Quetta, Karachi, Multan and Risalpur. (He also had the use of a Ford V-8 which he drove himself, or if not he had a driver, to get him to places where he couldn't use an aircraft.) His log book records that from the time he had first climbed into an aeroplane during the First World War to 31 December 1944 he had flown a total of 3,142 hours, 2,357 as pilot and 785 as an air gunner, observer or passenger.

No.223 Group's ORB gives a very real sense of a busy group, even though away from the mainstream of South-East Asia Command activity, and it is worth presenting a snapshot of its contents as a way of illustrating Hal's responsibilities and the units he ultimately had administrative control of.

November 1944. No.117 (Transport) Squadron moved to Risalpur. No.194 (Transport) Squadron moved to Basal. Hal flew with his predecessor, Group Captain Horner to Gujrat, Chaklala and Basal to inspect the units at these airfields. No.7 Squadron IAF arrived at Peshawar for conversion training from the Vengeance to the Hurricane. No.343 Glider Wing Headquarters formed at Fatehjang to administer and operate three glider squadrons. Air Marshal Leslie Hollinghurst, AOC Base Air Forces South-East Asia, arrived at Peshawar for a two day visit and flew with Hal in Beechcraft Expeditor HB164 to Miranshah, Kohat and Basal to inspect units there. The Expeditor was newly delivered to Peshawar (another three were to follow) and it was immediately apparent that the greater speed and range of the aircraft would considerably reduce flying time. One of the aircraft was put at the disposal of Lieutenant General Finnis who accompanied Auchinleck on a tour of the stations on the North-West Frontier. The other aircraft on the Communications Fight were an Avro Anson and two Percival Proctors (although they were unserviceable due to 'woodwork defects' and would be replaced by two Harvards). The first four Hurricane IICs for No.7 Squadron arrived on No.151 OTU. On the 13th Hal was in Delhi at BAFSEA to attend a conference on Training and Administrative matters. There were two cases of poliomyelitis on base which necessitated those suffering being flown to Rawalpindi in a hand-operated iron lung for further treatment.

December 1944. An Afghan military mission visited No.151 OTU as part of a ten-week tour of military establishments of India Command, the mission, which was accompanied by British military officers, being headed up by Lieutenant General Muhammad Umar Khan, Chief of the General Staff of the Afghan Army. Hal and Wing Commander Jones, OC of the OTU received the Afghans who watched an air display put on for their benefit. A training conference was held at Peshawar in connection with the reorganisation of No.151 OTU. This was convened under AVM Meredith Thomas, AOC RAF India, with Hal as his deputy, where the main topic was the difficulty in recruiting sufficient suitable aircrew candidates to meet Indian Air Force requirements and the difficulties

A Beechcraft Expeditor of Peshawar's Communications Flight, August 1945.

of converting to the Hurricane and Spitfire by pilots of Nos.7 and 8 Squadrons IAF because of the necessity of imposing a time limit on the conversion course. Hal received a letter from BAFSEA raising concerns over the inadequacy of flying control facilities at many of the airfields under the command of No.223 Group in view of the continuous and ever-increasing flow of reinforcement aircraft. A court martial at Kohat found four airmen of the Indian Air Force guilty of the theft of arms and ammunition at that station and they were imprisoned up to a maximum of five years.

January 1945. In late 1944 and early 1945 Glider Squadrons were formed and based in No.223 Group's area of jurisdiction for training purposes. The RAF.MOD website concisely explains the complex but brief story of Glider Squadrons in India at this time.

Six squadrons, numbered 668 to 673, were formed in India for airborne assaults in South-East Asia. Each was to have had an

December 1944. The Afghan military mission which visited Peshawar as part of their extensive tour of India Command.

establishment of eighty Hadrians and ten light aircraft, the personnel consisting of RAF pilots surplus to current requirements and pilots from the Glider Pilot Regiment. On 16 November 1944, No.668 formed at Calcutta and No.669 at Bikram followed by No.670 at Fatehjang on 14 December 1944. It was later found that No.669 had been formed at the wrong airfield and since No.671 was due to form there, No.669 was renumbered No.671 on 31 December. On 1 January 1945, No.669 re-formed at Basal where it should have formed in the first place. The three squadrons, Nos.668, 669 and 670, were part of No.343 Wing. A second wing, No.344 comprised Nos.671, 672 and 673 Squadrons. On 16 November 1944, No.672 formed at Bikram, where No.673 joined it on 1 January 1945; on the same day No.669 had been re-numbered No.671 to complete the wing. Until the end of the war, the squadrons undertook sporadic glider training and

courses in jungle warfare, but were never used in operations due
to the Japanese surrender. On 25 October 1945 Nos.671 and 673
disbanded, followed by Nos.668 and 669 on 10 November. The
two remaining squadrons, Nos.670 and 672, disbanded on 1 July
1946.

Glider squadrons apart, No.147 Staging Post was formed at Peshawar
and No.148 Staging Post at Chaklala to provide staging facilities for
transport aircraft on the Delhi/Peshawar/Delhi route. No.436 (RCAF)
Squadron, flying the C-47 Dakota, formed at Gujrat where Air Marshal
Lloyd Breadner, who was AOC-in-C RCAF in the UK, visited them.
The Royal Canadian Air Force Overseas Headquarters in London was
responsible for Canadian airmen serving outside Canada during the
Second World War. It had no operational authority but rather liaised
with the Air Ministry on matters of personnel and administration. As a
matter of interest the Air Marshal was promoted on his retirement at the
end of 1945 to Air Chief Marshal, the first Canadian to hold this rank.

The perils of flying for the busy Communications Flight were high-
lighted in early January when bad weather over the North-West Frontier
caused some disruption. Sir George Cunningham, the Governor of the
North-West Province, was flown to Thal in an Expeditor but a return
became impossible due to a deterioration in conditions. Sir George had
to return to Peshawar by road but the aircraft couldn't take off until the
next day and even then it was found to be impossible to cross the hilly
country between Thal and Peshawar so had to divert into Kohat. On the
following day the Expeditor took off again but encountered icing conditions at 2,000 feet above ground level and was forced to return to Kohat.
It finally landed back at Peshawar three days after leaving.

February 1945. On the 21st Hal flew to Karachi to meet the new
Allied Air Commander in Chief South-East Asia Sir Keith Park and
inspect units under No.223 Group's command. New Zealander Park
is best remembered for commanding No.11 Group prior to and during
the Battle of Britain, responsible for the fighter defence of London

and south-east England, after which he served as AOC Air HQ Malta
and Commander in Chief of Middle East Command before moving to
SEAC.

Shortly after he had arrived at Kandy, in true Sir Keith Park fashion,
he made what he termed a 'short' address to the staff there, to explain
his working system and what he hoped to achieve. He was, he said,
keen to simplify everything – paperwork and organisation primarily –
so that 'the lower formation, the fighting chaps, do not get confused'.
(He and his staff formed the higher formation of course.) He acknowledged that there was a complex command system. 'I have already
landed at five airfields in ACSEA and at two of them the Commanding
Officers stated that they did not know exactly who their masters were.'
He continued:

> There have been a lot of changes throughout the Command in
> the past year. It has been unavoidable. The progress of the war
> has required many changes in organisation and nomenclature.
> These changes often cause confusion to the staff of a lower for-
> mation. Too many changes of organisation and titles get people
> confused and bemused and after a bit they lose interest in the
> higher formation which is a pity because the higher formation
> has its uses and can be more than helpful to squadrons in the
> fighting line. So the first principle is to simplify our organisa-
> tion, to put the brakes on changes of title and organisation for
> the benefit of the lower formations.

Having made his point, Sir Keith moved on to 'concentrating on absolute essentials.'

> Papers should come in and be handled, filtered and flow through
> the Headquarters rapidly. I always contended that Hitler's
> secret weapon at the beginning of the war was our British Staff
> paperwork, our own bumph … . We have got to have paper but

let it flow fast and evenly and cut out the non-essentials and what is known in peacetime as 'red tape.' Reducing the paperwork to absolute essentials will allow you fellows more time to get out and visit units to see what is happening in the Command … . The farther away one gets from the Tactical Units in the line the greater the tendency to become inflexible in ideas. It is very hard being a long way from the majority of units to keep one's mind really flexible.

The final specific point made by the Air Chief Marshal concerned manpower, the shortage of which he conceded was always going to be a headache but which he could see no solution to and so 'unfortunately we will have to exercise economy in man power throughput this year'.

Park's address also reveals an interesting view of the Air Ministry and the way it worked.

When I was appointed to this job I was called to the Air Ministry for what they were pleased to call 'consultations' which consisted of six days in London dashing from one Department of the Air Ministry to another, to be greeted in this way – 'I am delighted to meet you, delighted to brief you. Here is a little brief we have prepared for you.' And everywhere the paper grew and when I came away after six days it was with two very spacious briefcases full of briefs. I thought it was a bit of a bind until I started to read and I frankly admit that Air Ministry Departments had taken definite trouble and if any of you have the time and inclination to look at the briefs you will be surprised to learn how much they know about this Command – surprised at the intimacy of their knowledge of every phase of activity in this Command. The significant point is that they do know and are interested very much in what is going on out here, and secondly that they are flat out to co-operate and assist us 100%. I know many of you have the notion that Air Ministry thinks that the people out here are not achieving all that they could. Bellyaching signals that one can easily dictate at the end of a long day and signed in a hurry can spoil the mutual confidence that exists between us and the Air Ministry. Let us keep the Air Ministry with us and not have any friction. Air Ministry's goodwill of us is frightfully important and it is something for you chaps to guard very jealously and I for one will try to remember to set a good example by never sending a belly aching signal to Air Ministry.

Just as the assembled staff officers thought Sir Keith had come to a conclusion he made one further observation.

Finally, with the example set by the Supremo [Mountbatten] there is no need to express the necessity for teamwork. He is a shining example of a successful commander who believes first and foremost in good teamwork … throughout the Command. Friendly co-operation with our American Allies is of vital importance at all times and everywhere. Teamwork here within headquarters is important but more important between us and the lower formations. The lower formation always think that the higher formation is 'sitting pretty' and the higher formation usually knows that the lower formation is having a much easier time than they are having.

And so the address came to an end. 'Thank you one and all for your attention and obvious interest: now let us get on with the job.'

*

Hal entertained another high-ranking visitor to Peshawar in February a couple of days after meeting Sir Keith when the Inspector General of the Royal Air Force, Sir Edgar Ludlow-Hewitt, arrived by air and then went on to inspect Fatehjang, Chaklala and Risalpur with Hal. An inspection of cookhouses and meals was carried out at all stations and the standard of messing was found to be generally good.

It was reported that the cost of building an all-weather runway strip and aircraft pen at Razmak had increased from 4.29 lakhs to 7.80 (1 lakh equals 100,000 rupees) thanks to unsettled and hostile conditions, including sniping at labour, the murder of the contractor, the murder of the 'concrete association representative' and the wounding of the Assistant Garrison Engineer. Furthermore there was tribal dispute over the ownership of the land. Hal oversaw this and other new airfields in the North-West Frontier Province and Baluchistan, checking that they were properly built as, all other problems apart, local contractors were apt to skimp the cement used on runways and other defence works. 'There was the famous case of the anti- tank "dragon's teeth" obstructions in the Khyber Pass floating gently down the first spate! They were wooden, painted over with cement,' wrote Hal and you can imagine the smile on his face as he did so.

Harvard IIB FE483 was involved in a landing accident when, landing in a strong and gusty wind, the starboard oleo leg sheared and the aircraft suffered Cat. A damage. And Hurricane IIC LD986 was taxiing back to dispersal when it struck a 10-inch wall protecting a culvert, suffering Cat. B damage. The accident was considered to be pilot error. Spitfire VIII JF743 crashed on the bombing range and the IAF pilot was killed when he failed to pull up from a steep bombing dive. Another Spitfire JG679 was involved in a taxiing accident in a strong wind when it ended up on its nose with damage only sustained by the propeller. At the end of the month Hurricane IV LF454 force-landed on the bombing range when it ran out of fuel. The pilot had, contrary to regulations, taken off on reserve tanks and when the engine stopped he switched to main tanks but was unable to restart it. The next day LF432 pulled out of a dive too late and the port main-plane hit the ground. The aircraft and pilot survived. On the same day LD790 force-landed at Risalpur when the pilot was unable to lock the undercarriage in the down position and the Hurricane suffered Cat. A damage. Attrition was obviously high at Peshawar and there were accidents of varying severity month by month but a lot of hours were flown with No.151 OTU flying 1,919 during February. In addition to losing aircraft to accidents, during the month Peshawar was ordered to prepare twenty Hurricane IICs for return to operations (as opposed to training). They would be replaced by Spitfires.

March 1945. Changes were afoot and Hal flew to BAFSEA at Delhi to discuss points on proposed re-organisation which would mean the disbandment of No.223 Group. It had been suggested that a new Group should form in Peshawar under AIR HQ India and if this were to happen No.223 and HQ North-West Frontier Wing would be disbanded and the new HQ would be responsible for air operations on the North-West Frontier, administration of units on the North-West Frontier under similar terms of reference to those followed by No.223 Group, and Indian Air Force training from EFTS to OTU stages 'if it is decided to hand over control of air training to AIR HQ India'. The ORB then goes on to state 'details of this reorganisation are not yet crystallised but it may be that RAF base Karachi may then come under HQ 227 Group'. It seems that the change proposed would duplicate to a large extent what 223 Group was already doing. Keith Park's remarks about 'too many changes of organisation' spring to mind.

Hal met Keith Park again during March 'to discuss current matters'. He also accompanied the Deputy Under Secretary of State to the Air Ministry on a tour of the Karachi area, and at BAFSEA in Delhi discussed accommodating WAAFs at No 1 Hill Depot during the summer. No.1 WAAF Hill Depot was subsequently formed which could accommodate sixty. No.10 RAF General Hospital was established at Karachi under the administrative control of 223 Group. No.7 Squadron IAF moved from Kohat to Imphal and Base Headquarters Karachi was redesignated HQ RAF Base Karachi. Action was taken to declare RAF Stations Fatehjang, Basal and Gujrat prohibited areas as the local magistrate had refused to take action against trespassers. The average serviceability of all aircraft of the Group was only 67 per cent, although that of the Communications Flight was near 100 per cent and during March flew 35,200 air miles. Station buildings were undergoing something of a facelift with repair, refurbishment and repainting, especially of the Khyber and Trenchard barracks at Peshawar very much in evidence. The Link Trainer section, which had long struggled on in an unsuitable building, was rehoused in a newly-built one.

April 1945.   There were inevitably social commitments for Hal at Peshawar. His bungalow was too large for him alone so he invited two of his group captains to share it. 'We found we could not spare time to run the place properly so one of the group captains suggested an Army wife who was temporarily a 'grass widow' to act as hostess. Her husband approved and the arrangement worked well. The same arrangement was adopted in other parts of India'. Colonel Irving Dooh of the Chinese Army was one who was entertained by Hal during the month when he visited No.151 OTU, also Major Chen of the Chinese Air Force who arrived to study flying training and methods of ground instruction. The major's visit had been organised by SEAC and he was on the station for ten days. He flew for several hours as a passenger in a Harvard. The Club at Peshawar was also a great amenity for visiting VIPs as well as personnel based there. It was residential with swimming pool, squash and tennis courts. 'The kite hawks used to dive down as we had snacks beside the pool and sail away with claws grasping our sandwiches!'

North American Harvard at Peshawar in August 1945.

The first of the season's hill parties left for No.1 Hill Station at Lower Topa with seven parties comprising one seventh of the personnel of each section being away for three weeks. With the arrival of the hot season working hours across the board were modified with the training programme starting at 06.00 each day from May with maintenance personnel starting at 05.45 and finishing at 14.30. Lectures for the day ceased at 13.00. Station HQ soldiered on without changing their working hours – were their buildings adequately cooled by ceiling fans? Temporary sun shelters were erected on the airfield for the benefit for those who had no option but to work in the open and for the guards on duty around the perimeter.

The Communications Flight suffered its first fatal accident when Expeditor KJ483 crashed into a hillside in very bad weather; the two RAF crew and five passengers died.

A letter was received from BAFSEA during the month referring to spraying from the air with DDT as part of anti-malarial measures in North-West India. Hal was against this, for apart from the fact he felt that there wouldn't be any problem with controlling mosquito breeding areas by ground measures, local tribesmen might interpret spraying from the air as a hostile act.

May 1945. On the 8th as many base personnel as possible crammed into Base HQ for Hal to announce the end of the war in Europe and the programme for the following two days, declared official holidays, was made known. This included, on the 9th, a special dinner for all airmen served by officers and senior NCOs. 'The remaining pig, reared at Lower Topa, had been killed a few days previously in anticipation of the end of hostilities. There was therefore an ample supply of pork for the celebration dinner. Fresh and tinned fruit, nuts and 100 cigarettes per man obtained from welfare sources helped to make the event a great success.' Everyone was obviously elated by the cessation of hostilities in Europe but 'mindful of the fact that there is still a long and bitter struggle to be waged against the Japanese before victory is complete, the airmen expressed the view that the celebrations should be restrained and should consist mainly of a break in the normal routine with special meals but with a minimum of ostentation.'

These views were respected. A few days after the dinner there was a drumhead thanksgiving service held on the football ground attended by the Governor and Lady Cunningham. A Victory Parade in the city of Peshawar consisted of a drive past by Army and RAF units. A week later, Hal flew to Delhi for a conference of group commanders.

One of the OTU pilots narrowly escaped disaster when in Spitfire VIII MT558. He was taking evasive action during a dog-fighting exercise and pulled out violently from a high speed dive causing wrinkling and displacement of the main-plane surfaces and distortion of the fuselage, fin and rudder. In the cockpit the pilot's seat had collapsed and the starboard rudder cable was severed with the seat preventing movement of the rudder bar anyway. The pilot was censured for 'over enthusiasm in completing such a manoeuvre.' In another far less serious incident but embarrassingly for him, the Station Commander, Group Captain M.V.Delap, swung to starboard when landing in a Harvard. The aircraft turned through 180 degrees and the port tyre burst, the port oleo bent and the wingtip touched the ground. The cause was judged to be the Group Captain's inexperience in controlling a Harvard from the rear seat.

June 1945. There was a sad beginning to the month when Hal drove to Rawalpindi to attend the funeral of Lieutenant General Sir Henry Finnis, General Officer Commanding-in-Chief North-Western Army, who had died suddenly. Everyone especially felt the sadness of the occasion with the war now over in Europe at least and the general unable to enjoy the just rewards of peace. Concerned with the continuing high number of training accidents, Hal convened an 'accidents meeting' with No.151 OTU where it was decided that as ground discipline had a definite bearing on flying accidents, stricter ground discipline would be enforced and the accident rate review every two weeks. RAF Station Korangi Creek was disbanded. A temperature of 116° F was recorded at Peshawar and over three days there and at Risalpur, Basal, Fatehjang and Chaklala, forty-eight cases of heat exhaustion were recorded, with the death of one officer.

July 1945. At the end of the month ACM Sir Keith Park and Lady Park flew in an Avro York to the North-West Frontier again, starting their visit at Samungli airfield Quetta where Sir Keith addressed the airmen of the two RIAF squadrons resident there. The next day he lectured at the Staff College at Quetta before moving on to Peshawar where he was met by Hal, the new Station Commander, Group Captain E.G.Campbell-Voullaire, and other high-ranking officers. Here he again addressed the airmen, this time of HQ 223 Group and RAF Peshawar before spending the evening with Hal at Group HQ. Hal accompanied Sir Keith and his wife on to Chaklala in the York the next morning. He and the Air Chief Marshal then transferred to a Dakota along with twenty paratroopers who were dropped over Chaklala airfield.

An Expeditor was used to evacuate an Indian Air Force officer who had suffered severe burns in an aircraft accident to the RAF Hospital at Karachi. The flight routed via Quetta to avoid the hot weather which

In July 1945 ACM Keith Park visited Peshawar with his wife.

Sir Keith with Hal and the new station commander, Group Captain Campbell-Voullaire.

would be encountered if refuelling at Multan. A little late in the day it was discovered that a general-purpose stretcher couldn't be loaded into an Expeditor and there was no oxygen for the sick man when being flown for an hour over 12,000 feet. At a malaria conference at BAFSEA Hal's objections to spraying DDT in the area under his jurisdiction were over-ruled although it was agreed that RAF Peshawar itself would not be sprayed but only the breeding area outside the perimeter, in other words a half-mile-wide belt around the cantonment.

Sir Keith addressing the airmen at Peshawar.

The form of the Saturday morning colour-hoisting parade was reorganised with the flag mast being moved from Trenchard Barrack Square to the front of the Hurricane hangar in the technical area of the camp. Henceforth, the parade took the form of a Wing Parade with station personnel forming up in three squadrons on their own parade grounds, later marching as a squadron to form the Wing Parade in the area facing the flag. After the colour-hoisting ceremony and general salute there was a march past with the Station Commander, and sometimes Hal, taking the salute. 'The airman's prerogative of grumbling has not been overlooked in this matter of parades,' states the record. 'But in spite of this a marked improvement in the general turn-out has been noticed and a greater degree of smartness both among the officers and airmen has been apparent.' Everyone likes a good parade!

August 1945. No.223 Group and the North-West Frontier Wing were disbanded with effect from the 15th and No.1 (Indian) Group was formed to take over part of its duties. A few days before, Hal flew to Ambala where he inspected the station and took the salute at a passing out parade in the evening. This was Hal's last official engagement before he departed.

*

Towards the beginning of this biography, we quoted from Hal's letters to his mother from the Western Front. Now, towards its conclusion, we can draw on his letters to Nora back home in England in which he describes life as he experienced it on the North-West Frontier, a quite different experience of course from that of almost everyone serving below him, that is Park's lower formations. For Hal these were experiences as far removed from the Western Front as it was possible to get. For example, he took a short period of leave in Swat, which since 1926 had been a princely state aligned to the Raj by treaty and which, following the independence of Pakistan in 1947, acceded to that country. It was, and is, a place of great natural beauty.

> The party consisted of a political officer, his wife and daughter, his brother, myself, a bearer and an armed driver. We went in two cars. I drove my Ford V-8. We left the morning after a Hunt Ball not feeling very bright but before lunch we stopped to inspect a sugar factory. We saw the whole process from sugar cane growing to the granulated sugar flowing into the sacks. Then via a hydro-electric plant we arrived that evening in the capital of Swat state [Saidu Sharif]. When the Swat River Hydro Electric scheme was being debated one of the Indian ministers who had only a very hazy idea of how the plant worked and was against the whole project anyway, suddenly exclaimed 'but how do you know that all this electricity you talk about is in the waters of Swat?'
>
> The sentry at the fort where we stayed was holding a baby in one arm and his rifle with the other! We were entertained in

royal style by the *Wali*'s [custodian's] eldest son in a lovely house fitted out in the most modern style with every convenience. The food was perfect. Next day we had a chickaw shoot over a very rough mountain side. [Perhaps Hal meant *chukar*, a type of partridge.] Imagine a rough rocky mountain side with some 200 beaters advancing in line all making noises and throwing stones to put up the birds. Birds did get up but I was so occupied in climbing that I only got one. Got back very tired to lunch at 4pm. That evening the old Wali of Swat took us on a drive round part of the State and gave us wonderful views of the snows [on the Hindu Kush mountains]. He speaks no English but is a fine old man – an absolute dictator. Next day we had a duck shoot in a ten-mile wide valley with snow-covered mountains on all sides. I shot five duck all flying high. We shot from concrete hides covered in straw. It was good fun. Lunch was well run in a big stone shooting lodge. We sat down to a hot meal before roaring wood fires – and they were needed.

We left next day via a wonderful pass where the snow was thick and lunched at a bungalow built like a fort beside one of the large irrigation canals. We stayed there a few nights, each day visiting local notables each of which entertained us to food and tea. The best tiffin was *pilau*, roast chicken eaten in the fingers and chapatti with cream and honey. The honeycomb had the tree branch on which it was made still stuck in it. Then oranges and green tea. We fed ravenous fish with chapatti. They were twelve-inches long and ate out of your hand. They fought to get at the food with heads well out of the water.

In another letter Hal told Nora of his meeting again with Archibald Wavell who since Hal first knew him in 1942 had been appointed Viceroy and Governor-General of India.

I met the Viceroy recently when he came into my area. He looked very well and was in great spirits. He remembered my name (perhaps he was briefed) and we had quite a conversation about the job I was doing. He presented Victoria Crosses and new Colours to a regiment. The first VC went to a Gurkha, a fine looking chap, Terai hat well on one side of his head, grey shirt, khaki shorts and green stockings. His belt carried his bayonet and kukri [knife] polished to perfection. The second VC was posthumous and was received by a little girl of 11 years who would have been his wife if the receiver of this the highest decoration for bravery had lived. She was accompanied by her aunt and a colonel and was dressed in a pale purple sari with gold embroidery. To see the little figure receive the great decoration in the palm of her hands and then kiss it brought a lump to my throat and tears to my eyes which continued during a fine march past by a Gurkha Battalion. After a stand up lunch we saw the presentation of new Colours to the Battalion.

Tiffin with a mullah was the subject of another letter.

I was out with Sir George Cunningham, the Governor of the Province, recently and we dropped in on a mullah for tiffin. We started on dishes of nuts in one room then moved to the dining room where there must have been over 300 dishes on the table. After soup we went on to *pilau*, highly spiced chicken, chicken boiled in sugar and chapattis etc. Sweets were cornflour coloured with beetle blood and about twenty sweetmeats like sugared orange peel, sugar cane etc. Then we went back to the first room and found the tables loaded with fruit and pots of green tea. We drove home feeling as if we were full of cotton wool.

On another occasion with the Governor they toured Islamia College, one of the oldest higher education institutions in Pakistan, founded in 1913.

The students live in houses each built like a square fort in the grounds. There is only one entrance and it is locked and barred at 9pm. The master in charge sleeps in a room over the gate. Students go there at six or seven and can stay until eighteen years if they wish. The college has its own farm, flour mill, bakery etc. and is self-contained like a small town. I saw flour being ground and found it very hot to touch as it came from the mill. The baking of the flour into chapattis was amusing. The bakers sat on the floor. The men making the bread worked hard measuring quantities and producing row after row of little round cakes. They make 2,000 a day. The ovens consist of chambers below the floor with only a small round hole at the top. The bakers sat on the floor beside the little round holes through which one could see glowing embers of charcoal in the bottom of the oven. They worked quickly snatching cakes from the boards, flattening them on a dirty little cushion and, leaning down into the oven, they slapped the cakes against the side of the oven where they stuck. The cushion was out again and another cake on its way in a shorter time than it takes to tell. The bakers picked the baked cakes off the walls of the oven with tongs. It was fun to watch. Some of the cakes were at full arm's length inside the oven.

The Jamrud Fort is located at the mouth of the Khyber Pass.

I was honoured to be invited by one of the crack Indian Army units to lunch inside Jamrud Fort to meet their Colonel in Chief, the Maharajah of Patial. I had a spirited conversation with him about helicopters and rockets. I found him well up to date in these matters. He is allowed many wives and had just had 3 sons and 2 daughters born to him in one week!

Hal also wrote to Nora describing his pride to be appointed a Commander of the British Empire in the New Year's Honours list of 1945. He could add this honour to the Military Cross awarded in 1918 and the Cloud and Banner Decoration with Special Cravat which would be awarded by the Chinese in 1946. Nora and John accompanied

Hal to Buckingham Palace when he returned to England when King George VI invested him with the CBE.

*

The war in Europe ended on 8 May 1945 and that against Japan on 2 September 1945.

> Both these great events called for celebrations of every kind and hopes of early repatriation and demobilisation for those concerned. I addressed the men on parade at Peshawar airfield in a prepared speech which I hope was appropriate to the great occasion. As I had by then completed my overseas tour I was due to be amongst the first to be repatriated. When handing over to my successor [Group Captain Wingate] I was amused to find that my bearer had sold all the moveable parts of my cycle in the bazaar and substituted 'country-made' parts. He got into trouble for this!

Hal flew back to the UK in an Avro York at the end of August, landing at Hurn Airport, Bournemouth, after a twenty-three-hour flight via Basra, Cairo and Luqa.

> Need I say what a joy it was to be reunited with Nora, John, Michael and Richard and to see the enchanting little house at Thornton-le-Dale [in Yorkshire] that Nora had bought.

But India had taken its toll.

> I was run down in health when I arrived home and but for Nora's excellent feeding and creative work in the fresh air I don't think I would have survived very long.

But with Nora caring for him, with the fresh clean air of Yorkshire to aid his full recovery and with his family around him Hal found a new lease of life away from the RFC and RAF, to which he had devoted almost thirty years, a life he could look back on with pride, satisfaction and a sense of real accomplishment.

His legacy is what he left behind in writing and photography which has enabled us to see at first-hand what the Royal Air Force was really like in all the places he served from Ireland to India.

Afterword

Along with many contemporaries Hal was retired from the active list of the RAF in 1946 and transferred to the Reserves, although after some thirty years in the armed services he felt he had had enough and so was glad to embrace civilian life. Living in peaceful Thornton-le-Dale with a family he had seen little of during the wartime years he settled down to tending the garden and tinkering with his succession of cars. Well, more than tinkering actually as before each journey, however short, however long, a full RAF-style engineering check was conducted to make sure the vehicle was fit for the road. He also became involved in amateur dramatics – he had always enjoyed the theatre as his memoir and diaries show, but that was from an audience perspective, not as a participant. However, he was persuaded to take on the role of Professor Higgins in *Pygmalion* and the family considered it to be his finest hour on the stage.

But Hal also wanted to take on some responsibility and he became a Justice of the Peace and ultimately Chairman of the Bench at Northallerton. He was appointed Chairman of the Governors at Lady Lumley's School in Pickering and also became involved with Civil Defence matters, visiting Yorkshire communities to advise what could and should be done in the event of nuclear attack. In addition he worked for the Royal Air Force Benevolent Fund.

After an active retirement Air Commodore Henry George Crowe MC CBE CBD (SC) died peacefully in April 1983. Nora, who was a little younger, died in February 1991.

Appendix

Hal left lists of the aircraft types he had flown during his RFC and RAF days. A selection follows.

Airco DH.9 – a single-engined biplane bomber with an unreliable engine resulting in heavy losses over the Western Front.

Airco DH.9a – a development of the unsuccessful DH.9 with a strengthened structure and an American V-12 Liberty engine. Known to all as the Ninak, it served in large numbers with the RAF following the end of the war both at home and overseas where it was used for colonial policing in the Middle East.

Airco DH.10 Amiens I – an unsuccessful prototype medium bomber powered by two pusher Puma engines.

Airco DH.10 Amiens III – a redeveloped Amiens I and successful medium bomber powered by two tractor American Liberty V-12 engines.

(Note: Airco went into liquidation after the end of the First World War and its aircraft designer, Geoffrey de Havilland, formed his own company in 1920, after which all types were known as de Havillands.)

Airspeed Oxford – a twin-engined aircraft used for training British Commonwealth aircrews in navigation, radio-operating, bombing and gunnery.

Avro 504K – a two-seater biplane briefly used as a front-line bomber but which excelled as a trainer, production of which during the First World War totalled 8,970 (the most produced aircraft of that war) and continued for almost twenty years thereafter. The 504K could take either a Clerget 9, Gnome Monosoupape or Le Rhône 9J engine.

Avro 504N – a redesigned post-war trainer for the RAF with an Armstrong Siddeley Lynx engine.

Avro Aldershot – a bomber biplane powered by a single Rolls Royce Condor engine and carrying a crew of three. Fifteen were built.

Avro Andover – a single-engined biplane developed from the Avro Aldershot and built as a successor to the Airco DH.10 on the Cairo to Baghdad air route. Four were built, three as flying ambulances and one as a transport.

Beechcraft Model 18/C-45 Expeditor – over 4,500 Expeditors and Beech 18s saw military service as light transports, light bombers and as an aircrew trainer for bombing, navigation and gunnery and photo-reconnaissance.

Boulton and Paul Defiant – an interceptor designed and built as a so-called 'turret fighter' without any forward-firing guns.

Bristol Blenheim – a three-seat twin-engined light bomber powered by two Bristol Mercury VIII radial engines. Seven marks of Blenheim were built in total.

Bristol Bulldog – a single-seat biplane fighter powered by a Bristol Jupiter engine.

Bristol F.E.2b – a two-seat biplane fighter and reconnaissance aircraft, often simply called the Brisfit, which remained in military service into the 1930s.

Bristol Fighter Mk IV – a structurally-strengthened version of the Bristol F.E.2b.

de Havilland DH.60 Cirrus Moth – a 1920s Cirrus-engined two-seat touring and training aircraft

de Havilland DH.60G Gypsy Moth – de Havilland replaced the original Cirrus engine of the DH.60 with a Gipsy I engine.

de Havilland DH.80A Puss Moth – a three-seater high-wing monoplane built for private use. A few were impressed for communications duties during the Second World War.

de Havilland DH.82 Tiger Moth – a 1930s biplane operated extensively by the RAF as an *ab initio* and primary trainer.

de Havilland DH.85 Leopard Moth – a three-seat monoplane built as a successor to the Puss Moth and sometimes used as a communications aircraft during the Second World War.

Fairchild 24 – a four-seat single-engined monoplane light transport aircraft adopted by the United States Army Air Corps as the UC-61 and by the RAF as the Argus.

Fairey IIIF – built in two versions, either as a two-seat general-purpose biplane or a three-seat spotter-reconnaissance biplane, both versions powered by a Napier Lion W-12 engine.

Fairey IIIF Mk IV – a two-seat general-purpose aircraft powered by a Napier Lion XIA W-12 engine.

Fairey Gordon – a two-seat light day-bomber and utility aircraft.

Gloster S.19 – the prototype of the Gloster Gauntlet fitted with a Bristol Jupiter radial piston engine

Gloster Gauntlet – a single-seat biplane fighter. The Gauntlet II had a Bristol Mercury engine.

Gloster Gladiator – the RAF's last biplane fighter aircraft.

Handley Page 0/400 HP 12 – a biplane bomber of the First World War and the largest aircraft that had been built in the UK at the time, powered by two Rolls Royce Eagle VIII engines.

Hawker Audax – a variant of the Hawker Hart designed for army co-operation work.

Hawker Demon – a fighter variant of the Hawker Hart.

Hawker Fury – a biplane fighter which was the first interceptor in RAF service to be capable of more than 200mph.

Hawker Hart – a two-seater biplane light bomber aircraft with a Rolls Royce Kestrel IB engine.

Hawker Hart Fighter – a fighter version with a Kestrel IIS engine used by No.23 Squadron, later redesignated as the Demon. Six were built.

Hawker Hurricane – a Rolls Royce Merlin engined single-seat monoplane fighter aircraft ordered into production in 1936. It went on to down 60 per cent of enemy aircraft during the Battle of Britain and served in all major theatres during the Second World War.

North American Harvard – a single-engined advanced trainer used to train pilots of the Royal Air Force and other air forces of the British Commonwealth during the Second World War. As the T-6 Texan, it was used to train pilots of the USAAC/USAAF and the US Navy.

Percival Proctor – a radio trainer and communications aircraft.

Percival Vega Gull – a 1930s British four-seater touring aircraft. A small number were used by the RAF on communications duties during the Second World War.

Royal Aircraft Factory R.E.7 – a two-seat light bomber and reconnaissance biplane. The RE designation refers to Reconnaissance Experimental.

Royal Aircraft Factory R.E.8 – a two-seat light bomber and reconnaissance biplane.

Royal Aircraft Factory R.E.9 – two R.E.8s were modified with equal-span wings and a larger fin and rudder but showed no advantage over the standard RE.8 and didn't enter production

Royal Aircraft Factory N.E.1 – a single engine pusher biplane prototype night fighter. Only six were built. The N.E. designation refers to Night Experimental.

Royal Aircraft Factory B.E.2c – a major redesign of the original BE.2 to make a very stable aeroplane enabling the crew to concentrate fully on reconnaissance duties. The BE designation refers to Bleriot Experimental.

Royal Aircraft Factory B.E.2e – superseded the BE.2c with new wings and tail-plane to improve performance. A new engine was expected to improve it even further but the improvement didn't materialise.

Sopwith Bulldog – an unsuccessful prototype British two-seat fighter intended to replace the Brisfit.

Stinson Reliant – an American single-engined high-wing monoplane of the 1930s designed for the civilian market but also used by the United States Army Air Corps during the Second World War when it was designated the UC-81.

Supermarine Southampton – a biplane flying-boat with twin Napier Lion engines mounted between the wings.

Supermarine Spitfire – a Rolls Royce Merlin engined fighter built in many variants (there were twenty-four marks of the aircraft plus Seafires) using several wing configurations which was produced in greater numbers than any other British aircraft ever and was the only British fighter in continuous production throughout the Second World War.

Vickers FB.5 Gun Bus – a two-seat pusher biplane armed with a single Lewis gun operated by the observer in the front of the nacelle. It was the first aircraft purpose built for air-to-air combat and was thus the world's first operational fighter aircraft. The FB designation refers to Fighting Biplane.

Vickers Valentia – a cargo aircraft built for the Royal Air Force, the majority built being re-engined (with the Bristol Pegasus) conversions of the earlier Vickers Victoria.

Vickers Vernon – a development of the Vickers Vimy Commercial which, powered by Napier Lion engines, entered RAF service in 1921 as its first dedicated troop transport.

Vickers Victoria – a biplane freighter and troop transport aircraft powered by Napier Lion engines which first flew in 1922.

Vickers Vildebeest – a large single-engined biplane used as a light bomber, torpedo-bomber and in army co-operation roles.

Vickers Vimy – a heavy bomber of the First World War and post-First World War era powered by two Rolls Royce Eagle VIII engines. The Vimy also achieved success as a civil aircraft. Alcock and Brown made the first non-stop crossing of the Atlantic in June 1919 in one.

Westland Lysander – an army co-operation and liaison aircraft with exceptional short field performance.

Westland Wallace – a two-seat general purpose biplane with a Bristol Pegasus engine, developed as a successor to the Wapiti.

Westland Wapiti – a two-seat general-purpose Bristol Jupiter-engined biplane which remained in service with the RAF in India until 1942.

******

Hal lists the following as aircraft he was flown in as a crew member or passenger.

Airspeed Envoy, Avro Anson, Avro York, Consolidated PBY Catalina, de Havilland DH.89 Dragon Rapide, de Havilland DH.95 Flamingo, de Havilland DH.86 Express, Douglas Boston, Douglas C-47 Dakota, Handley Page HP.42 , Lockheed Hudson, Lockheed Model 14 Super Electra, Lockheed Model 10 Electra, Lockheed Model 18 Lodestar, North American B-25 Mitchell, Percival Q.6 Petrel and Short Empire flying boat.

Bibliography
and
Acknowledgements

My sincere thanks to Dr Michael Crowe for making his father's memoir, photographs, log books and letters available.

Various internet sites to garner information about places and people mentioned in Hal Crowe's memoir, Wikipedia providing additional links.

RAF Operations 1918–1938 by Chaz Bowyer: William Kimber 1988.

Ian Alder at the RAF Museum Reserve Collection.

The 74(F) Tiger Squadron Association photographic archive.

Aviation History September 2002 issue.

Winged Promises by Dr Vincent Orange, The Lord Deramore, AVM Deryk Stapleton and Wg Cdr Edmund Donovan: RAF Benevolent Fund Enterprises 1996.

Biggin on the Bump by Bob Ogley: Froglets Publications 1990.

Reggie. The Life of Air Vice Marshal R L G Marix CBE DSO by John Lea: Pentland Press 1994.

The raid on Collinstown airfield March 1919. http://www.anphoblacht.com/contents/4709.

Winged Crusaders by Michael Napier: Pen and Sword 2012.

The Imperial War Museum for descriptions of army kit in 1916.

The National Archive for access to AIR and WO documents relating to Air Commodore Crowe's career.

Fairey IIIF. Interwar Military Workhorse by Philip Jarrett. Ad Hoc Publications 2009.

Bristol Aircraft since 1910 by C H Barnes: Putnam 1988.

De Havilland Aircraft since 1909 by A J Jackson: Putnam 1987.

Avro Aircraft since 1908 by A J Jackson: Putnam 1990.

Hawker Aircraft since 1920 by Francis K Mason: Putnam 1991.

Tony Brooks and his research into pre–World War II camouflage.

Siege Within the Walls by Stewart Perowne: Hodder and Stoughton 1974.

From Peace to War : Royal Air Force Rearmament Programme 1934–1940 by Martin Waligorski. Published on line.

The Air and Space Magazine: The Smithsonian, July 2011.

The Red Eagles – A History Of No.23 Squadron, Royal Air Force, 1915–1994 by Peter Rudd. Privately published 1995.

Notes for RAF Officers Proceeding to India for the First Time. Air Ministry 1921.

Journal of the Air Forces. India Command Edition. 1942–1945.

The Mountbatten Papers: *South East Asia Command 1943–1946.*

The Great Bombay Explosion by John Ennis. Berkley Publishing 1959. See also www.youtube.com/watch?v=GuD3esOUlvc.

Colonial Film. www.colonialfilm.org.uk.

And thanks as well to my editor, Richard Doherty, who saved me from a few embarrassing mistakes! Any remaining errors are mine and mine alone.

Index

NAVAL, MILITARY AND AIR FORCE FORMATIONS AND UNITS

ENGINES
Engine Manufacturers

Engines

PEOPLE

(*Where known, ranks shown of those in service are those ultimately reached by the individual.*)

PEOPLES, PLACES, GEOGRAPHICAL

GENERAL INDEX